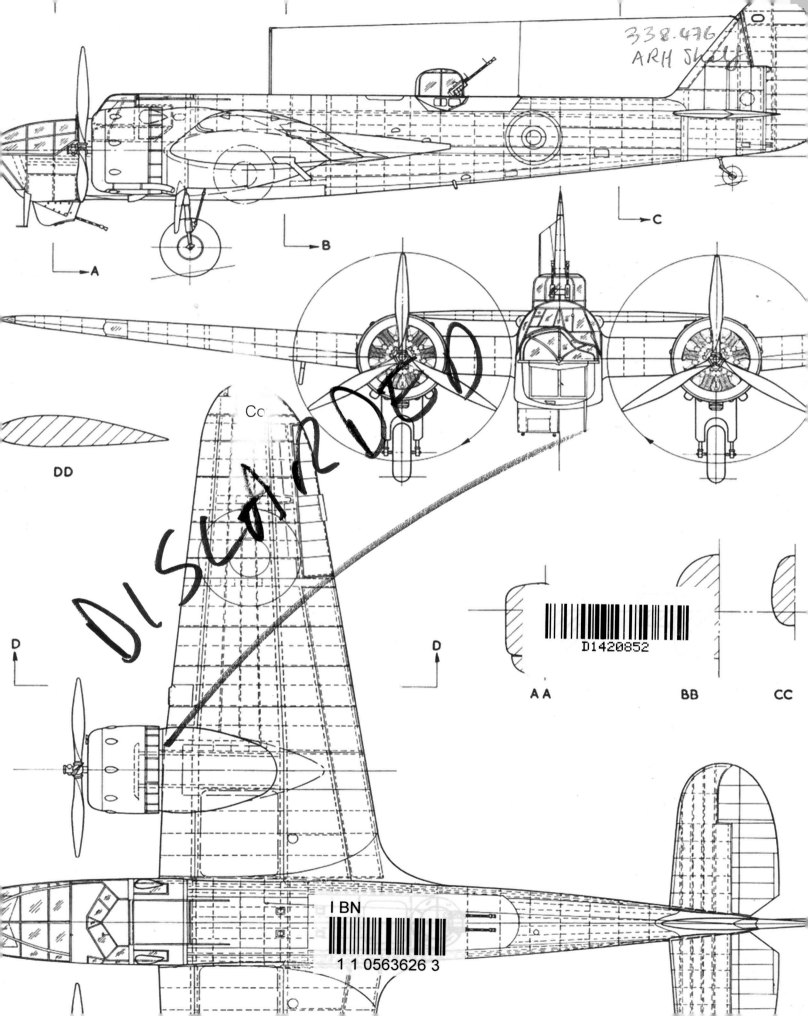

338.476
ARH SU...

A

B

C

DD

Co

D   D

AA   BB   CC

D1420852

I BN

1 1 0563626 3

Take Flight

Portrait of Sir George White at Dale Vicarage, Milford Haven by Frank Eastman, originally commissioned for presentation to the Royal Aeronautical Society by the Bristol Aeroplane Company in 1953 but purchased by Sir Stanley White (Sir George White Bt).

Take Flight

Celebrating Aviation in the West of England Since 1910

Andrew Kelly and Melanie Kelly

Bristol Cultural Development Partnership

Published by:

Bristol Cultural Development Partnership (BCDP)

Leigh Court, Abbots Leigh, Bristol BS8 3RA

Design and typesetting by Qube Design Associates Ltd
Printed in England by Butler Tanner & Dennis Ltd

2010

ISBN 978 0 9550742 3 3

We are grateful for the support of Component Coating and Repair Services Ltd, which has
kindly sponsored this publication:

A project of Bristol Creative Projects (trading as Bristol Cultural Development Partnership):

Take Flight is published as part of the BAC 100 celebrations marking the centenary of the
founding of the Bristol Aeroplane Company.

Home of the British Aviation Industry

www.bac2010.co.uk

We would like to thank all those who have provided illustrative material for this book.
They are credited by each image. No image in this book should be reproduced without the
permission of the holder of the reproduction rights. Images of Beaufighter, Blenheim, Bulldog
and Bristol Fighter on endpapers from Bristol Aero Collection.

[Sir George White, Chairman, said] that for some time past both his brother and himself had been directing their attention to the subject of aviation which was one hardly yet ripe for practical undertaking by such a company as the Bristol Tramways Company, but yet seemed to them to offer promise of development at no distant date; so much so that they had determined to personally take the risks and expense of the endeavour to develop the science both from the spectacular and commercial or manufacturing point of view.

If, as they believed, they could make the headquarters close to Bristol, they would give their own city a prominent place in the movement nationally, and secure for the Tramways Company a very important source of new traffic, as of course, they would take care that the centre of attraction was located upon the Company's system, and it was obvious that the public interest in the subject would attract enormous crowds from the whole of the West of England and South Wales to witness the numerous demonstrations that would take place.

Incidentally he might say that they had on order several aeroplanes of the best designs hitherto produced, and the intention was to develop a British industry making Bristol its headquarters. (Loud applause).

– from Report of Proceedings at the Annual General Meeting of the Bristol Tramways & Carriage Company held at the Grand Hotel, Bristol, 16 February 1910

Contents

The Shuttleworth Collection's
Bristol Fighter in flight with a
RB199-powered Tornado, c 1994
(Bristol Aero Collection).

Introduction

On 30 July 1910 a Bristol Boxkite biplane, built by the newly formed British & Colonial Aeroplane Company at Filton, took off from Larkhill in Wiltshire, home of the company's first flying school. That pioneering flight was the start of a remarkable journey that today sees the West of England as one of the foremost centres of aerospace engineering and advanced technology in the world.

Women in the British & Colonial machine shop working at lathes to make component parts, c 1917 (detail) (private collection).

The British & Colonial Aeroplane Company and the Bristol Aeroplane Company, known to generations as 'the BAC', were founded in February 1910 by Sir George White, a Bristol stockbroker. He was also one of the country's great transport entrepreneurs and a leading philanthropist. The industry he worked hard to establish and to transform from a speculative venture into a viable concern continues to make a significant contribution to Bristol and the region.

It has employed hundreds of thousands of people, including three or more generations of the same family; had a major impact upon the physical, economic, cultural and social development of the areas in which its factories are located; established links around the globe through business connections and the opening up of world travel; and not only led innovation in aviation but also diversified into the building of buses, boats, cars, satellites, missiles, mobile phones and prefabricated buildings, among many other products.

This book is published to coincide with the BAC 100 programme in 2010 marking the centenary of the founding of the British Aeroplane Company. It celebrates the achievements of the past and looks forward to tomorrow. Filton is unique among the historic sites that formed the cradle of British aviation in the early years of flight – the others being Farnborough, Brooklands and Hendon – in that its industry is still active and remains a major employer. This is a sometimes complicated history because of the various mergers, take-overs and transfers of assets that have taken place over the last century. However, there is a distinctive, unbroken lineage that can be traced back to 1910 and looks set to continue for many decades to come.

In the first 50 years alone, before the name 'Bristol' was lost from airframe and aero-engine production, BAC and its associated companies produced around 15,750 aircraft of 85 different designs, of which only ten per cent were not originated in-house. Among

them were production aircraft like the Bristol Fighter, the Blenheim, the Beaufighter and Britannia, as well as one-off and development aircraft such as the record-beating Type 138A and the fondly remembered but financially doomed Brabazon. A further 8,320 Bristol aircraft were built elsewhere under subcontract or licence. All this was achieved before the technological triumph of Concorde, the last complete airliner built in the West of England, and the success of the Airbus fleet, the wings of which are now designed and partly built in Filton. There is also an extraordinary range of world-conquering aero-engines including the Bristol Jupiter, Hercules and Proteus, the Olympus and the RB199.

Today, 43,000 skilled workers are employed in aerospace in the South West, the majority based in the West of England.[1] The South West region is home to major facilities belonging to nine of the 12 largest aerospace companies in the UK as well as a comprehensive logistics chain of around 800 suppliers, specialist manufacturers and research and development organisations. The research and development capability is enhanced by links with the region's top-rated university research departments and specialist agencies. This present-day expertise and the industry's future aspirations are based on a strong foundation of decades of achievement, much of it attributable to BAC.

Brabazon on its approach at Farnborough, c 1950 (George Rollo). The Cody Tree in the foreground is thought to be where pioneering designer and pilot Samuel Cody tied his aeroplane to test its engine power.

Take Flight aims to provide an accessible, informative and engaging overview of the variety, significance and impact of the aircraft, engines and other pioneering technologies that have followed in the wake of BAC's founding. It seeks to appeal to the general reader who is a novice when it comes to the principles of flight and the BAC story, as well as to those looking for a lasting reminder of BAC's achievements, with which they may already be familiar.

Take Flight does not attempt to provide a complete chronology of the company, nor detailed technical specifications of every aircraft or aero-engine that has been produced, nor the name of every licensed subcontractor or every airline operator to purchase BAC products. Other books provide this, of which the most authoritative is still widely believed to be C H Barnes' *Bristol Aircraft*, first published in 1964 and last revised in 1988. There are also books in print on individual West of England aircraft. Some of this previously published material has been drawn upon during the research for *Take Flight* and the BAC 100 programme. Another invaluable resource has been the work of the members of Filton Community History. Over the last few years this group has been conducting in-depth interviews with former employees of the local aviation industry through an extensive oral history project, building up an archive of original audio recordings and transcripts. These provide insight into the working conditions and social life of the employees as well as details of the projects developed by the companies. The authors are also grateful to those individuals who have helped during the researching, fact-checking and proofreading stages of writing this book, many of whom have shared their personal experiences of working in aviation.

Take Flight has six main sections. 'The Pioneers' tells the story of how BAC was founded and of the first decade of its development, when it operated under the name of the British & Colonial Aeroplane Company. It places this story within the wider context of the development of heavier-than-air flight over several centuries, with particular reference to the pioneers associated with the West of England and surrounding areas. 'Technological Achievements' demonstrates how BAC and its associated companies were at the forefront of several major technological innovations and also adapted the innovations of others.

Concorde during its assembly phase in the Brabazon hangar at Filton, c 1972 (detail) (Rolls-Royce plc). Four of the seven Filton production Concordes are shown in various stages of finish.

It includes simple explanations, suitable for those with limited technical knowledge, of how aeroplanes stay airborne, how pilots control their aircraft and how different types of engines work. 'The Workforce and the Community' looks at the West of England's aviation industry from the perspective of those thousands of people employed within it, as well as the physical and social changes it has brought to the area. 'Worldwide Connections' shows the global significance of what has been achieved by BAC and others in terms of doing business overseas and developing world travel, particularly with regard to the civil airliner market. 'War in the Air' looks at the aviation industry's contribution to defence, warfare and aerial combat. 'Into the Future' is a look ahead to some of the aviation projects currently in the pipeline, with a particular focus on steps taken to minimise the environmental impact of flight.

Although the main focus of the BAC 100 celebrations (and therefore of this book) is the thread that links British & Colonial and the Bristol Aeroplane Company in 1910 to Airbus, BAE Systems, GKN, MBDA, Rolls-Royce and others today, the stories of Parnall, Gloster Aircraft, Rotol, Dowty and Westland are also touched upon. They too have contributed to the building of the West of England's impressive reputation in the field of aviation. In addition, although the celebrations largely concentrate on activities in the Filton and Patchway area, reference is made, where appropriate, to the locations of other BAC facilities including Weston-super-Mare, Whitchurch and some of the shadow factory and dispersal sites used in World War Two.

In 1940 BAC celebrated its 30th anniversary. The words of *The Aeroplane* magazine published 70 years ago could still serve in 2010 for the centenary celebrations:

> the history of the Company is in some danger of appearing primarily as that of a commercial success. There is a more romantic side to the development of this great firm, for in itself it epitomises, perhaps more completely than any other, the tale of British aeronautical progress... This anniversary marks more than the successful completion of three decades of a new engineering industry. It celebrates the triumph of a consistent policy, of fearless financial enterprise, of patient and persistent research and development, and of a faith in the soundness of convictions which in their inception were little short of inspiration.[2]

Artist's impression of the forthcoming
Taranis Unmanned Combat Air
Vehicle (BAE Systems).

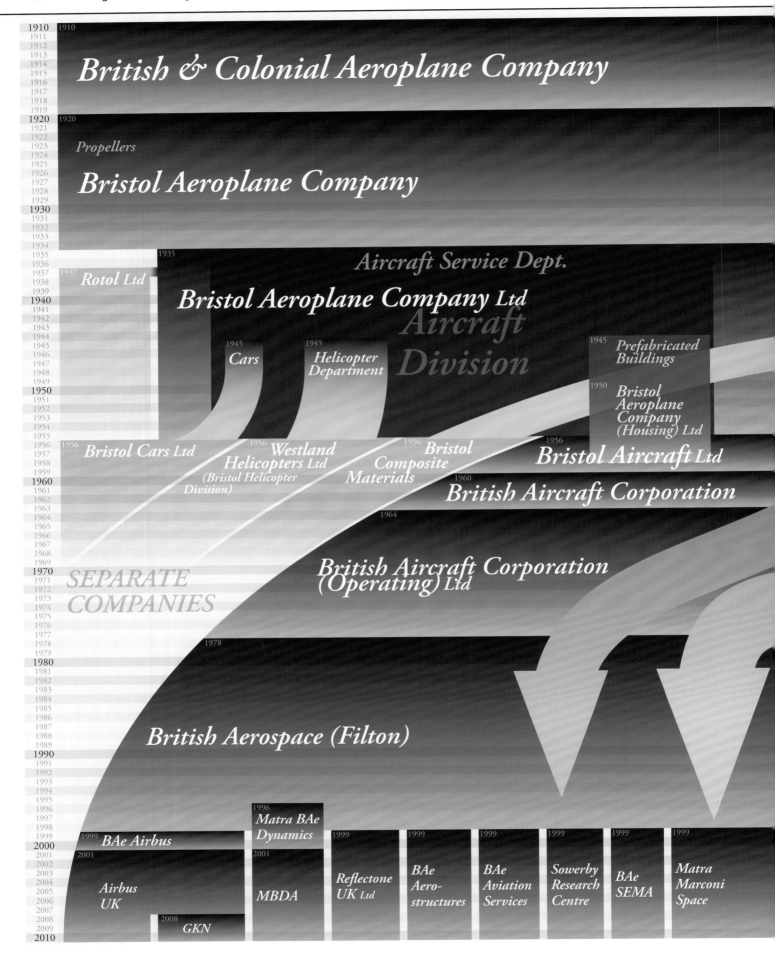

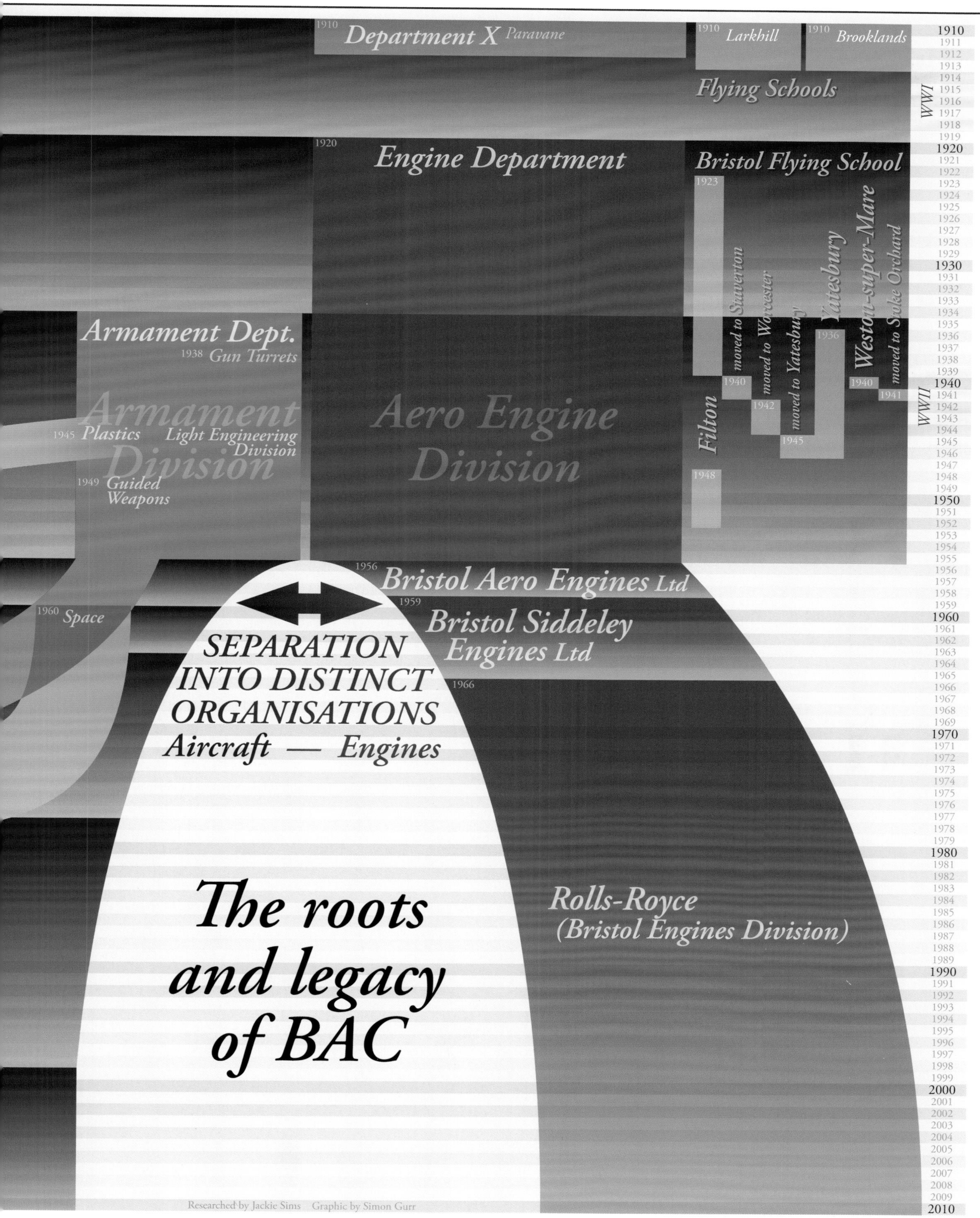

1910 Department X *Paravane* 1910 *Larkhill* 1910 *Brooklands* 1910

Flying Schools

WWI

1920 Engine Department Bristol Flying School 1920

1923

Armament Dept.

1938 *Gun Turrets*

Armament

1945 Plastics Light Engineering Division

Division Aero Engine

1949 *Guided Weapons* Division

moved to Shaverton

moved to Worcester

moved to Yatesbury

Yatesbury

Weston-super-Mare

moved to Stoke Orchard

Filton

1940 1936 1940 1941

WWII

1942

1945

1948

1956 Bristol Aero Engines Ltd

1960 *Space* 1959 Bristol Siddeley

SEPARATION Engines Ltd

INTO DISTINCT

ORGANISATIONS 1966

Aircraft — *Engines*

The roots

Rolls-Royce

and legacy (Bristol Engines Division)

of BAC

Researched by Jackie Sims   Graphic by Simon Gurr

1910 1911 1912 1913 1914 1915 1916 1917 1918 1919 1920 1921 1922 1923 1924 1925 1926 1927 1928 1929 1930 1931 1932 1933 1934 1935 1936 1937 1938 1939 1940 1941 1942 1943 1944 1945 1946 1947 1948 1949 1950 1951 1952 1953 1954 1955 1956 1957 1958 1959 1960 1961 1962 1963 1964 1965 1966 1967 1968 1969 1970 1971 1972 1973 1974 1975 1976 1977 1978 1979 1980 1981 1982 1983 1984 1985 1986 1987 1988 1989 1990 1991 1992 1993 1994 1995 1996 1997 1998 1999 2000 2001 2002 2003 2004 2005 2006 2007 2008 2009 2010

Timeline

The following timeline shows key events in the history of West of England aviation, concentrating on the BAC lineage, alongside other important events of the period, mainly of a technological nature.[3]

Year	BAC Event	Elsewhere
1910	19 February: George White's four aviation companies registered – British & Colonial Aeroplane Company name used for initial operations. March: Zodiac shown at Olympia. June: Sheds erected for Larkhill Flying School. 30 July: Boxkite's first flight. 21 September: Students enrol at Brooklands Flying School. 24 September: Boxkite at Autumn Manoeuvres. 14 November: Boxkite flights from the Downs. 15 November: announcement of sales to Russia. December: Start of sales tour of India and Australia.	First US airshow. JTC Moore-Brabazon is Royal Aero Club's first certificated pilot. Baroness de Laroche in France is world's first qualified female pilot. Claude Grahame-White makes Europe's first night flight. Louis Paulhan wins *Daily Mail* London-Manchester challenge. Charles Rolls makes first double crossing of Channel. Rolls killed at Bournemouth airshow. First flight over Swiss Alps. First flight over 100km an hour. Grahame-White wins Gordon Bennett International Air Race. First mid-air collision. First take-off from deck of a ship. First floatplane flight.
1911	18 February: Stanley White made Managing Director. 14 March: War Office places first order for Boxkites. December: Frank Barnwell joins company.	Air Battalion Royal Engineers formed. First flight of Curtiss floatplane. First London-Paris non-stop flight. First wartime use of aeroplane.
1912	Henri Coanda appointed Chief Designer. February: First overseas flying schools set up. August: Coanda designs submitted to War Office trials at Larkhill.	Royal Flying Corps founded. Military use of monoplanes restricted. First enclosed cabin aeroplane. First all-metal aeroplane. First flight over 100mph. First parachute drop from aeroplane. Wilbur Wright dies. Monocoque (single shell) construction introduced. First recorded recovery from a spin.
1914	23 February: Scout's first flight. 14 June: Larkhill flying school closed for mobilisation. 30 September: tuition ends at Brooklands.	World War One begins. First Zeppelin raid (Antwerp). First British air attack on Germany.
1916	9 September: Fighter's first flight. 22 November: death of Sir George White.	First test of a flying bomb. Battle of the Somme.
1917	July: MR1's first flight. 8 November: Visit from King George V and Queen Mary.	First London blitz. Russian Revolution.

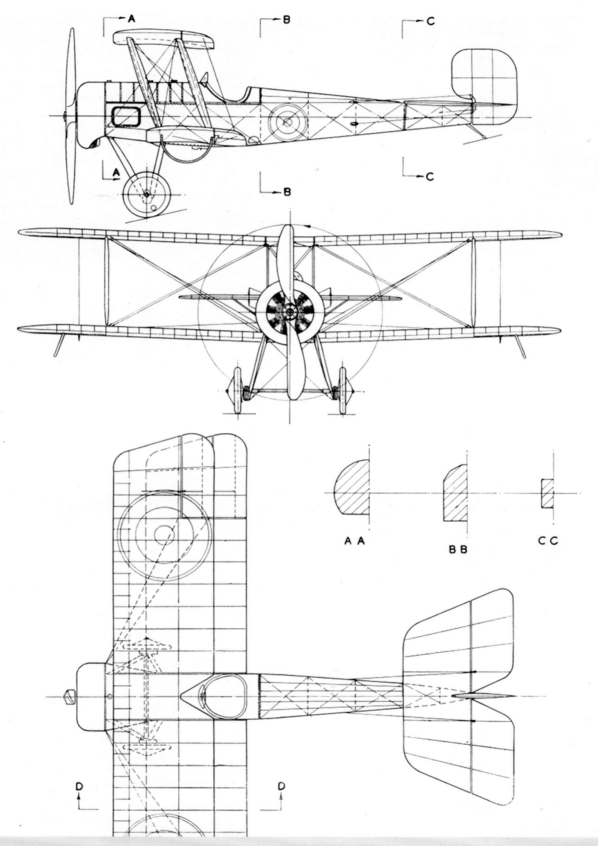

Plan drawings of Scout Type 1-5 (Bristol Aero Collection).

Year	BAC Event	Elsewhere
1918	13 August: Braemar's first flight. 25 October: Cyril Uwins joins company. 12 December: M1C makes double crossing of Andes.	Red Baron killed. Armistice. Cosmos Engineering takes over Brazil Straker at Fishponds.
1919	28 November: Bristol Babe's first flight.	First regular airmail and passenger services. First Atlantic crossings. First Britain-Australia flight.
1920	23 March: British & Colonial Aeroplane Company formally wound up having transferred assets to Bristol Aeroplane Company. July: Pullman airliner shown at Olympia. July: Cosmos Engineering team and assets acquired.	First flight with practical retractable undercarriage.
1921	Jupiter air-cooled radial starts production.	First test-sinking of battleship by aerial bombing.
1925	May: Archibald E Russell joins company. First Jupiters delivered to RAF.	First University Air Squadron formed at University of Cambridge.
1927	17 May: Bulldog's first flight.	First solo transatlantic flight.
1929	26 May: Jupiter powered Junkers sets new altitude record.	First flight of Dornier Do X flying boat.
1932	Perseus sleeve-valve cleared for flight. 6 September: Vespa powered by Pegasus sets new altitude record.	Imperial Airways London-Cape Town service begins. First female solo transatlantic flight.
1933	3 April: Westland Wapitis powered by Pegasus fly over Everest.	First flight of Boeing 272, first modern monoplane airliner. First solo flight around the world.
1934	11 April: Caproni powered by Pegasus sets new altitude record. 14 May: diesel altitude record set by Phoenix in Wapiti.	Breguet's helicopter's first flight.
1935	BAC floated as a public company. 12 April: Britain First (Type 142)'s first flight. 23 June: Bombay's first flight.	Start of rearmament programme in UK.
1936	January: first run of Hercules. April: New Filton House opens. 25 June: Blenheim's first flight. 28 September: Type 138A sets altitude record. 30 October: first service flight of C Class Empire flying boat (Pegasus engines).	First helicopter flight of over an hour. Hindenburg disaster.

Farndon's picture of Blenheims in formation from the BAC 40th anniversary calendar (Bristol Aero Collection).

Year	BAC Event	Elsewhere
1937	Rotol set up to specialise in design and manufacture of airscrews. March: Blenheim enters service with RAF. 16 June: Start of Bermuda-New York service by Empire flying boat (Perseus engines). 30 June: Type 138A regains altitude record.	Bombing of Guernica during Spanish Civil War.
1938	2 August: Death of Frank Barnwell. 15 October: Beaufort's first flight. November: Vickers Wellesleys set world distance record with Pegasus engines.	First flight of pressurised transport aeroplane. Germany occupies Austria.
1939	17 July: Beaufighter's first flight. 5 August: first scheduled transatlantic mail service flight completed by Empire flying boat (Perseus engines). 4 September: Blenheims make first bombing raid on German fleet.	First turbojet flight. World War Two begins. BOAC formed. Air Transport Auxiliary formed.
1940	April: First Beaufighter prototypes delivered to RAF. 25 September: Major daylight bombing raid on BAC.	First successful flight by single-rotor helicopter. Start of British Strategic Air Offensive against Germany. Evacuation of Dunkirk. Battle of Britain.
1942	Over 52,000 employees on payroll. Roy Fedden leaves company. Bristol Aeroplane Company Welfare Association (BAWA) formed.	First jet combat aeroplane. First long-range missile.
1945	Helicopter division formed. 30 July: First tenant moves into BAC-built pre-fabricated bungalow at Shirehampton. 2 December: Freighter's first flight.	VE Day. Atomic bomb dropped. VJ Day.
1946	Car division begins production.	Pan-Am starts scheduled New York-London service.
1947	British Messier set up as subsidiary. Bill Pegg joins company. 27 July: Sycamore helicopter's first flight.	International Civil Aviation Organisation established.
1948	Bristol Theseus becomes world's first turboprop engine to pass type test. Stanley Hooker joins company. Lockleaze pre-fab school erected. 14 July: Silver City begins first car ferry service using Freighter.	Berlin airlift.
1949	Guided Weapons Department formed. 4 September: Brabazon's first flight.	Maiden flight of Comet. NATO formed.
1950	7 February: 26 Bristol aluminium schools sent to Australia. May: Prototype Olympus has first run.	Korean War begins.
1951	19 July: first successful flight of Bloodhound missile.	First direct unrefuelled crossing of the Atlantic by jet.

Year	BAC Event	Elsewhere
1952	3 January: Type 173 twin-engined, twin-rotored helicopter's first flight. 16 August: Britannia's first flight.	First all-cargo air service across the North Atlantic.
1953	4 May: Altitude record set in English Electric Canberra (Olympus engines).	First woman to fly faster than the speed of sound. Korean War ends.
1955	Apprentices' school opens. January: First run of Proteus 755. 29 August: Altitude record set in Canberra (Olympus engines). 30 December: Britannia formally handed over to BOAC.	Helicopter lands on summit of Mont Blanc. London Heathrow Airport Central becomes operational.
1956	1 January: Bristol Aero Engines Ltd, Bristol Cars Ltd and Bristol Aircraft Ltd formed from BAC's main divisions.	Suez crisis.
1957	August: Britannia makes first non-stop Atlantic crossing and first US coast-to-coast flights by turboprop airliner. 6 November: Downend crash.	Sputnik 1 put into orbit. The dog Laika launched in Sputnik 2.
1959	1 January: Bristol Aero Engines Ltd and Armstrong Siddeley Motors Ltd form Bristol Siddeley Engines Ltd (in effect from 1 April). 2 September: First run of Bristol Siddeley BS53 Pegasus, the first vectored thrust Vertical Take-Off and Landing engine.	Astronaut capsule for NASA's Mercury programme tested.
1960	June: Bristol Aircraft Ltd joins Vickers-Armstrong and English Electric to form British Aircraft Corporation. 21 October: first tethered hover of Pegasus.	Sputnik 5 makes 18 Earth orbits.
1961	Bristol Siddeley absorbs Blackburn and de Havilland engine companies. September: first Pegasus transition from vertical take-off to flight to vertical landing (P1127).	The first non-stop flight between UK and Australia. First man in space.
1962	14 April: Type 188's first flight. 26 April: launch of Ariel 1 satellite. 29 November: BAC and Sud Aviation sign agreement for Concorde project. 2 December: Vulcan runway fire.	First US astronaut orbits Earth. Telstar launched. Cuban Missile Crisis.

Year	BAC Event	Elsewhere
1964	January: death of Sir Stanley White. 27 March: launch of Ariel 2. 1 May: Type 221 first flight. 17 July: World land speed record broken by Bluebird CN7 car (Proteus engine). 27 September: TSR2's first flight.	First female solo flight around the world.
1966	Bristol Siddeley merges with Rolls-Royce.	First man-made vehicle soft lands on Moon's surface.
1967	First launch of Sea Wolf guided missile. Space work transferred from Stevenage. 4 January: Donald Campbell killed in attempt at breaking water speed record in hydroplane Bluebird K7 (Orpheus engine).	Boeing awarded contract for design of a US Super Sonic Transport. Apollo I capsule destroyed on launch pad by fatal fire.
1969	9 April: Concorde's first Filton flight. 18 April: First Harrier delivered to RAF (Pegasus engines); enters service in May. 5 May: Harrier wins *Daily Mail* London to New York Air Race.	First man sets foot on Moon.
1971	US Marine Corps AV-8A Harrier enters service. Rapier ground-to-air missile system enters service. 4 February: Rolls-Royce goes into receivership before being nationalised as Rolls-Royce (1971) Ltd. September: RB199 first run. 28 October: launch of Prospero. 11 December: launch of Ariel 4.	Apollo 14 and 15 Moon landings.
1974	4 August: RB199 first flight in Tornado.	Maiden flight of 'Gerald Heineken', the world's largest hot air balloon.
1976	21 January: Concorde enters service.	Salyut space station launched.
1977	29 April: British Aircraft Corporation nationalised and becomes part of British Aerospace, trading as such the following year.	Trial of Freddie Laker's Skytrain service to New York.
1978	Sea Harrier enters service with Royal Navy. August: 100,000th Concorde passenger carried by British Airways.	UK government announces it has acquired a 20 per cent interest in the Airbus Industrie's A310.
1979	Concorde 216 completed (the last Filton Concorde). Sea Wolf ship-borne anti-aircraft and anti-missile system introduced into Royal Navy.	Soviet invasion of Afghanistan.
1981	British Aerospace formed as public limited company (plc).	Space shuttle Columbia launched for its first mission.

Year	BAC Event	Elsewhere
1982	Sea Harriers shoot down 21 Argentine jets without combat loss in Falklands War. June: RB199 operational with RAF.	First Airbus A310 completed.
1985	July: Giotto launched.	First launch of space shuttle Atlantis.
1986	30 April: first Filton-built wings for the Airbus consortium's A320 despatched. 11 August: Westland Lynx with two Rolls-Royce Gem60 engines sets world's helicopter speed record at 400.87kph (Gems built at Patchway since 1992).	Space shuttle Challenger explodes 75 seconds after take-off.
1987	Rolls-Royce privatised.	British Airports Authority privatised.
1989	14 August: Harrier with Pegasus 11-61 engine sets time-to-height records.	Space shuttle Atlantis launches Jupiter probe.
1993	Rolls-Royce Leavesden closes and UK helicopter engine business moves to Patchway.	First B2 Stealth bomber is delivered to the USAF.
1997	December: last Pegasus built.	New balloon distance record set by Steve Fossett.
1998	ASRAAM (Airborne Short Range Anti Aircraft Missile) delivered to RAF.	RAF relinquishes nuclear role.
1999	Rolls-Royce Defence Aerospace established at Filton. January: British Aerospace merged with GEC's Marconi Electronic Systems business. November: BAE Systems formed.	Rolls-Royce acquires Vickers plc for its marine businesses. NATO embark on systematic bombing campaign against Serbian forces in Kosovo.
2001	July: Partners in Airbus Industrie form Airbus SAS (BAE Systems holds 20 per cent). 7 November: Concorde resumes transatlantic service after Paris crash.	Hijacked aircraft crashed into the World Trade Centre and Pentagon. War on Terror begins in Afghanistan. Space station Mir ends its 15-year mission.
2003	26 November: Concorde 216's final flight.	Launch of Second Gulf War. Space shuttle Columbia disintegrates. Centenary of Wright brothers' flight.
2005	April: Airbus A380's first flight.	First non-stop solo flight around world.
2006	September: BAE sells its 20 per cent stake in Airbus leaving it wholly owned by EADS.	Space shuttle Discovery conducts two-week mission to International Space station.
2008	GKN buys Airbus' Filton wing-making facility.	Centenary of British flight.
2010	Centenary of BAC.	

'Meeting d'Aviation Nice',
France, 1910 (Science and
Society Picture Library/Science
Museum Pictorial).

Section 1:
The Pioneers

The BAC story began on 19 February 1910 when transport entrepreneur Sir George White formally entered the aviation business by registering the names of four new companies: Bristol Aeroplane Company Limited, British & Colonial Aeroplane Company Limited, Bristol Aviation Company Limited and British & Colonial Aviation Company Limited. Behind that historic moment lay centuries of dreams and experimentation which had reached a tentative fruition less than seven years previously with the Wright brothers' flight at Kitty Hawk.

Portrait of Sir George White, 1905 (Airbus).

One of the world's oldest stories is the legend of Icarus and his fatal attempt to escape the island of Crete using wings of wax and feathers made by his father, Daedalus. The moral of Icarus' fall was that humans were overreaching themselves in their attempts to fly because the gods had destined that they should be earth-bound. However, the desire to emulate the birds would not go away and many, mainly fanciful, attempts continued to be made.

Among the most popular methods was climbing to the top of a tower or other high place, strapping on a pair of artificial wings, jumping off and frantically flapping, hoping for flight before hitting the ground. There were two flaws in this. First, humans do not have enough strength to support their weight in flight – unlike birds, which have the perfect combination of a light skeleton and powerful musculature in their chest with which to beat their wings. Secondly, birds do not flap their wings straight up and down as they fly, as those early imitators thought. They reach forward to grasp the air with each downward stroke to achieve thrust. They also position their wings to harness aerodynamic forces that provide them with lift and the ability to soar and glide.

The turning-point in endeavours to achieve human flight came in the fifteenth century with the application of scientific reasoning. Maurice Davy of the Science Museum said: 'The realization that flight was a physical phenomenon and not a manifestation of the supernatural was the beginning of a long period of speculation as to the means whereby it could be achieved.'[1] The inventor, artist and scientist Leonardo da Vinci's treatise on flight (c 1505) was based on 'the fundamental idea... that human flight was possible by the mechanical imitation of nature...'.[2] Unlike most of his predecessors, da Vinci made a close study of the flight of birds before seeking to design his own artificial wings and flying machines. He realised the importance of establishing a centre of gravity before attempting movement, the significance of the curvature of a bird's wings, and the need to research the properties of the air and its currents. Like many, he was perhaps distracted by the notion that flapping wings were the key and he made drawings of flapping-wing machines called ornithopters, but he also drew what are thought to be the first pictures of parachutes and helicopters. With access to the appropriate materials and equipment, some of his theoretical designs might have worked in practice.[3]

Initially, more success lay in lighter-than-air flight with large kites and hot-air, gas and hydrogen balloons. The first aeronauts were a cockerel, a sheep and a duck which were launched in a Montgolfier brothers' balloon on 19 September 1783 from the gardens of the royal palace of Versailles. The first humans to make a flight were Jean-François Pilâtre de Rozier and the Marquis d'Arlandes, who flew across Paris in a Montgolfier balloon on 21 November that same year. The first balloon ascent in Britain took place on 15 September 1784 and was made by the flamboyant Vincenzo Lunardi, the Daredevil Aeronaut, who was secretary to the Neapolitan ambassador to the Court of St James. Unlike the Montgolfier brothers, who had started their extensive research by conducting experiments with paper bags held over open fires, Lunardi had little scientific knowledge. He thought adding rowing oars and flapping wings to the basket of his balloon would enable him to maintain his flight should the wind drop or his envelope deflate. Nevertheless, he was a sensation, making several ascents around the country until falling from public favour when a bystander was killed at an exhibition he held in Newcastle-upon-Tyne on 27 August 1786.

Both kites and balloons lacked thrust, meaning that they were largely dependent on air currents to move and that their pilots had limited means of controlling direction. Gliders also lacked thrust, but Otto Lilienthal's experiments in the late nineteenth century did have the advantage of developing the use of manual controls. He made the first piloted, controlled flight in 1891, travelling a distance of ten metres in his glider. The airships of the late nineteenth century possessed both propellers to provide thrust and rudders to provide control, and they continued to be used alongside aeroplanes for passenger travel until at least the 1930s.[4] All these precursors to the aeroplane contributed to the gradual accumulation of knowledge over centuries and were part of the risk-taking and trials that eventually led to heavier-than-air flight – the transport revolution Sir George White wanted to develop further.

In setting up his business in the West of England in 1910, White provided the latest stage in over a thousand years of aviation history based in and around the Bristol area. The pioneers who preceded him were a fascinating collection of eccentrics, one-offs and genuine innovators. Among these were King Bladud, legendary founder of Bath, who was said to have learnt to fly using feathered wings as part of his exploration of magic. Eilmer,

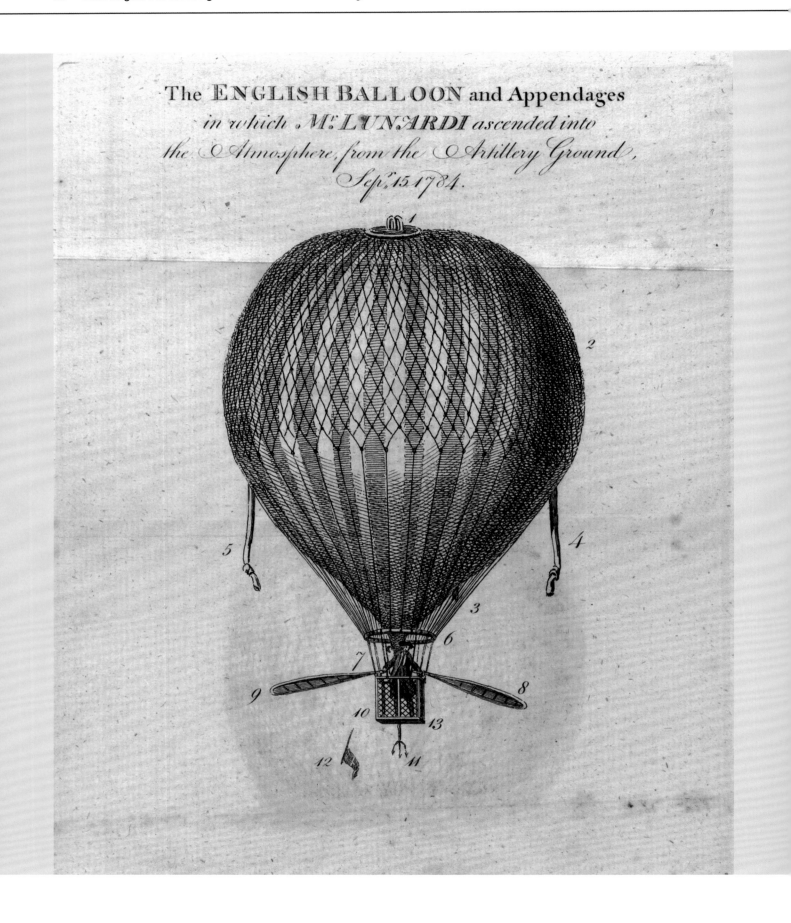

The ENGLISH BALLOON and Appendages *in which* Mr. *LUNARDI* *ascended into the Atmosphere, from the Artillery Ground, Sepr. 15 1784.*

Illustration from Vincenzo Lunardi's *First Aerial Voyage in England*, 1784 (University of Bristol Library, Special Collections).

an eleventh-century monk at Malmesbury in Wiltshire, made a partly successful glide from the abbey tower using wings that were probably made from Somerset willow covered in ecclesiastical cloth. His subsequent crash landing was attributed to the absence of a tail. The experiments with kite-power of Bristol's George Pocock, schoolteacher and evangelist, included the kite-drawn carriage, the charvolant. The vehicle could carry six people and travel at 25 miles an hour. In addition, Pocock toured the islands of the Bristol Channel by kite-propelled boat and lofted his daughter from the bottom of the Avon Gorge to the Bristol Downs in a wicker chair suspended from a kite. The gorge was also the scene of Courtney's great Flying Leap in 1826. Billing himself as The Great Funambulist, Courtney slid down a wire from the top of the Clifton cliffs to the river on the other side of the gorge, giving the illusion to the crowds below that he was airborne. Another quirky character was the mysterious Steeple-Jack who, in the 1860s, stopped by in Bristol and used kites to reach the tops of smoking factory furnaces so that he could repoint them.[5]

More influential in the development of the aeroplane were William Henson and John Stringfellow, who were based in Chard in Somerset. They were inspired by the work of the aeronautical thinker Sir George Cayley, sometimes referred to as the Father of British Aeronautics, whose brief trials with a manned glider had proven that artificial flight was at least *theoretically* possible. Davy describes Cayley as 'the first man of science to apply his mind fully to the problem of mechanical flight and to attempt to explain mathematically its fundamental principles'.[6]

Henson and Stringfellow were both manufacturers involved in the local lace trade. They shared an interest in powered, fixed-wing flight and discussed ideas on how this might be achieved. On 29 September 1842 Henson was granted provisional protection for his patent for an Aerial Steam Carriage, a passenger-carrying, steam-powered flying machine. The completed specification was filed on 28 March 1843, by which time Henson had moved from Chard to London.[7] While D E Colombine, an attorney and a partner in the venture, tried to raise funds to form a company to exploit the patent, Stringfellow suggested he and Henson build a model version at their own expense. Stringfellow had previously been promised the work of building the full-scale machine once funding was secured and had grown impatient with the wait. The extent of Stringfellow's involvement in the original patent is unclear, but it is generally accepted that he had at least improved the design, particularly with regard to its engine.

Henson and Stringfellow conducted their experiments between 1844 and 1847 with limited success; they never managed to get their model to make a sustained flight. When their model was exhibited at the Science Museum in 1907, Henson was credited as the inventor of the aeroplane, as it was now known, with the date of his achievement given as 1842. The model had propellers, fixed wings, rudders, elevators and a wire-braced structure. The wing span was about seven metres (20 feet), but it was intended that the span of the final version would be nearly 46 metres (150 feet), with a laden weight of around 1,360kg (3,000lbs). Save for the absence of a facility for maintaining lateral stability (for example, wing warping, ailerons or flaps), the model was, according to Davy, 'in all essentials... the counterpart of the modern aeroplane'.[8]

Henson abandoned the work for good and in 1848 emigrated to the US, where he later tried his hand at airship design. That same year, Stringfellow, who had continued his research alone, gave his own steam-powered model its first trial flight at Chard, covering a distance of about 12 metres (40 feet). With further improvements, the model was able to fly over 36 metres (120 feet) at trials at Cremorne Gardens in London. The model was able to climb under its own power once it had detached itself from its launch wire, leading to claims that this was 'the first power-driven self-supported flight in world history'.[9]

In January 1866 the Aeronautical Society of Great Britain was founded, marking 'the beginning of the systematic record of aeronautical study and achievement in this country'.[10] Francis Herbert Wenham, a marine engineer who had worked in Bristol with Isambard Kingdom Brunel, delivered his paper 'Aerial Locomotion' at the society's first meeting on 27 June that year. In the paper, which he had written seven years earlier, Wenham explained why a long, narrow wing was the best type for providing lift and how the lift would be increased if the wings were superimposed – set one above the

Depiction of Courtney's Flying Leap, 1826 (left) (Special Collections, Bristol Central Library).

'Charvolants travelling in various directions with the same wind' from George Pocock's *The Aeropleustic Art, or Navigation in the Air by the use of Kites or Buoyant Sails*, 1827 (above) (Special Collections, Bristol Central Library).

other. Wenham's work inspired Stringfellow to resume his own experiments for the first time since 1848 (in the meantime he had been involved in other ventures, including photography). Stringfellow built a working model demonstrating Wenham's principle of superimposed planes for the UK's first Aeronautical Exhibition, held in June 1868 at the Crystal Palace. He also exhibited a steam engine which won the Aeronautical Society's £100 prize for the lightest engine in proportion to its power from any source.

Stringfellow's problem, according to his biographer Ronald Birse, was that 'his model aeroplanes suffered from the twin disadvantages of being too large to be fully tested indoors, and not stable enough to be tested out of doors'.[11] Although unable to demonstrate a free flight because of the lack of space, witnesses at the exhibition reported that the wire along which his propeller-driven triplane travelled was seen to rise, suggesting the possibility that the model would be able to gain height under its own power in the right conditions.

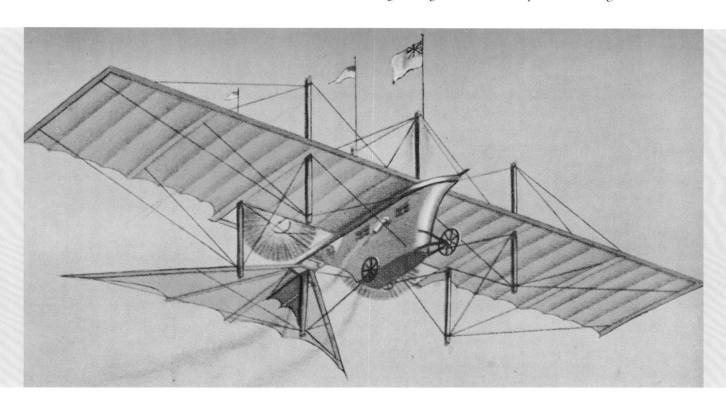

Artist's impression of Henson's Aerial Steam Carriage reproduced in M J B Davy's *Henson and Stringfellow*, 1931.

Stringfellow used his prize money to build a dedicated workshop where he could continue his experiments, but failing eyesight curtailed his plans. He died on 13 December 1883.

The Henson-Stringfellow model was purchased for the nation and donated to the Science Museum by another West of England figure prominent in early aviation. This was the well-connected Patrick Alexander, a philanthropic aeronaut from Bath, described by one commentator as a 'zestful dilettante'.[12] Alexander met most of the key aeronautical experimenters around the turn of the century. These included Lilienthal; Wenham; Hiram Maxim, who funded his research with his popular amusement ride, The Captive Flying Machine; Percy Pilcher, the Bath-born disciple of Lilienthal; Octave Chanute, the great aeronautical communicator and confidant of the Wright brothers, who Alexander also met; Alexander Graham Bell, who constructed enormous tetrahedral kites and who also sponsored the first flight in Canada; and Samuel Pierpont Langley, Secretary of Washington's Smithsonian Institution and designer of the steam-powered Aerodrome, which failed to fly in 1903. Alexander also witnessed the first flight of a Zeppelin airship in 1900. He became a member and patron of aeronautical clubs and societies, and poured his inherited wealth into visiting aviation experts. He spread knowledge of their achievements around the world, having, at that time, the leisure and money to indulge his passion.

In September 1902 Alexander organised a gathering in Bath to celebrate the centenary of the first balloon ascent from the city. His guests included some of the country's leading aeronauts, among them Major Baden Baden-Powell, President of the Aeronautical Society; showman, pilot and designer Samuel Cody; and Charles Rolls, motor car promoter and aviator. He showed the group his experimental workshop at Batheaston where he was developing propeller-driven gas balloons and a wireless telegraphy system, among other inventions. They also saw a demonstration of Cody's war kites at Bannerdown. In 1909 Alexander provided a £1,000 prize for the development of a lightweight engine suitable for aviation. The prize was to be awarded by the Aerial League of the British Empire, of which he was a founding member. It was won by the Green engine, manufactured by Aster Engineering Ltd. This was used by Cody when he won the Michelin Cup Trophy in December 1910.

During World War One, Alexander volunteered to promote the military value of aviation on both sides of the Atlantic, and was appointed to the Meteorological Office at Falmouth by the Air Ministry. However, by the war's end, with his inheritance exhausted and his ideas overtaken by the developments in flight achieved by others, Alexander was no longer a man of influence. He ended his days as a teacher of aeronautical engineering at the Imperial Service College, Windsor, of which he had been a benefactor. He died in poverty and his name was soon forgotten outside a small, specialist circle. He does, however, retain a physical link to modern aviation as his original experimental workshop at Combe Down is now part of the site of Cross Manufacturing, specialists in seals used worldwide by the aerospace industry. The company was founded by Roland Cross, a former employee of the British & Colonial Aeroplane Company, who knew Alexander as a child.

A mix-up over a telegram sent to his New York hotel meant Alexander missed the opportunity to witness the Wright brothers' success at Kill Devil Hills near Kitty Hawk on 17 December 1903. They achieved the world's first sustained, powered and controlled heavier-than-air level flight. It seems obvious today that this was a major advance, marking the

Photographs of Stringfellow's 1848 and 1868 models reproduced in M J B Davy's *Henson and Stringfellow*, 1931.

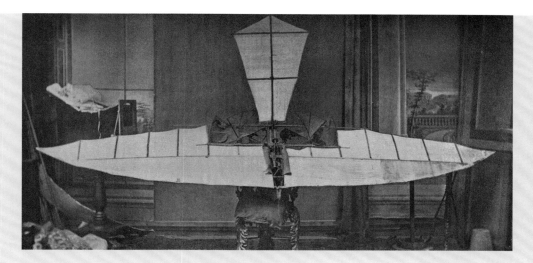

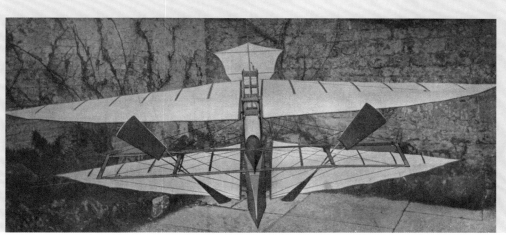

beginning of modern aviation. However, it took some time for the significance of the event to be appreciated by more than a select few and, in the absence of reporters and a large crowd of witnesses, for sceptics to believe that it had even happened. European designers were certainly slow to pick up on what the Wrights had accomplished, and continued with their own independent experiments. It was only when Wilbur Wright came to Hunaudières in France in 1908 to give public displays of controlled flight that the brothers' influence began to spread.

Henri Farman, an Englishman who adopted French nationality, was the first successful European pilot, setting a new official distance record of 771 metres (2,530 feet) in a Voisin-Farman I on 26 October 1907. On 13 January 1908 he flew the first officially recorded European circular flight of 1km, winning a 50,000 franc prize. The UK was lagging behind France at this stage in the development of aviation. Cody, an American who had originally come to the UK with his touring Wild West music-hall show, made the first powered flight in Britain on 16 October 1908, travelling 424 metres (nearly 1,400 feet) at Farnborough. He flew in British Army Aeroplane No 1, a biplane of his own design.[13]

The first accredited flight by a *British* pilot in Britain was by John Theodore Cuthbert Moore-Brabazon in his Voisin biplane at the Isle of Sheppey on 30 April 1909. To put the difference between British and French achievements at this period into perspective, on 23 July 1909 Edwin Alliott Verdon Roe accomplished a straight-line flight at Lea Marshes of about 274 metres (900 feet) in his self-built triplane, making him the first Briton to fly in Britain in a British-designed aircraft (his manufacturing company A V Roe & Co was founded in January 1910). Two days later, on 25 July 1909, Frenchman Louis Blériot made the first flight across the Channel in his Blériot Type XI monoplane, winning the prize of £1,000 that had been offered by the *Daily Mail*. However, after a slow start, by the time war broke out in 1914, Europe was starting to match the Americans and the British were starting to match the French.

Sir George White is thought to have first read of the Wrights' exploits in 1904. This was not an immediate *Eureka*! moment but the start of a gradual, carefully considered development of an interest in flight as a business proposition. Although an expert in commercial transport, White was not an engineer or scientist and, despite his interest in aviation, he never learned to fly. The key to his success was that he recognised the value of patience and the need to undertake thorough research, consulting suitably qualified experts, before embarking on a new enterprise. At the Annual General Meeting of the shareholders of the Bristol Tramways & Carriage Company on 16 February 1910, three days before registering his aircraft businesses, he finally felt able to announce his investment in aviation. Harry Harper, former aviation correspondent for the *Daily Mail*, who had met White, recalled in 1952:

Patrick Alexander and his guests, including Charles Rolls and Samuel Cody, take a tour of his Batheaston workshop, 1902 (facing page, left) (private collection).

Wilbur Wright, c 1903 (facing page, right) (Rolls-Royce plc). Sir George White and his wife travelled to Pau in France to see him fly in early 1909.

Samuel Cody at the controls of his Aeroplane No 1 in the Farnborough flight shed, 1908 (right) (Science and Society Picture Library/Science Museum).

Sir George had reduced the problem to a factual basis, as was his habit. Land and sea transport, he reminded me, was already near a limit of economic speed. But speed in the air promised to be another proposition altogether; the possibilities it offered made the future of flying almost illimitable, as far as he could see. And then there was the immense and more immediate scope in military and naval operations.[14]

Having registered four company names, White chose to operate initially as the British & Colonial Aeroplane Company. According to company chronicler C H Barnes, this was to avoid 'premature adoption of the name "Bristol"... [which] might well prejudice a later application for its registration as a trade mark'.[15] Most of the £25,000 private capital had been raised by the founding directors: £10,000 each from White himself and his younger brother, Samuel, and £2,500 from his son, (George) Stanley. The remainder came from his nephews, Henry White Smith (Secretary) and Sydney Ernest Smith (Manager), sons of his sister Georgina. The company's head office was at Clare Street House, Bristol, which was also home to some of White's other business interests: George White & Co, Stockbrokers, the Western Wagon & Property Company Limited, Bristol Tramways & Carriage Company Limited and Imperial Tramways Company Limited. The manufacturing workshop was based in two sheds leased from Bristol Tramways at its Filton depot. Filton, then a small rural community in the county of Gloucestershire, was the company's northern terminus and the shed had previously served as a building and maintenance depot for motor buses. British & Colonial later acquired Filton House for its general offices.

White's company represented a major shift in aviation. Other pioneering companies of this period had been set up by 'engineers or enthusiasts who were still engaged in developing and testing experimental models... Few of them... shared White's ambition of building aeroplanes on a commercial scale, and none of them could rival his business acumen or contacts'.[16] Few others also had access to the level of private investment White and his family were prepared to put in. British & Colonial started out on a financial footing 'which must have made the mouths of struggling pioneers like A V Roe and the Short Brothers water'.[17] The capital value was doubled at the beginning of 1911 and again at the end of the year because of increasing demand for the company's aircraft. By February 1913 the share capital had risen to £250,000 to cover further expansion of the Filton site.

White initially intended to build existing aircraft under licence rather than develop new designs. He was interested in the work of the Société Zodiac in France, and Sydney Ernest Smith and Herbert Thomas (another nephew who was shortly to become Works Manager) were sent out to meet the company directors. It was agreed that a Zodiac biplane, designed by Gabriel Voisin, would be shown on the British & Colonial stand at the Olympia Aero Show in March (a Zodiac monoplane was also to be displayed, but it was never delivered). The main sections of the biplane arrived at Filton, where they were checked over by newly appointed Engineer and Works Manager George H Challenger and his assistant Collyns Pizey, both former employees of Bristol Tramways.

An agreement was drawn up by Émile Stern, the company's Paris agent, for British & Colonial to assemble six of the biplanes under licence, including the one already sent over, and the Zodiac trademark was added to the company letterhead. After Olympia, the Zodiac was sent to Brooklands airfield in Surrey, where the company was leasing a shed for test flights. It was assembled and an engine fitted before it made its first short, demoralising hop on 28 May 1910, the test pilot declaring it to be underpowered and unimpressive. The five additional Zodiacs already under construction at Filton were scrapped and British & Colonial sued for compensation. The company hastily dropped the Zodiac trademark and adopted instead the famous Bristol scroll, which soon came to be 'universally recognized as a label of excellence'.[18]

This brief set back was possibly caused by White and his colleagues being taken in by the high-quality finish of the Zodiac products, failing to appreciate that their performance had already been surpassed by others. It was suggested that British & Colonial adapt a design from the Farman brothers' company instead and this provided the basis for the first Bristol biplane, commonly known as the Bristol Boxkite. White had seen Farman biplanes at the Rheims international airshow in August 1909. In his adaptation of the aircraft, Challenger combined the Farman's basic structure with some of the more refined and stylish Zodiac-type fittings. It is likely that the Farmans were annoyed by the infringement of their copyright – and

Sheds at the main entrance to the British & Colonial on Homestead Road, Filton, 1910 (above left) (Airbus).

Zodiac at Olympia, 1910 (above right) (Bristol Aero Collection).

there was a short-lived proposal to sue British & Colonial – but they were generally happy with the publicity generated and, according to Barnes, remained friendly with the company.[19]

Despite cold and windy weather, a brief but spectacular demonstration flight was given on Durdham Downs on 14 November 1910, the first time the Boxkite had been seen by the Bristol public. In an official statement issued to the *Evening Times* and *Echo* ahead of the display, White and Herbert Ashman (Vice President of the West of England Aero Club) wrote: 'We feel sure that the spectators will be... willing to do everything in their power individually, by the exercise of patience, restraint and good order, to ensure the success of this novel entertainment for Bristolians.'[20] By this stage, two aircraft a week were being produced at Filton and 16 had been completed by the end of the year.

1910 was a significant year for flight, and not just in Bristol: developments in the capabilities of aircraft were advancing swiftly. The first floatplane was designed and flown in France by Henri Fabre on 28 March and the first aeroplane took off from the deck of a ship on 14 November, marking the beginning of the aircraft carrier. The first aeroplane with two engines instead of one was being tested, and Henri Coanda, a name later associated with British & Colonial, built the first full-size, jet-propelled aircraft.

More and more people were learning to fly, though it remained largely the preserve of wealthy amateurs, professional engineers and those associated with the military. Moore-Brabazon became the first person to attain a Royal Aero Club certificate, qualifying on 8 March 1910. The second certificate was awarded to Charles Rolls, who made the first double crossing of the English Channel on 2 June. Five weeks later, on 12 July, he became the first Briton to be killed in an aeroplane crash when his biplane collapsed mid-flight at the Bournemouth airshow. The Baroness de Laroche became the world's first qualified female pilot on 8 March and Edith Maud Cook became the first British woman to fly solo. Cook died at a display in June when she attempted to jump out of a balloon using a parachute.

Bristol scroll.

The Milan Aviation Meeting, Italy,
1910 (Science and Society Picture
Library/Science Museum Pictorial).

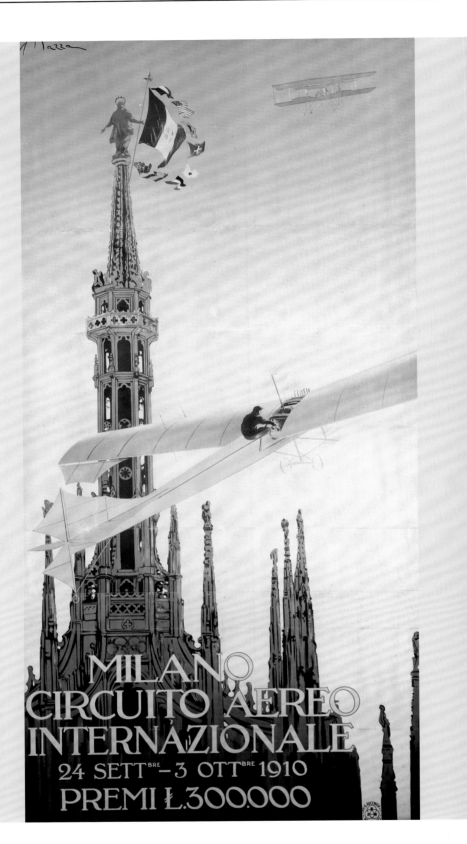

Watercolour showing the final form of the Short Brothers aircraft as flown by John Moore-Brabazon on 25 March 1910 (Science and Society Picture Library/Science Museum Pictorial).

Colour lithograph by Marguerite Montaut showing Louis Paulhan's Farman biplane flying above railway tracks on 27-28 April 1910, on his way to becoming the first aviator to fly from London to Manchester (Science and Society Picture Library/Science Museum Pictorial).

1910 fashion advertisement
(© Victoria & Albert Museum,
London, donated by H L Sparks, Esq).

Claude Grahame-White made the first night flight in Europe on 28 April 1910 during a
Daily Mail-sponsored challenge to be the first pilot to fly from London to Manchester. He
was using a Farman biplane, as was French pilot Louis Paulhan who went on to win the
race and the £10,000 prize. World records set that year included Maurice Tabuteau's non-
stop distance flight of 586km (363 miles) and Georges Legagneux reaching the altitude of
3,100 metres (over 10,000 feet). Léon Morane became the first person to fly at more than
100km an hour (around 66 miles per hour). Georges Chavez from Peru made the first
flight over the Swiss Alps, but unfortunately his triumph was short-lived as he was fatally
injured when his Blériot monoplane crashed on landing. On 2 October at Milan the first
mid-air collision occurred between two aeroplanes. One of the pilots involved was Bertram
Dickson, who was associated with British & Colonial. He flew one of the Boxkites that
took part in the Autumn Manoeuvres of 1910 and joined the company in January 1911 as
a technical adviser and the representative for London and the Continent.

Outside of aviation, 1910 marked the final years of La Belle Époque, Europe's golden age
of political stability, scientific advancement and the flowering of modernist arts. It was also
the end of the Edwardian period in the UK with the death on 6 May of King Edward VII,

Aerial views of Filton, 1916
(Bristol Aero Collection).

who was succeeded by his son, George V. Halley's Comet re-entered the inner solar system
for the first time since 1835. The Girl Guide movement was started by Lady Baden-
Powell, while suffragettes continued to fight for the right to vote. The luxurious ocean liner
Olympic was launched in Belfast by the White Star Line. Marie Curie published her work
on radioactivity. Florence Nightingale died at the age of 90. A revolution began in Mexico.
Mount Etna erupted. Some of Britain's first cinemas were opened and a little-known
London comic called Charlie Chaplin left England to seek his fortune in America. Average
life expectancy in the UK was 54 for women and 50 for men, and the 1911 census recorded
a total population of around 37 million people, compared with the 60 million of 2010.

Within a year of its founding, British & Colonial at Filton had become the world's biggest
aircraft factory, expanding steadily until the major surge in production necessitated by
World War One. The payroll rose from around 80 in 1911, to 200 in 1914, to over 3,000
by 1918. With some of its leading designers and pilots leaving for wartime appointments
with the Admiralty, Royal Flying Corps and Royal Naval Air Service, and many skilled
workers enlisting, it was sometimes difficult for the remaining workforce to keep up with
government demand. These large contracts covered the manufacture of BE2s, designed
by the Royal Aircraft Factory at Farnborough, and, later, Bristol-designed aircraft. A
bonus scheme introduced in June 1915 helped with both the recruitment and retention
of workers, and in August 1916 aviation was recognised as an essential wartime industry
which meant that part of the labour force could be excused conscription.

Alcock and Brown's biplane used on their transatlantic crossing is on display in the Science Museum in London (Science and Society Picture Library/Science Museum).

After the war, British & Colonial was able to retain much of its profit by going into voluntary liquidation and transferring its assets to the previously inactive Bristol Aeroplane Company (BAC) – a discontinued business that transferred its assets to a new trading company paid less in Excess Profits Duty. Having long insisted that its aircraft always be referred to with the 'Bristol' prefix, on 9 February 1920 the company entered the next phase of its story by adopting new Articles of Association under the name of BAC. BAC's share capital was increased from £100 to £1,000,000, of which £553,000 was secured by the British & Colonial assets.

In aviation generally, the war had brought the rapid development of aircraft design and manufacture. Once peace had been restored, there was the chance to seek many new opportunities. In April 1913 the *Daily Mail* had announced a transatlantic race, with a prize of £10,000 to be awarded to the first to make a direct crossing. The challenge was suspended during the war but taken up again soon after the Armistice. In May 1919 a Curtiss flying boat captained by the American pilot Albert Read became the first aircraft to cross the Atlantic. However, this was not a non-stop flight and was therefore ineligible for the prize. Read and his crew flew from Long Island, USA to Plymouth, England, breaking the journey down into several stages requiring over 57 hours of flying time. The transatlantic crossing was made from Newfoundland to Lisbon on 16 and 17 May via the Azores. The *Mail* prize was won a few weeks later when British aviators John Alcock and Arthur Brown flew a Vickers Vimy biplane direct from Newfoundland to Ireland on 14-15 June with a flight time of 16 hours and 27 minutes. The following month the Royal

Bus and car bodies under
construction at Filton, c 1920
(Peter Davey: Bristol Tram
Photograph Collection).

Air Force's R34 made the first direct transatlantic crossing by airship during a flight from
Scotland to New York. Another long-distance record set that year was the first flight from
Britain to Australia, which was completed on 10 December in a Vickers Vimy.

In its first decade, British & Colonial Aeroplane Company had successfully managed its
wartime expansion as well as the challenge of a downturn in business when the war ended.
By 1918 it had, according to Barnes, 'the best-equipped factory in the country, covering 8
acres of floor space, and had the pick of 3,000 operatives, including an exceptionally skilled
toolroom staff'.[21] After the war, not only was there little demand for new aircraft from
customers but there was also a stockpile of surplus military aircraft available. The Ministry
of Munitions formally terminated all existing contracts for Bristol Fighters on 26 November
1918. Later the Air Board agreed to accept most of those already in production and British
& Colonial was able to scrape by for a few years with this and other small contracts, mainly
for experimental aircraft. It was also able to keep a core body of staff employed during this
period because of Works Manager Herbert Thomas' success in diversifying production. He
sought out 'coach-building contracts from the motor-car industry, and eventually set up
a production line of bus and coach bodies for the Bristol Tramways Company and saloon
bodies for Armstrong Siddeley cars which lasted through the worst of the lean years'.[22] This
was an early example, repeated later at other slack periods, when other uses were found
for the company's skilled workforce, tools and machinery. Ten years after its founding, Sir
George White's company looked set for a stable and possibly spectacular future.

Sir George White

Sir George White was a businessman and stockbroker fascinated by the commercial possibilities of transport. Chairman of a number of transport-related businesses, he had the skill to work one company to the benefit of another, for example in his use of the resources of the Bristol Tramways & Carriage Company in the setting up of British & Colonial.

His many interests also meant he had wide-ranging professional and social dealings with Bristol's leading figures, providing him with the necessary connections to raise the capital or political support for his ventures. A self-made man, he had the personality and capabilities suited to an entrepreneurial environment. His biographers state:

> The cogency of his arguments, coupled with his personal charm, made him a popular and respected figure with opponents and employees as well as business associates... His driving ambition and boldness in experiment were ideally balanced by hard-headed realism and sound judgement. It is these qualities that mark him out as one of Bristol's most distinguished businessmen of modern times.[23]

Autochrome of Sir George and Lady White in a garden, possibly in France, c 1909 (detail) (Sir George White Bt).

White was the second son of painter and decorator Henry White and his wife Eliza (née Tippetts), a former domestic servant. He was born at the family home in Cotham on 28 March 1854 and attended St Michael's National School. He married Caroline Rosina Thomas on 14 June 1876 and they had two children, George Stanley (always referred to by his second name) and Daisy May. In addition to his business interests, White served as a Conservative councillor and was a JP. In 1906 he refused the offer of a safe Parliamentary seat in West Bristol as he had no interest in backbench life. His extensive charitable work included major fundraising initiatives for the Red Cross and the Bristol Royal Infirmary, and in 1904 he was made a baronet in recognition of his public service. He died suddenly at his home, Old Sneed Park in Stoke Bishop, on 22 November 1916. He was interred at St Mary's Church in the vault he had built for Caroline, who had died the previous year.[24]

White began his working life in 1869 when he left school to become a junior solicitor's clerk at the firm Stanley and Wasbrough. Shortly after his arrival, Stanley and Wasbrough became involved in tramways, which many saw as the solution to city congestion and a cheaper and more efficient alternative to horse-drawn omnibuses. To set up a tramway service over an economically viable area was a time-consuming business that involved obtaining local, county and parliamentary consent and the approval of the Board of Trade regarding standards and fares. The traditional narrow, winding British streets also created considerable problems for the laying out of track. The Tramways Act of 1870 simplified some of the administrative procedures, and Stanley and Wasbrough,

acting on behalf of a London syndicate, proposed setting up a service in Bristol. Their main rival for this scheme was Waring Brothers, an engineering firm, but Bristol Corporation (later Bristol Council), wary of public transport being in private hands, opposed both plans, choosing to build their own line, which ran from the city centre to the suburb of Redland. Completed in 1874, this was described as 'one of the shortest and least promising tramways in the country'.[25] Aware that the Corporation, having built the line, now required someone to operate it, Stanley and Wasbrough offered to lease it from them and also to add more routes to the service. The offer was accepted and the new Bristol Tramways Company was registered on 23 December 1874 with William Butler, a

Sir George White inspecting Boxkite prior to flight on the Downs, November 1910 (Bristol Aero Collection).

local tar distiller, as its first Chairman. As a result of his work on the proposals, the scheme's promoters recognised White's potential and appointed him Company Secretary on a part-time basis at £150 per annum. White saw that his future lay in business rather than the law and left the solicitors in 1875 to form George White & Co, Stockbrokers. He joined the Bristol Stock Exchange the following year but remained the tramway company's Secretary.

By the 1880s Bristol had 'an integrated, though not fully developed, tramway network', operating over seven routes including the original Redland one which had now been purchased from the Corporation.[26] White opposed the Corporation's ban on Sunday operation as he wanted people to have access to the Downs and other leisure facilities on their day off. He was defeated on that point – a rare failure as he usually won the argument when he emphasised the public benefit of a service. He also failed to get the tramway extended into Clifton as the residents did not want the 'nasty, low inhabitants of Bristol [coming] up into our sacred region'.[27] Because of these objections, Clifton continued to be served only by horse-drawn omnibuses.

Between 1886 and 1891 the number of passengers carried by White's network rose from 5.5 million per annum to 11.2 million. Despite the growth in business, tramways were becoming generally known for their 'dirty, crowded carriages and irregular service'.[28] As alternatives, other cities experimented with steam-powered trams, which ended up creating even more dirt and noise. Edinburgh introduced an electric cable system but this was considered unsuitable for Bristol. White consulted his friend James Clifton Robinson, a leading tramways expert, who reported to the company board in 1893 on the benefits of electric traction: larger carriages, improved speeds, faster turnarounds, the ability to cope with steep gradients, cleanliness and quiet. On his recommendation, work began on a new electrified line to Kingswood. This was completed in October 1895 at a cost of £49,981, making Bristol the first city in Britain to operate electric trams under Board of Trade regulations. The whole network had been electrified by 1900, with a new depot and tramcar building works built at Brislington, and passengers and profits doubled, justifying the initial high capital outlay.

White became a leading figure in other transport schemes including the proposed Bristol & London & South Western Junction Railway, which was submitted for Parliamentary approval in November 1882 as an alternative to the Great Western Railway's (GWR) Bristol to Paddington route. White was on the board of the Bristol & North Somerset Railway, whose tracks would be

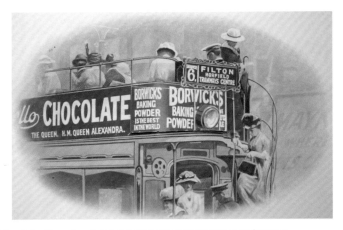

Illustrations from a brochure printed by Edward Everard c 1910 for Bristol Tramways' Advertising Department showing different advertising rates on the trams (Special Collections, Bristol Central Library). The company boasted the advertisements would be seen by 400,000 prospective customers. Rates ran from four shillings a week for a side panel to 3d a week for a door plate. Everard was Sir George White's brother-in-law.

VICTORIA ROOMS.

Illustration from the *Official Handbook of Bristol Tramways* showing a horse-drawn omnibus and electric tram at the Victoria Rooms, Bristol, c 1905 (Bristol Record Office).

used for the section of the proposed route that would run from Bristol to Radstock. The proposal was supported by local businesses and the Corporation (a rarity for the two groups to be in agreement). However, the GWR lobby was too strong and the bill was defeated, with the promoters agreeing not to propose a rival route for another ten years. Despite this disappointment, White's involvement in the project enhanced his reputation in the local community and his connections with civic and commercial leaders.[29]

In 1886 White set up the Bristol Cab Company to operate horse-drawn cabs from Bristol Temple Meads station. The following year the business was merged with Bristol Tramways to form the Bristol Tramways & Carriage Company. Although lacking the official title until 1894, White acted from the outset as the company's Managing Director and in 1900 became its Chairman. By 1914 the company was operating 17 tramway services, 15 omnibus services and a fleet of tramcars, motor buses, charabancs, taxis, vans, lorries and commercial vehicles. It had depots at Bath, Cheltenham, Gloucester and Weston-super-Mare in addition to Bristol and Filton. Rather than distributing the increased profits to shareholders, a substantial reserve was built up to fund the ongoing maintenance of the extensive system.

White's company was also manufacturing road vehicles by this time. Originally, motor buses had been purchased for the company's use from Thorneycrofts, Fiat and Berliet, but

they struggled with the Bristol hills and White decided it would be preferable for Bristol Tramways to build its own. The first completely Bristol-built bus went into service on 12 May 1908. It was the Bristol C40, which was used on the No 18 route to Clifton. In 1912 another building was acquired in Brislington and became the Motor Constructional Works (later Bristol Commercial Vehicles Limited) where taxis and lorries were also built (White had introduced Britain's first motor taxi service in 1908).

A series of long-running disputes between the Corporation and Bristol Tramways began to come to a head in the late 1890s. The concerns about the network being in private hands resurfaced during a period when other cities were opting for municipal control. Under the terms of the 1870 Act, the Corporation 'were empowered to purchase privately owned undertakings after 21 years, or subsequently at seven year intervals'.[30] As the business

became profitable, this became increasingly attractive. A Tramways Purchase Committee was set up in January 1897, but White was in a position to resist this pressure for a while as the 21-year rule only came into effect after the most recent extension to the route: this would be 1913. In the meantime the Corporation gathered its evidence.

A report by the National Civic Federation of New York's Municipal and Private Operation of Utilities (1907) concluded that municipal services performed better than private ones in terms of the management of assets, customers and staff. The research was not strictly applicable to Bristol as the data were based on services that were not comparable in scale, structure or history to those of the city, and the researchers did not have access to Bristol Tramways' records. However, councillors welcomed its conclusions as they accorded with their own. In July 1913 the report was submitted of a Council-commissioned

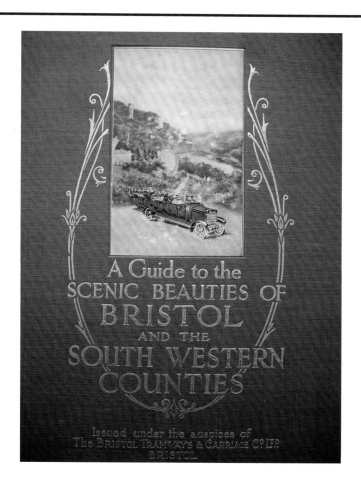

review of the viability of Council ownership of the city's public transport system. Once again, the findings were in favour of municipalisation and the Council's Act for outright purchase of Bristol Tramways & Carriage Company's assets received Royal Assent in August 1914. The Council offered £670,000 but White countered that the company was worth £2m. The Council started backtracking and, in any case, with the war now on, had other matters to deal with.

Control of Bristol Tramways & Carriage Company passed to the Thomas Tilling Group of Bus Companies in the 1930s, which in turn came under the control of the state-owned British Transport Commission in 1948. The last Bristol bus chassis left the works on 3 October 1983.

The first Bristol bus, 1908 (facing page) (Bristol Vintage Bus Group).

Cover of Bristol Tramways' guide to tours of the South West with advertisement for Bristol motor coaches, 1925 (above) (Special Collections, Bristol Central Library).

Sir Stanley White

Sir George White's son, Stanley, was a founding director of the British & Colonial Aeroplane Company and its Managing Director from 1911, a position he subsequently held with the Bristol Aeroplane Company. He was the Deputy Chairman of the BAC holding company from 1955 until his death in January 1964. Like his father, he retained a keen interest in the business to the end. He was succeeded to the baronetcy by his son, George Stanley Midelton White, later Chairman of Bristol Cars.

In an editorial referring to White relinquishing the office of Managing Director, the company magazine *Bristol Review* wrote:

> When Sir Stanley was first appointed, it was to take charge of what was then no more than an interesting offshoot of another and quite different business. It had been his task to guide and mould its fortunes through all the storms of war and peace, and now, as he hands over the executive task, the 'off-shoot' stands as one of the greatest concerns in the world aviation field.[31]

White had come into aviation at a time of piano wire, wood and Egyptian cotton and in his 44 years at the helm saw his company move on to puddle-welded stainless steel and Mach 2, from the Boxkite biplane to the beginnings of the supersonic Concorde.

White was an unassuming man who avoided the limelight. To the workforce he could sometimes appear a stern and autocratic figure, generating a mixture of respect and fear. However, he was generally regarded as a man of principle who would give encouragement when needed, praise when deserved and stand up for the company against government ministers if they acted against BAC's interests.

He was a keen horseman and an enthusiast for motor cars. His father bought him a Panhard Levassor in 1903 for his 21st birthday. Fifty years later the car took part in the London-Brighton vintage car rally. He never learnt to fly (at the insistence of Sir George, who could not risk losing him in an accident), but was a passenger on some of the first flights of the Boxkite, being flown over Clifton during the famous public display at the Downs in November 1910. He took a number of aerial photographs in the early days of flight, including several of Bulford Camp on Salisbury Plain with which he aimed to convince the military of their vulnerability from above.

He took an active part in research and development on early aircraft and maintained a thorough understanding of the later ones. Many of the great pioneer pilots and aeronautical engineers stayed with him at Hollywood Tower, Cribbs Causeway – the house which his father had given him as a wedding present. Before 1914 these included Henri Jullerot, Bertram Dickson, Gordon England and Louis Breguet. Photographs show White and Lieutenant Charles Dennistoun Burney carrying out pioneering experiments on model aeroplanes and hydrofoils in the secrecy of the Hollywood estate. White is said to have been offered a peerage for his achievements during the First World War, but modestly turned it down.

Portrait of Sir Stanley White, 1952 (Airbus).

Bristol Boxkite

The failure of the Zodiac scheme brought forward the need for British & Colonial to develop its own aircraft designs.

Adapting the widely praised Farman biplane, George H Challenger made the drawings for the first two Boxkites – officially called Bristol-Challenger Biplanes. His introduction to aeronautics is thought to have begun in Paris in 1908 and he met Wilbur Wright, presumably at Sir George White's behest, in October that year. The threatened copyright suit by the Farmans was withdrawn when lawyers pointed out the improvements Challenger had made to the original design and the superior quality of the British craftsmanship.

One of the most striking features of the Boxkite is the contrast between the apparent flimsiness of the open structure and the solidity of the traction engine that powers it. Challenger's first Boxkite (designated No 7 as it was the company's seventh aircraft, the first six being the Zodiacs) used a 50hp, four-cylinder, water-cooled Grégoire engine, while the second (No 8) had an eight-cylinder ENV (the letters referring to the French pronunciation of its V-shaped configuration) built by the London and Parisian Motor Company. Émile Stern arranged for a 50hp Gnome air-cooled rotary engine to be sent over from France for Challenger to try. This replaced No 7's Gregoire when it was re-assembled for the Boxkite's maiden flight. After the dismal debut of the Zodiac when it struggled to get airborne at Brooklands, it was heartening to see the new aircraft make a successful ascent of about 46 metres (150 feet). Impressed by its performance, British & Colonial became the sole agent for Gnome in the British Empire with an agreement set up by Stern. The first shipment arrived in Filton in April 1911. A 70hp Gnome was used on later models of the Boxkite and the company also experimented with a Renault 60hp on the instruction of the War Office, who wanted to compare performance. In 1910 a Boxkite could be bought for £1,100, of which £600 covered the cost of the engine.

Plan drawing of the Boxkite from three viewpoints (Bristol Aero Collection).

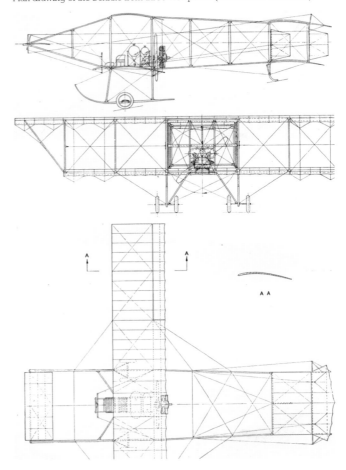

F W Merriam in Boxkite at Brooklands, c 1910 (private collection).

The aircraft was offered by Sir George White to Captain Scott for his 1910 Antarctic Expedition and to Richard Haldane, Secretary of State for War; both offers were politely declined. More welcome was the offer to lend two Boxkites for the 1910 Autumn Manoeuvres on Salisbury Plain. This was an opportunity to educate potential customers as to the practical value of heavier-than-air flight, which many still considered a novelty. The Manoeuvres were a major military exercise involving a series of large-scale mock battles and other exercises through which the command could ascertain the most effective ways of deploying its forces on the ground.

On 24 September Captain Bertram Dickson, acting on behalf of the 'Red Army', flew across the terrain in Boxkite No 7, locating the 'Blue Army' and thereby becoming the first British pilot to undertake a reconnaissance flight. Dickson was subsequently captured when he landed in 'enemy territory' to make his report by telephone. According to on-the-spot reporter Harry Harper, Dickson was not too perturbed by this as he 'had managed to get his information through and had the satisfaction of knowing that the aeroplane... had already more than justified itself'.[32] Dickson was later questioned by the Home Secretary, Winston Churchill, about the flight. Churchill was reported as charging across the field on horseback trying to keep up with the aircraft.

Among those to read of Dickson's exploits in Harper's report was the actor Robert Loraine, who in August 1910 piloted the first aeroplane to land on the Isle of Wight and on 11 September became the first pilot to fly across the Irish Sea. He volunteered to fly Boxkite No 8 for the Blues. The aircraft was fitted with a Thorne Baker radio, which Loraine used to transmit simple messages about his observations using a Morse key, making this the earliest example in the UK of an air-to-ground wireless transmission. (The first air-to-ground audio

M. Tetard. in Flight on Durdham Downs

radio transmission took place at Brooklands in 1911 in a Flanders monoplane.) The communication from the ground was made by hand-held lamp signals.

The Boxkite had been displayed at the first Scottish airshow, held at Lanark in August, and on 14 November Bristolians finally had a chance to see the aircraft in flight in a display at Durdham Downs by No 12A and 14, piloted by Maurice Tétard, Henri Jullerot and Leslie Macdonald. The event was arranged under the auspices of the Bristol and West of England Aero Club, of which Sir George White was President, providing welcome publicity for both the company and aviation in general. The *Bristol Times* and *Mirror* reported: 'During the afternoon many thousands of people assembled upon the Downs in the hope of seeing a flight and though the weather conditions were far from favourable, those who arrived before three were not disappointed.'

It continued:

At 2.45 the machine was brought out of the hangar, and the excitement then grew intense... Owing to the vastness of the crowd, and the way they had surrounded the machine, it appeared as if there would be some difficulty in getting a start... M Tétard, the famous French aviator, took his seat upon the biplane. He ran it over the grass towards the Stoke Road for a considerable distance, and then, turning, rose swiftly into the air. He steered for the Sea Walls and then took a wide sweep round the Downs in the direction of the Reservoir. After wheeling back towards the hangar, he started on another circle of a very wide radius, and eventually came back to earth, lightly as a bird...

It was evident to the spectators that during a large part of the flight the aeroplane was badly buffeted by the

THE BRITISH & COLONIAL AEROPLANE Co's BI-PLANE "THE BRISTOL" FLYING OVER THE AVON GORGE. NOV. 12. 1910.

Postcards of the Bristol Boxkite at the Downs, 1910 (private collection).

wind, and it spoke volumes both for the skill of M Tetard and the quality of the biplane that he was able to give so fine an exhibition under such adverse weather conditions.[33]

The following day Henry White Smith announced to the British & Colonial directors that sales of eight military versions of the Boxkite had been agreed with the Russians, making this the first British aircraft to be exported. In total, 22 Boxkites were sold abroad. The Filton works had been expanded by early 1911 so that five aircraft could be laid down at a time for assembly. On 14 March 1911 the War Office announced the order of four Boxkites, marking the official start of the company's long-lasting business association with the British military.

Seventy-six Boxkites were built at Filton and the Brislington tramworks, of which 60 were the extended military versions which could carry up to three people. There were also two one-off versions: a racer built for Tétard to fly in the Circuit of Europe race in 1911 and a variation built by Gabriel Voisin in 1912. The Boxkite had been a triumph for the company, quickly establishing the Bristol name, but, with the fast-moving developments in aviation in these early years, it was 'soon eclipsed by faster, lighter and handier monoplanes of equal power'.[34] Three replicas were made for the film *Those Magnificent Men in Their Flying Machines* using the original drawings, one of which is on display at Bristol's City Museum and Art Gallery.

Challenger went on to design the Bristol Glider (1910), the Bristol Monoplane (1911) and the Bristol Biplane Type T (1911). He left the company in the spring of 1911 to join Vickers Sons and Maxim Limited.

The early pilots

For Sir George White to make a commercial venture out of the embryonic business of aviation, he needed to develop a viable market. He also had to ensure there were enough trained pilots to fly the aircraft the company sold. He established a flying school operation soon after setting up as a manufacturer, as well as a chain of air stations (early airports) from Filton to Shellbeach on the east coast.

The first of White's schools opened at Larkhill, Wiltshire in June 1910. It was based in three tin sheds which were erected by British & Colonial. The War Office leased the company the site along with flying rights over an area of 2,284 acres.[35] An additional group of hangars was soon added, with a strategically positioned gap between them so their presence would not interfere with the sun's rays falling upon the altar of Stonehenge at the summer solstice. The five remaining sheds are now used as stores by the Larkhill Garrison and are probably the world's oldest surviving aerodrome buildings.

White had chosen the site to secure contracts from the military – just the type of substantial, dependable market that could make his venture a success. The Bulford and Tidworth army camps on Salisbury Plain were close to the airfield and activities at the school attracted the wary interest of the War Office, which was still sceptical about the military value of heavier-than-air aviation. The triumph of the Boxkite's performance at the Autumn Manoeuvres removed some of that doubt.

The Bristol Flying School at Brooklands in Surrey took its first pupils on 21 September 1910. These were Lieutenant H M Maitland, who later broke both his legs when his Bristol biplane stalled and crashed on Salisbury Plain, and Captain Herbert F Wood of the 12th Lancers, later of Vickers.[36] Initially, officers had been forbidden to learn to fly by the War Office because of the high risk of casualties. When the ban was lifted, officers still had to pay privately for their tuition as the War Office was not yet prepared to subsidise them, but they were offered preferential rates at the Bristol schools. Brooklands therefore drew its pupils from a pool of 'Army officers, foreign visitors, and our own politicians – the classes most likely to buy, or to influence the buying of aircraft'.[37] Boxkites were used for primary instruction at both schools, with Bristol-Prier monoplanes later used for advanced work.

In 1910 the Royal Aero Club (RAC) introduced its Aviators' Certificates. These were recognised internationally as proof of a pilot's competence as they were endorsed by the Fédération Aéronautique Internationale (the RAC was the UK's representative on that distinguished body). Seven

Advertisement in *Flight*, 10 February 1912, for the Bristol Monoplane and Flying Schools.

The "Bristol" Military

Monoplane

(Two Seater.)

ADOPTED BY

HIS MAJESTY'S WAR OFFICE

AND

OTHER EUROPEAN GOVERNMENTS

THE FASTEST PASSENGER-CARRYING MONOPLANE (80 H.P. WITH GNOME)
YET PRODUCED.

FLAWLESS CONSTRUCTION   PERFECT STABILITY AND CONTROL

TUITION IS GIVEN AT THE
"BRISTOL" FLYING SCHOOLS,
AT
SALISBURY PLAIN AND BROOKLANDS

WHICH SECURE MORE CERTIFICATES. AND GIVE MORE THOROUGH
AND RAPID TUITION. THAN ANY OTHER SCHOOL

WRITE FOR PARTICULARS TO

THE BRITISH & COLONIAL AEROPLANE CO., LTD.
FILTON. BRISTOL.

Photograph of the Royal Flying Corps balloon at the Bristol Flying School, Larkhill by T L Fuller, 1912 (© J T Fuller).

certificates were awarded that year to pupils trained by the Bristol schools. One recipient was White's 18-year-old nephew (on Lady White's side), Herbert Thomas, making him the youngest qualified pilot in the world. An injury sustained in an accident with a propeller shortly after he qualified meant he was unable to join the Royal Flying Corps when war broke out.

By the end of 1911 nearly half of Britain's certificated pilots had been trained at the Bristol schools. The first of these was Bristol-born Leslie Macdonald, who was awarded certificate No 28 on 12 November 1910 at Brooklands. Macdonald was later drowned when he was working as a test pilot at Vickers. Flying then was strange, dangerous and unpredictable: aeroplanes were untried, fragile and aerodynamically questionable. Every flight brought a strong possibility of death.

The first pilots to be killed on duty on Salisbury Plain were Captain Eustace Broke Loraine and Staff Sergeant Richard Wilson, who died when their Nieuport monoplane crashed on 6 July 1912. Their deaths are commemorated by a stone cross at Airman's Corner on the A360. Wilson had achieved his RAC certificate at Larkhill on 18 June 1912 in a Bristol biplane. More fatalities on the Plain followed, including Major William Hewetson, who was killed on 17 July 1913 in a Bristol-Prier monoplane while attempting a figure-of-eight manoeuvre as part of his pilot's qualification. He was a member of the Indian Army who had come to the UK for flight training.[38]

In addition to teaching at the Bristol schools, pilots were employed by British & Colonial to give customer demonstration flights and to fly aircraft for development and production tests. The company also called upon members of the Royal Flying Corps, free-lancers and

Group of British & Colonial pupils, instructors, pilots and other staff at Larkhill photographed by T L Fuller, 1912 (© J T Fuller). The pupils are Mr Lywood (1), Captain Lucina (2), the Australian Vincent P Taylor (3), Mr A V Bettington (21) and a group from Turkey: Lieutenants Saffet (4), Fethi (6), Aziz (7), Abdullah Ali (16) and Fazil (17). The Turkish pilots could well have used their training against the Allies in World War One. The instructors and pilots are Mr E Harrison (5), Henri Jullerot (14), Collyns Pizey (15), Harry Busteed (19), Geoffrey England (23) and James Valentine (24).

Commanding Officers of the Filton Aircraft Acceptance Park when necessary. Among the early aviation stars used by the company was Douglas Gilmour, who was described as 'the most daring and skilful British pilot of the day'.[39]

Pilots of Gilmour's calibre and renown brought welcome publicity for the fledgling business. Having flown Boxkites at Larkhill, Gilmour was loaned one to compete in the 1910 Michelin Cup. He added his own ENV engine to the aircraft but was eventually beaten in the contest by Samuel Cody. Among his accomplishments, Gilmour was the first aviator to fly over Portsmouth, demonstrating the threat to the Royal Navy fleet of aerial attack by 'bombing' the submarine depot at Fort Blockhouse with oranges. He died on 17 February 1912 when he crashed in the Old Deer Park at Richmond after taking off from Brooklands for a cross-country flight in seemingly perfect conditions. His Blériot aircraft was donated to his old school, Clifton College, where it was suspended from the rafters in the gymnasium.

Collyns Pizey from Clevedon, Challenger's one-time assistant, was sent to Larkhill to learn to fly and chose to stay on at the school rather than returning to Filton's experimental department. He took charge of teaching there when Maurice Tétard, the Chief Flying Instructor, resigned. In September 1913 Pizey left England to take up an Admiralty appointment as Flying Officer to the British Naval Mission to Greece. In this role he carried out experimental and instructional work needed for the organisation of the Greek Naval Air Service. He died in Athens on 11 June 1915.

Gordon England was one of a group of new recruits brought in by British & Colonial in 1911 to fill the gap that opened up as the original intake of French pilots returned home. He was given the opportunity to develop his own biplane designs but left the company in 1912 with the intention of extending his knowledge of international aviation. England's younger brother, Geoffrey, was killed on Salisbury Plain on 5 March 1913 during a test flight for a Bristol-Coanda monoplane. Edward Hotchkiss, a leading trainer at Brooklands and a volunteer pilot for the Royal Flying Corps Special Reserve, had also been killed in a Bristol-Coanda monoplane in a previous accident in September 1912.

The company's first full-time test pilot joined British & Colonial on 19 January 1917. This was New Zealander Captain Joseph Hammond, who had been the first pilot to achieve a Royal Aero Club certificate at Larkhill (No 32). He was later killed in trials for the American version of the Bristol Fighter. Flight-Lieutenant Cyril Uwins replaced him as Chief Test Pilot on 25 October 1918. Uwins had come to the company's attention ferrying Fighters to France and he went on to fly over 50 Bristol prototypes, starting with the Scout F.

By 1912 military flying schools were being set up overseas on the Bristol model using Bristol aircraft and Bristol instructors, but business at home and abroad was interrupted by World War One. On 2 June 1914 Larkhill was closed to allow for the mobilisation of the Royal Flying Corps. Shortly afterwards, Royal Engineers built an encampment of wooden huts on what had previously been the airfield to house thousands of troops. The school's aircraft, instructors and pupils were transferred to Brooklands, which came under War Office control on 17 August 1914 (tuition continued to 30 September). By this time 308 of the UK's 664 RAC certificated pilots had been trained by British & Colonial and 80 per cent of the country's qualified pilots had been trained on Bristol aircraft. The Bristol Flying School was reformed at Filton in 1923 and continued to operate until 1953, although it was relocated during World War Two.

Photograph of what is believed to be Chief Flying Instructor Collyns Pizey with his wife and students at Larkhill, c 1911 (facing page) (Bristol Aero Collection).

Preparations for encampment at Larkhill photographed by T L Fuller, 1914 (below) (© J T Fuller).

Henri Coanda

The Coanda Effect refers to the tendency of a moving fluid, either liquid or gas, to attach itself to a curved surface and flow along it rather than following a straight line in its original direction.

It can be most easily seen by holding the back of a spoon close to – but not touching – a stream of water running freely out of a tap. Providing the angle is not too sharp, the stream will deflect from its vertical fall in order to run down the back of the spoon. The tendency found practical application in the field of aerodynamic design. It was discovered by Romanian designer Henri Coanda, who used it as a basis for a patent registered in the 1930s entitled 'Procedure and device for the deviation of a fluid inside another fluid'.

Many years before this, in 1912, Coanda was appointed British & Colonial's Chief Designer. Sir George White had been impressed by his design for an aeroplane that 'employed a ducted fan instead of an airscrew' along with 'many other ingenious features'.[40] This ambitious but unsuccessful attempt to achieve jet-propelled, heavier-than-air flight was displayed at the Paris Salon in October 1910. Coanda was initially employed at British & Colonial to make improvements to the Bristol-Prier monoplane and this experience led to the building of a series of prototype monoplanes of his own original design.

In August 1912 the War Office held trials at Larkhill following an open invitation to submit designs for aircraft in various categories. The overall winner was to be purchased for the Army. The tests included 'speed and ease of assembly, capability of being transported as a road vehicle on tow, taking off and landing in rough country, climb to height

Coanda monoplane, c 1912 (Bristol Aero Collection), with its now rather odd-looking, pram-like undercarriage. For many years aircraft were tail-wheel equipped, which gave more stable taxiing.

Bristol Coanda TB8 tractor biplane, c 1915 (Bristol Aero Collection).

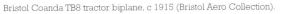

Henri Coanda

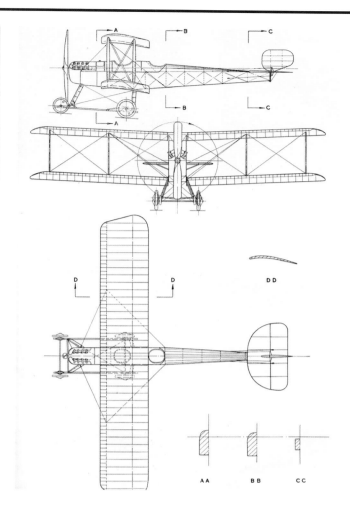

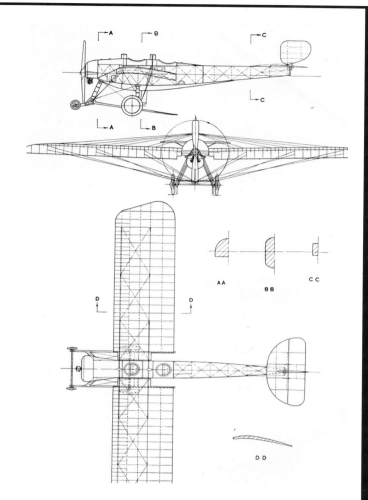

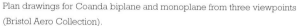

Plan drawings for Coanda biplane and monoplane from three viewpoints (Bristol Aero Collection).

times, altitude and speed tests'.[41] British & Colonial entered two Coanda monoplanes for the trials, along with two biplanes designed by Gordon England. Although they were not overall winners, the monoplanes gave an impressive performance and were bought by the War Office. In September a temporary ban was introduced on the use of monoplanes by the Royal Flying Corps' military wing following a spate of accidents. The ban, which remained in place until February 1913, meant British & Colonial was unable to exploit fully this sales opportunity. The Admiralty had been exempt from the ban, however, and British & Colonial was also able to continue to sell monoplanes abroad. According to *The Aeroplane*, some were used by Bulgaria in the First Balkan War of 1912.

When Gordon England left British & Colonial, Coanda took over biplane design in addition to his monoplane work, and his new projects included two sea planes. The most successful Coanda aircraft built by the company was TB8 ('TB' stands for 'Tractor Biplane'), which was displayed at the 1913 Paris Salon. This started out as a conversion of a military monoplane and developed into what is thought to be the first purpose-built bomber in the world to use a prismatic bombsight. It had a rotating rack capable of carrying 12 ten-pound bombs. The company produced 53 of these aircraft, which were used mainly for training purposes rather than in action.

In October 1914 Coanda moved to France to work for Delaunay-Belleville and later returned to Romania where he became his country's Minister of Science. Romania's international airport is named after him.

Frank Barnwell

British & Colonial and later BAC owed much of their success to the airframe designs of Frank Barnwell. Barnwell was born in Lewisham in 1880 and educated in Edinburgh.

He undertook a ship-building apprenticeship before setting up Grampian Engineering & Motor Co Ltd at Stirling, where he worked alongside his elder brother, Harold. Since boyhood the two had been experimenting with their own aircraft designs and on 28 July 1909 at Causewayhead near Stirling they made the first all-Scottish powered flight with their prototype No 3 biplane. On 30 January 1911 they won the Scottish Aeronautical Society's £50 prize for the first all-Scottish aeroplane to fly at least half a mile. With Harold at the controls, their prototype No 6 flew between Causewayhead and Bridge of Allan.

The Barnwells abandoned their private ventures in December 1911 when Frank joined British & Colonial's Department X, which was housed at 4 Fairlawn Avenue, Filton. Barnwell was working with Clifford Tinson (who had joined British & Colonial from A V Roe) and naval Lieutenant Charles Dennistoun Burney. This was a top secret project, independent of both Henri Coanda and Gordon England. It was financed by the Admiralty and its main aim was to develop a sea-going floatplane that utilised Burney's design for a hydrofoil undercarriage. This resulted in the building of the prototype Burney X1, X2 and X3, which were of limited success.

Portrait of Frank Barnwell, c 1920 (Airbus).

Barnwell was invited to stay on at Filton after the Burney project was abandoned. He was now partnered with Harry Busteed, who had originally been hired by the company as a pilot but had shown an aptitude for design. They developed the high-speed single-seater Scout A, also referred to as the Baby Biplane, which had its maiden flight on 23 February 1914. It was the smallest biplane on show at Olympia in March – hence its nickname – and only one prototype was produced. Two Scout Bs were built and differed slightly from the A version, but of greater significance was the Scout C, which was the first Bristol Type (Bristol Types 1 to 5 were all variants of the Scout). Orders for this aircraft were received from the War Office in November 1914 and from the Admiralty in December. In total, 161 Scout Cs were built by British & Colonial. Production was initially centred on the Brislington works as Filton was stretched to capacity by production of the Royal Aircraft Factory-designed BE2 fighter.

By the time the initial Scout orders were being fulfilled, Barnwell had left British & Colonial and joined the Royal Flying Corps. He had seen little opportunity to continue his work as a designer at Filton because of the Royal Aircraft Company's monopoly on military contracts at the start of the war. However, when it became apparent that the BE2 was consistently out-performed by Fokker monoplanes and unable to cope with the threat from Zeppelin airships, the government invited tenders for the design of a new, more effective fighter to replace it. Barnwell returned to British & Colonial in August 1915 and was made Chief Designer. He had been released on indefinite unpaid leave from the Royal Flying Corps having attained the rank of Captain. Initially the Scouts were not armed, having been designed for a purely reconnaissance role, but pilots in the field adapted them for offensive use by carrying carbine rifles and Lewis guns. In response to

the government requirement, Barnwell now designed the Scout D. This was completed in November 1915 and had a synchronised Vickers machine gun to fire through the spinning propeller disc. Barnwell also made improvements to the fuel tank to prevent the leaks that had previously resulted from excessive vibration. Over 200 of this aircraft were produced.

In July 1916 Barnwell started work on designs for a two-seater, single-engined biplane which developed into the F2A. This saw extensive service in its subsequent variant, the F2B, known as the Bristol Fighter. He also designed the Twin Tractor, a twin-engined biplane fighter (possibly the first of its kind), which did not go beyond the prototype stage, and a series of M1 monoplanes, which had limited service because of continuing concerns about single-wing safety. Two prototypes of his Type MR1 Metal Biplane were built for evaluation purposes (Barnwell wrote off the second one when he hit a tree on a flight to Farnborough in 1919). He began designs for what became the Braemar Bomber, intended for use in bombing raids on Berlin, but passed them to Wilfred T Reid, then British & Colonial's Chief Draftsman. Barnwell's post-war sporty Babe, which had its maiden flight on 28 November 1919, was the smallest aircraft built by company. Only three prototypes were produced, one of which was a monoplane

Scout C, c 1915 and Scout D, 1916 (Airbus).

Rodney Hall employees with Frank Barnwell at centre between Wilfred T Reid and Leslie Frise, November 1918 (facing page) (Bristol Aero Collection). Roland Cross, founder of Cross Manufacturing, is two places to the left of Reid.

Babe Mark 3, 1920 (above) (Airbus).

configuration. Barnwell had anticipated demand from former Royal Flying Corps pilots looking for leisure aircraft to fly, but the private commercial market was still in its infancy and there were in any case nearly as many ex-military machines available to buy as there were ex-military flyers.

Barnwell left the company again on 1 October 1921, this time to take up a technical commission to the Royal Australian Air Force. He cut short his stint in Australia and returned a final time to Filton in 1923, where he enjoyed a productive partnership with engine-designer Roy Fedden.

Barnwell was seemingly unaware of his own shortcomings as a pilot. After so many accidents, BAC refused to let him fly company aircraft because he was uninsurable. He died on 2 August 1938 testing a small, wooden monoplane built for his private use by a syndicate based at Whitchurch. Barnwell was interested in designing light single-seaters suitable for the Civil Air Guard. He was killed on his second test flight. The Barnwell family also suffered the loss of his three sons, who were all killed while serving in the Royal Air Force during World War Two. Barnwell's brother, Harold, had been killed in 1917 in an accident at Vickers, where he was Chief Test Pilot.

Parnall & Sons

World War One brought new companies into the aviation business in the West of England, particularly those with experience in carpentry as aircraft were primarily constructed from wood at this time. Of these, one of the most successful was Parnall & Sons.

Parnall & Sons was a Bristol-based shopfitting and cabinet-making firm which had been taken over by the national Avery group in 1898 but had retained its name. The company had acquired use of the Coliseum building on Park Row in Bristol for aircraft manufacture near the start of the war (the building had been opened in 1910); they had secured Admiralty contracts to build Avro 504s and Short Brothers' 827s, among others, building around 600 aircraft in total. In addition to the Coliseum, works at Mivart Street in Eastville, Belmont Road in Brislington and Quakers' Friars were also used for production. After initial assembly, the aircraft were dismantled and towed or transported to the No 5 (South Western) Aircraft Acceptance Park at Filton for final assembly and flight tests. British & Colonial, Gloucestershire Aircraft and Westland also tested their aircraft there.

Most of the wartime aircraft built by Parnall were made to the designs of others but did include two original designs of their own, the unsuccessful Scout and the more significant Panther, a naval spotter designed by Harold Bolas in response to an Admiralty specification. Bolas had joined Parnall in 1917 and the Panther had its maiden flight the following year. Initially the company was offered two contracts to produce over 300 of the aircraft, but the signing of the Armistice and a dispute between parent company Avery and the Air Ministry led to their cancellation. The first contract was later reissued and offered to British & Colonial. This was a welcome opportunity to keep the firm in the aircraft business at a time when other contracts were drying up, and 150 Panthers were built at Filton between 1919 and 1920. The Panther had a hinged fuselage for easier shipboard storage. In the event of its ditching in the sea, it could utilise air floatation bags and a hydrovane, a wing-shaped float fitted between the wheels that generated lift when submerged in water. The Panther first entered service on the Royal Navy aircraft carriers *Argus* and *Hermes*.

With Parnall & Sons returning to its shopfitting and cabinet-making after the war, Managing Director George Parnall resigned in 1920 to form his own firm, George Parnall & Company, as he was keen to continue in the aviation business. He initially leased production space in the Coliseum and his aircraft were tested at Filton in an agreement with BAC. In 1925 the company moved its operations to Yate, taking over the former No 3 (Western) Aircraft Repair Depot. This had been constructed by German POWs during World War One and by 1918 was one of the largest aerodromes in the country. In 1935 Parnall retired and his company merged with Hendy Aircraft and Nash & Thompson to form Parnall Aircraft Ltd. This came to specialise in gun turrets and other

Parnall Panther, c 1919 (above) (Fishponds Local History Society).

Women workers at Parnall's Coliseum works, c 1917 (right) (Fishponds Local History Society).

Frame of Avro 504 in Parnall workshop, c 1917 (bottom) (Fishponds Local History Society).

components rather than complete aircraft. The final Parnall-designed aeroplane was the Parnall Type 382, completed in 1938. Major bombing raids in February and March 1941 at the Yate works led to the use of dispersal sites for some of its wartime production. After the war the company diversified into the manufacture of washing machines.

Meanwhile, in 1923 Avery moved Parnall & Sons into the former Cosmos engine factory at Fishponds, the assets of which had passed to BAC in 1920. The company continued in the high-quality fittings business and was one of the subcontractors hired by BAC to make the interior furnishings for the Britannia airliner, including bar units, toilets, bulkheads and galley units.

Charles Rolls

In 1910, the year Sir George White was establishing his aircraft business, Charles Rolls had the unfortunate distinction of becoming the UK's first aviation fatality. He was 32 years old and just establishing himself as a leading manufacturer of engines and motor cars through his company, Rolls-Royce. The name Rolls-Royce would frequently be linked with that of White's company over the coming years.

Charles Rolls in driving seat of Silver Ghost sitting next to Orville Wright with the brothers' agent, Griffith Brewer, at the rear with Wilbur, 1909 (Rolls-Royce plc).

In 1966 the two were officially united when Rolls-Royce merged with Bristol Siddeley (itself the result of the merger between Bristol Aero Engines and Armstrong Siddeley Motors) to run aero-engine production at the works at Patchway under the Rolls-Royce name.

Rolls was born at his family's London home in Berkeley Square on 27 August 1877. His father was John Rolls, the Conservative MP for Monmouthshire, who had been raised to the peerage as first Baron Llangattock in 1892. Unlike White, Rolls had been born into money, his family owning a large estate at Monmouth and other substantial assets. He was educated at Eton and graduated in 1898 from Trinity College, Cambridge where he had studied mechanical engineering and applied sciences.

From an early age, Rolls had been fascinated by machines and speed. He was a keen cyclist, earning a Cambridge cycling half-blue in 1896, and while still an undergraduate became one of the first people in the UK to own a motor car when he imported a 3.75hp Peugeot from France. On his first drive to Cambridge from London, he broke the Locomotive Act (1878) which limited self-propelled vehicles to a maximum speed of four miles per hour and required that someone walk in front of the vehicle waving a red warning flag. Over the next few years he became a popular and stylish figure on the drivers' club circuit, taking part in trials and races at home and abroad.

In January 1902 Rolls used his various society and business connections and £6,500 of his father's money to set up C S Rolls & Co, an agency for the sale of high-class petrol-driven motor cars, most of which were French imports. He had a business address in Fulham and opened a West End showroom in December 1903. At this time, motoring was still a hobby for the wealthy rather than an everyday experience for ordinary people. Keen to find a British manufacturer he could work with, in May 1904 Rolls and his business partner, Claude Goodman Johnson, travelled to Manchester to meet the engineer Henry Royce and test-drive his two-cylinder 10hp motor car. He and Johnson were so impressed with the car's performance that an agreement was soon drawn up making C S Rolls & Co Royce's sole agent.

Rolls was a flamboyant aristocrat, while Royce, his senior by 14 years, was from humble origins with little formal education. Despite their different personalities and backgrounds, they made a successful partnership. By 1905 Rolls was only selling British cars through his showroom, of which the star attraction was Royce's Grey Ghost, and on 15 March 1906 Rolls-Royce Ltd was founded with a starting capital of £60,000. Rolls was a fearless and skilful driver and he was able to secure good publicity for the company with his exploits. He broke the Monte Carlo to Boulogne record in a 20hp Rolls-Royce and demonstrated the speed of the Grey Ghost on the Empire City Track

Charles Rolls sitting in his Flyer at Bournemouth, July 1910 (Rolls-Royce plc).

in New York. By 1910 Rolls-Royce had a new factory in Derby and was making over 300 luxury cars a year.

Rolls had also developed an interest in ballooning, making his first ascent in 1901, and was one of the founders of the British Aero Club. On 1 October 1906 he represented the UK in the international Gordon Bennett balloon race from Paris, and won the gold medal for remaining in the air for the longest time. He made around 170 balloon ascents in total during his short lifetime.

Rolls was excited by news of the Wright brothers' aviation experiments and in 1908 had the opportunity to fly with Wilbur during a visit to Le Mans. Back in Britain, Rolls was friendly with the three Short brothers who had been in the aviation business since 1898 when they started manufacturing balloons. In early 1909 they established the UK's first aircraft factory at an airfield partly owned by Rolls at Muswell Manor in Leysdown, on the Isle of

Charles Rolls posing in Short Brothers' balloon, March 1908 (Rolls-Royce plc).

Charles Rolls flies over Dover Castle after completing his double-Channel crossing, June 1910 (Rolls-Royce plc).

Sheppey in Kent. In July Rolls drove the Wrights from London to meet the Shorts and, impressed by the factory set-up, the Americans agreed that the Shorts could manufacture six Wright Flyers under a UK licence. This production line made Shorts 'the first British company to manufacture aeroplanes in series'.[42]

Rolls had originally hoped to persuade the Rolls-Royce board that the company should manufacture the Wright aircraft, but he was outvoted by his fellow directors. He resigned in April 1910 when the board further frustrated his plans to get into aviation by opposing his decision to manufacture aircraft and balloon gearings for the War Office. The previous month he had offered to donate his Flyer to the War Office in the hope this would encourage them to follow the Wrights' proven designs rather than continue with their half-hearted experiments, but the response had been lukewarm.

Having regularly been in the news with his motor driving and ballooning, on 2 June 1910 Rolls made fresh headlines when he became the first person to make a non-stop return flight by aeroplane across the English Channel. The following month he took part in a flying event at Southbourne, near Bournemouth. He was again flying a Wright Flyer, this one French-built, but had made modifications to the landing gear and tail. He was killed on 12 July when the elevator he had added to the tail section broke up while he was preparing for landing and he crashed to the ground. He was buried in Llangattock-Vibon-Avel churchyard near his family estate of Hendre in Monmouth.

Joseph Anthony Powell using his mallet to make an adjustment to the air-cooled radial Jupiter engine, West Works, c 1921 (Rolls-Royce Heritage Trust).

Section 2:
Technological Achievements

The principle of heavier-than-air flight has remained much the same since 1910, but the technological means by which it is achieved has changed dramatically. Some of the changes could be seen as progress, some as just a different way of doing things; some were incremental, some sudden; some made life simpler, some more complex; some seemed to have been made for change's sake. They are indicative of how technology can evolve over time in a dynamic business like aviation.

There have been obvious variations in the types of materials used and the methods by which these are made and assembled, but also many more subtle, behind-the-scenes changes. Just one of these changes has been in the technical aids employed by the industry to carry out the wide range of mathematical calculations needed throughout the development and production processes. In addition to mental arithmetic and pencil and paper, there have been log tables, Faber Castell and Fuller slide rules, hand-cranked Brunsviga calculating machines, Marchant and Frieden electromechanical adding machines, and Facit pinwheel calculators. BAC's first digital computer was the English Electric DEUCE, purchased in the mid-1950s (English Electric was an aircraft company that diversified its output). From the 1960s there were huge IBM mainframe computers in use and for years staff would deliver their punch cards to the operators' offices one day and collect the results and analyse the findings the next. There were the first desktop digital calculators – it cost extra for ones that had a square root button in addition to plus, minus, multiply and divide – then hand-held pocket calculators like the Hewlett Packard 35 introduced in 1972. Some of the first desktop personal computers were being used by the company in the late 1970s, and they were followed by Apple Macs, iMacs, laptops and palmtops. The storage of data moved from cardex cabinets to magnetic tape, disks and file servers. Drawing boards in offices were gradually replaced by banks of computer screens. Rulers, callipers, manual micrometers and vernier gauges were joined by electronic devices that used laser beams for measurements accurate to a thousandth of an inch or less. Some of these devices were designed by Renishaw, one of many successful companies set up by former BAC apprentices.

BAC and its associated companies were not working in isolation and rather than being uniquely innovative, their experiments with and development of new technologies were

Woman sat at a large data-processing machine made by Hollerith at the Bristol Engine Division offices, 10 December 1958 (Rolls-Royce plc).

often the result of the gradual, piecemeal accumulation of knowledge from all parts of the industry. What could be distinctive was the application found for a procedure or material that had been originated by others and for which BAC might devise a new or better use. Such applications could give the company competitive advantage as well as push forward the technological frontier. Many employees signed the Official Secrets Act and operated under conditions aimed at safeguarding military, state and commercial confidentiality, including getting security clearance where appropriate. Probably most never gave it another thought and just got on with their work. Others would have been acutely aware of the implications of what was being achieved within the factory walls and of why this knowledge and expertise needed to be protected.

Sir George White wanted to set British & Colonial on a sound business footing, which meant working closely with paying customers rather than indulging in too many personal projects. His company – and later BAC – did have the ability to shape the nature of its products to a certain extent, but this freedom was offset by parameters established by the market. For much of the company's history, the market was essentially defined by government. Customers like the Air Ministry, in its various permutations, usually operated a specification process, identifying the type of aircraft required and giving companies the opportunity to say how this might be delivered and what the cost would be. The customer would then select two or three of the proposals to go forward to a prototype stage at the government's expense before making the final choice of supplier and setting up a production contract.

Frank Barnwell's departure for Australia after World War One was partly driven by frustration over the lack of interest in developing his Bullfinch design and other original proposals, which fell outside the specification process. According to C H Barnes, 'too little money was available from official sources and too many unused wartime aircraft were still held in store for any real enthusiasm to be shown for new projects by the politicians of the Air Ministry'.[1] The Ministry specified 'the basic type, total quantity and the rates of delivery' of its aircraft, although it generally did not get involved in the minutiae of the production side, leaving that to the industry to manage as it thought best.[2] BAC also secured a little leeway within some government specifications once the aircraft got to the prototype stage. This would only happen if the prototype design was not chosen by the government, in which case the company could develop its own variants to offer to other customers.

Potentially there was more design freedom in the civil than the military sphere, but BAC's experience of negotiating with British Overseas Airways Corporation (BOAC) over the contracts for Britannia in the 1950s showed that civil ventures also had their drawbacks. BOAC had a specific requirement for its airline fleet which, according to some, limited opportunities to sell Britannia elsewhere. BOAC and British European Airways were the UK's only airline companies at this time. In the US, there was a much bigger market as there were a number of major airline companies in operation to meet the demand for flights. Being such a vast country, flying was for many Americans a more convenient and quicker way to travel between major population centres than train or road. Manufacturers were therefore in a position to develop civil aircraft that more than one customer might want to buy.

To succeed as a business there is usually a need to balance a desire for innovation with commercial common sense. BAC would have had to bear a considerable financial risk if it had concentrated on purely speculative designs, building aircraft and then trying to find a buyer. Nevertheless, some of its ventures were private rather than customer-driven ones and it seemed able to make the most of opportunities that cropped up to experiment and try out new ideas with an eye to future applications. *The Aeroplane* said on the 30th anniversary of BAC's founding: 'there was a spirit of enterprise and persistence in this Company which secured for it a leading place in all the advances which took place in the emerging British Industry.'[3] In 1960, on the occasion of the company's 50th anniversary, *Flight* wrote: 'Heavy investment has often been more in search of technical achievement than in immediate commercial promise.'[4]

Designing and building an aeroplane is a long, complex business, which takes inspiration, imagination, hard graft, trial and error, team-work, luck and capital, among other things. There is an element of risk-taking and the acceptance of failure, although physical risks obviously have to be minimised when dealing with large civil airliners as too many lives are at stake. Flying is no longer a seat-of-your-pants affair as it sometimes was in the early years, but has to be carefully planned throughout. The complexity of the process increases as aircraft get bigger and faster and more environmentally sensitive. It can start from a brand new idea that no one has ever thought of. More often, the idea improves or builds on something that has gone before. Years might be spent in technology maturation and the running of parallel studies before a product gets from the laboratory to what is termed 'acceptable technology readiness' and a prototype can be launched for testing. More years will then be spent in full-scale development before the product is in service.

Comprehensive calculations and extensive documentation are required long before the company gets to the stage of making something that can be tested. In the commercial world, the customers' key questions are typically 'How big is it? How many passengers will it carry? What will its fuel consumption be? What will be its range?', so the aircraft needs to be sold on paper before committing further funds and moving on to the detailed design stage. The design team will then design the aircraft the customer wants and the development team will turn that design into a product that does all the things the designers have promised, liaising with various departments, teams and individuals across the company, as well as a band of subcontractors and partner companies, to achieve this.

Even if an individual project does not come to fruition, other applications can be found for what has been learnt during the investigation stages – that is how knowledge grows. BAC was described by *The Aeroplane* as 'essentially a designing firm', and research and experimentation continued to be a high priority even during periods of intense production.[5] Research lays the groundwork for potential future production and is an essential part of long-term planning.

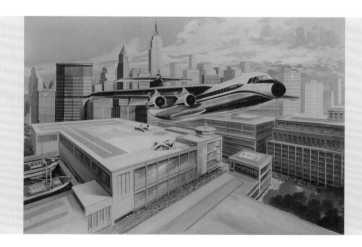
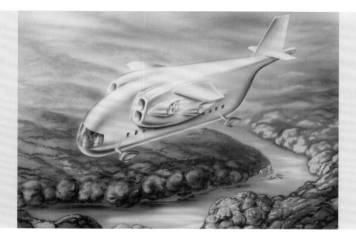

Artist's impressions from the late 1950s of aircraft capable of vertical or short take-off and landing which never got beyond the drawing board (Rolls-Royce plc).

Between the Bristol Fighter of 1917 and the Bristol Bulldog of 1927, around 30 prototype aircraft were built at Filton, of which only the Primary and Advanced Trainers went into full-scale production.[6] Prototypes and short-runs in the post-war period included the Tramp triplane, completed in 1921, of which two were built, but neither of which ever flew. The Tramp was a variation on the Pullman prototype airliner. The two completed aircraft were fitted with conventional piston engines but the original plan was to use steam turbines. The company also looked at the possibility of developing a flying boat version. The Brandon, which first flew in March 1924, was a variation on Wilfred T Reid's Bristol Ten-Seater biplane. One was built and it was thought it might have potential for troop-carrying, but it was found to be 'overweight with full payload' and was used instead as an air ambulance at Halton by the Royal Air Force.[7] The Brownie monoplane had its maiden flight in August 1924. It had a fuselage of high-tensile steel tubing, and two of the three built had metal wings. It was powered by the company's small, twin-cylinder Cherub engine. It performed well at the Air Ministry Light Aeroplane Trails of 1924 but could not compete with de Havilland's more commercial Moth as, according to Barnes, it 'was expensive to build and not rugged enough to stand up to normal light aeroplane club treatment, nor was it cheap to maintain and repair'.[8]

Bristol Brandon, April 1925
(Rolls-Royce Heritage Trust).

With these, as with any aircraft, there would have been testing throughout the development and, if appropriate, production stages. Hundreds, if not thousands, of tests are required for each assembled engine or airframe as well as for all the individual components both before and after they are installed. Tests can take place on paper, in laboratories, in specialist test facilities, in the air. There are tests to assess stress points, balance, reliability and safety, fuelling procedures, controls, hydraulic systems, synchronisation, reactions to variations in pressure, minimum distances of take-off and landing, rates of climb, stalling, weight distribution. For Britannia, a special outdoor water tank was built at Filton for fatigue tests, the water pressure replicating air pressure. A special altitude chamber was built to assess reactions to extreme heat and extreme cold, and the transition from one to the other. Temperature reactions are also tested on overseas flight tests in different climates. Pilots and flight observers usually complete snag sheets during such flights, with all the relevant personnel brought together for post-flight debriefings.

Another area of performance-testing involves assessing the maximum allowable take-off, landing and obstacle-clearing weight for operating at any given airport, runway, altitude and temperature. The data collected is compiled into a legally-binding flight manual. An aircraft's landing weight must be lower than its take-off weight. The burning of fuel during the flight will result in a loss of weight, but if the aircraft is still too heavy some fuel will need to be dumped prior to landing.

Key features such as the mechanics, radio, power unit and electrics have to be signed off before an aircraft can be put forward to the Civil Aviation Authority (successor to the Air Registration Board) for its Certificate of Airworthiness. If something fails or does not work as is intended at any test stage, it might be necessary to go right back to the drawing board before moving on. BAC prided itself that every individual production aircraft was also given an extensive test flight before its delivery to the customer, going well beyond the minimum requirement. However, customers may report back on aspects of the aircraft's performance long after it has gone into service. Any structural changes made by the manufacturer to an individual aircraft or series are likely to require re-testing for airworthiness.

One of the most important test facilities used in aeronautical design is the wind tunnel. For airframes, the normal procedure is to make a perfect scale model of the aircraft from such material as laminated mahogany, fibreglass, aluminium, brass, carbon fibre or silver. The models are either suspended by wires from an overhead balance or supported on what are called stinger mounts. Tests are run to measure lift, drag and side force, and degrees of pitching, rolling and yawing. The data collected over a series of tests is converted to coefficients and plotted on graphs. The resulting curves are then checked for anomalies

Illustration of low-speed wind tunnel from *The 'Bristol' Quarterly*, Autumn 1956 (Rolls-Royce Heritage Trust).

(if the curve is not smooth, it is an indication of a potential problem in performance). The wind tunnels are also used to test sections of aircraft such as the cowlings – the streamlined, removable coverings fitted around an engine when it is installed on an aircraft. Four or five years or more can be spent on this test stage.

Modern computer simulation using computational fluid dynamics software has reduced some of the need for wind tunnel tests, thereby cutting the maintenance and running costs of the facilities as well as shortening the test period. However, air can be an unpredictable force, particularly at lower speeds, so physical tests are still needed to assess potential performance and handling. A wind tunnel can throw up results that cannot be anticipated by computer prediction tools or mathematical modelling.

British & Colonial's first wind tunnel was built at Filton on Barnwell's insistence in June 1919. It was approximately 1.2 metres (four feet) square and open-ended. It remained in use until 1942, when it was destroyed after a German bomb exploded on the ground between it and an adjacent office building. A larger tunnel with a high-speed fan was built in 1937. This had an oval-shaped throat that was about 2.7 metres (nine feet) wide and had a closed circuit so that air flowed continuously round the system. When Barnwell's tunnel was lost, extra shifts had to be employed at the new one to keep up with the test schedule.

Hydrodynamic tunnel test of Concorde, c 1960s (Science and Society Picture Library/Science Museum). Exhaustive testing using a range of models was carried out in order to ascertain the ideal shape for the aircraft, and it became clear that a narrow delta wing would have sufficiently low drag for high-speed cruising and still have good handling characteristics at low speed and landing.

The construction of a supersonic (faster than the speed of sound) wind tunnel designed by the Guided Weapons Department was completed in 1952. It was a simple, blow-down type using pressured air from BAC's Turbine Test Station. Four years later a new, low-speed wind tunnel was opened and is still in use. Sadly for archivists, during the construction of these later tunnels, thousands of glass plates recording the history of the factory site since 1910 were broken up to form hard-core for the foundations.

For Concorde, much of the high-speed model-testing was done in the supersonic wind tunnel at the Royal Aircraft Establishment at Farnborough. The Aircraft Research Association transonic (equal to the speed of sound) wind tunnel at Bedford was also used, in addition to facilities at Filton, university sites and abroad. The British Aircraft Corporation found commercial uses for the low-speed wind tunnel at Filton once the Concorde work was finished, including tests for oil platforms, Richard Noble's record-breaking Thrust 2 racing car, the Ferrari Formula 1, a vertical axis windmill, lorries and golf clubs (although that was probably just a publicity stunt on the part of the manufacturers).

Like airframes, aero-engines are built to designer drawings. They are then run on test-beds to assess performance. Due to the likelihood of an engine catching fire during tests, it is standard procedure to have a crash tender on hand during the runs. This was especially important when the buildings were made primarily of wood and therefore at a high risk of combustion. If problems occur during the run, the engine might be stripped down, investigated, modified, rebuilt and re-run. As with the wind tunnel testing, this development stage could take years to complete before the engine performed as it was expected to, but the time-frame has been greatly reduced as modern spinning rigs are able to simulate months of running over a period of a few weeks. For type test certification, a pre-production engine built to standard has to run for 150 hours without developing any major mechanical problems. During the run, there are occasional shut-downs for oil and filter changes, and to check for debris. Production engines are run for at least three hours on test-beds and subjected to further runs and checks in an aircraft before going into service. Such attention to detail had to be set aside during World War Two: engines had to be ready for action as quickly as possible after a perfunctory test.

Specific tests are also carried out either during the development stage or when the engine is in production. These can be destructive and non-destructive tests to identify material or design failures, or tests that replicate failures caused by damage. A cut might be made in a turbine blade before a run to test whether it could pass safely through the engine without penetrating the turbine casing when it broke off. Two-inch ice cubes could be thrown at a running engine to recreate the impact of hailstones. Starlings and birds of other sizes (dead and defrosted) might be fired at the rotating blades from a compressed air gun to simulate bird strike at take-off.[9] High-altitude test plants are used to simulate the effects of low atmospheric pressure. Low-temperature start-up tests take place in refrigerated units. Outside test areas are usually surrounded by netting or similar protective material in case a blade or other item flies off. The windows of the observation chambers for indoor test-beds have triple-glazed toughened glass, sometimes supplemented by protective sheets of metal if an engine is to be deliberately destroyed to recreate an accident. The walls of the chamber are likely to be scarred and pitted from the impact of shattered pieces. In addition to the test facilities at Patchway, sites like Aston Down Airfield in the Cotswolds, the mud flats of the east coast and the United Kingdom Atomic Energy Authority at Aldermaston have also been used.

BAC could take some credit for leading the way in many areas of technological innovation, such as the use of materials. In a *'Bristol' Quarterly* article of the 1950s, for example, it was claimed that the company had brought about 'the general adoption of steel and, later, of aluminium as basic aircraft materials' during the previous two decades.[10] Looking even further back, Sir George White had commissioned a ground-breaking tubular-steel monoplane from the Voisin company as early as 1911, but it was too heavy to fly. Barnwell's MR1 military reconnaissance aircraft was an attempt to solve the problems of a shortage of Grade A timber stocks in World War One and the tendency of wooden airframes to warp in tropical climates. His solution was a riveted-duralumin, semi-monocoque fuselage. Duralumin was a strong, light-weight aluminium alloy first

Test-bed Centaurus at East Works early 1940s (above) (Rolls-Royce Heritage Trust).

Farndon's illustration of Bristol sleeve-valve on test-bed from the 40th anniversary calendar (facing page) (Bristol Aero Collection).

introduced in 1909 and used extensively by the Zeppelin company. In monocoque construction the load of the fuselage is carried by the structural shell, also referred to as a stressed skin, rather than by a rigid internal frame or truss (semi-monocoque structures retain some form of bracing). The method was probably first used in the Deperdussin Monocoque of 1912, a sports aircraft designed by Louis Béchereau. It is also used in the automobile industry and in architecture. For the MR1 Barnwell, using his shipyard experience, coated the aircraft's skin with a high-quality marine varnish to help reduce the effects of corrosion, but it was Reid who handled the details of its construction. The first prototype had wooden wings and made its maiden flight in July 1917. The second, completed the following year, had wings built by the Steel Wing Company in Gloucester, making it the first all-metal structured aircraft to fly in the UK.

Harry Pollard, a specialist in the use of high-tensile (high-strength) rolled-steel strips, joined BAC in the 1920s where he formed a team with Barnwell, Leslie Frise and Clifford Tinson to exploit this new technology. Steel-strip could provide lighter, stronger and cheaper airframes than traditional tubular construction, though it could require higher workforce skills. The steel would be delivered to the factory and then rolled on milling machines to the shape required. The method had been developed at the Structural Steel Department of Boulton and Paul Ltd in Norwich, which built the first twin-engined, all-metal biplane bomber, the Sidestrand, in 1926 (later versions used the Bristol Jupiter engine). Steel-strip was used on most of the Bristol airframes of the late 1920s.

In the early days, aluminium proved to be a variable material. Gradually the production of aluminium improved, becoming more uniform in quality, and the aircraft industry simultaneously acquired the skills to work with it. This partly explains the time gap between the first experiments in its use in aircraft construction and it becoming a standard material. A major breakthrough was the development of Alclad, a product trade-marked by the Aluminium Company of America. This is a material made from layers of coated sheets of aluminium alloy, rather like plywood. It was first used by BAC on the Type 133, which had its maiden fight on 8 June 1934. This cantilever monoplane with a stressed-skin fuselage was developed by Barnwell for the F7/30 fighter specification. There was a promise of substantial production orders for the aircraft, but it crashed during the test period and it was too late to build a replacement for the competition.

Light-alloy monocoque construction became the norm for aircraft manufacturers in the rearmament period of the late 1930s. Aeroplanes need to be as light and strong as possible while still retaining space for all the systems, cargo and passengers they need to carry. The fatigue load upon the aeroplane's supporting structure varies between the ground and the air, and in different types of air conditions. Cabin pressure also exerts a load. Light alloys reduce the amount of material that needs to be used in the structure and thereby reduces

MR1, 1917 (Airbus).

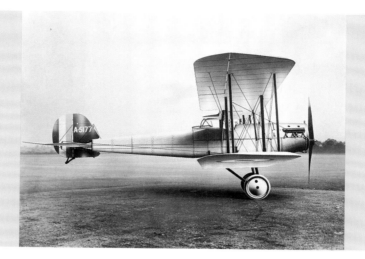

the weight without sacrificing strength. They can achieve the highest permissible stress level and 'an even distribution of stress throughout the component'.[11] However, they have a shorter lifespan than steel. There is therefore a need for a fail-safe (as opposed to fail catastrophically) design so 'that when failures occur they develop sufficiently slowly to be found by inspection before they become dangerous'.[12] This requires extensive research and became an area of expertise for BAC.

BAC also developed a particular expertise in undercarriages. The first practical hand-cranked undercarriage was probably that of the Dayton-Wright Racer developed in the US for the 1920 Gordon Bennett Cup. BAC had experimented with a similar design in the Bristol Racer of 1922. This was a project jointly led by Reid (who had recently succeeded Barnwell as the company's Chief Designer) and Roy Fedden. They aimed to design a high-speed monoplane that used a submerged Bristol Jupiter engine. The advantage of encasing the engine in cowlings rather than leaving it open was that it made the aircraft more streamlined and therefore subject to less drag. The Racer was constructed from a mixture of wood, metal and fabric-covering. According to *The Aeroplane*, it 'had almost everything which the modern monoplane can boast – cantilever wing, monocoque fuselage, retractable undercarriage and fully cowled engine'.[13] The undercarriage was operated by the pilot using a chain and sprocket gear, declared by Barnes to be the 'most striking feature of all'.[14] In retraction, the wheels lay flush within the wing and the legs and struts were concealed within specially designed grooves in the fuselage. Wind tunnel tests suggested the Racer could attain a top speed of at least 220mph, but it suffered from a series of design set backs and was scrapped after making seven rather shaky flights.

One of the main difficulties with retractable undercarriages is handling the aircraft during the transition from the wheels being down to them being up, and vice versa. This is likely to have caused the Type 133 monoplane crash. There were no appropriately equipped

The Bristol Racer, 1922
(Bristol Aero Collection).

trainers to help pilots learn to handle aircraft in these conditions, leading to a high level
of loss and damage, not helped by the absence of undercarriage warning lights. This was
seen in the early development of the Blenheim, where the undercarriage had a tendency to
retract one side at a time, throwing it off balance. This was solved by installing new doors
to the shell so it went up evenly. One unexpected problem during the latter stages of the
war was when Beaufighter torpedo bombers returned from their missions having been
unable to drop their loads because there had not been sufficient enemy ships to target.
Landing with the weight of the torpedoes still on board led to buckling, so bombs had to
be ditched in the sea before returning to base.

A Blenheim mock-up resting on jigs in order to test the starboard undercarriage mechanism, c 1942 (Bristol Aero Collection).

In 1947 BAC set up British Messier Limited as a subsidiary that would specialise in undercarriage research, marketing and production. The company was based on Cheltenham Road in Gloucester. It developed hydraulic-powered landing gear for use in the Brabazon, which was too big an aircraft to rely on manual operations (hydraulic systems were also used for some of its other controls). It also fitted Britannia with the first 4,000 psi hydraulic system used in a civil aircraft. Dowty Aviation in Cheltenham, which went public in 1936, also specialised in aircraft hydraulics. The company's founder, George Dowty, was a former employee of Gloster Aircraft Ltd. He designed the first internally-sprung wheel, which was introduced in 1937 on the Gloster Gladiator. Messier eventually merged with Rotol, another BAC subsidiary, and in turn became part of the Dowty group.

Fixed undercarriages continued to be used where appropriate, even when the problems with retractable ones had largely been solved. One of their advantages was that internal space on the aircraft was not needed for housing the retraction equipment, thereby leaving more room for passengers or cargo. Such an undercarriage was on the Bristol Freighter, the first post-war, purpose-built freight carrier and BAC's first successful commercial aircraft. The Freighter was initially developed as a private venture towards the end of the war (ie, without a prior specification being received). The design was shown to Air Staff who, recognising the potential, asked for the fuselage be enlarged so it could carry a standard three-ton army truck. Two prototypes were ordered. With the end of war and the loss of military interest, two further prototypes were produced for the Ministry of Supply with an eye on the civil market. The first of these flew in December 1945. The Freighter was 'a simple, rugged and exceedingly reliable flying box', with large, clam-shell doors at its nose for easier loading (a people-carrying variant called the Wayfarer had a fixed nose and seating for up to 32 passengers).[15] Major components for the aircraft were manufactured by Western Aircraft Limited (Canada), Harris and Sheldon Limited (Birmingham), Welsh Metal Industries Limited (Caerphilly) and Aviation Traders Limited (London).

E J N 'John' Archbold, who joined BAC shortly after World War Two to set up the company's first dedicated aerodynamics department, was killed along with six colleagues on 6 May 1949 when G-AIFF, a Type 170 Freighter, crashed into the sea off Portland Bill during propeller-testing. It is thought that the cause of the crash was rudder-lock. Before Archbold's arrival, aerodynamics had come under the Technical Office run by Archibald E Russell. The department's early life was largely spent working on the Britannia project.

By 1954 BAC was completing a Freighter or Wayfarer a week and over 200 were built in total before production ended in 1958. Early sales were disappointing, but the aircraft went on to provide a reliable bread-and-butter income; it was simple to build and cheap to operate. Customers included Silver City Airways, who used it on their Cross-Channel airborne car ferry services, the Argentine Air Force, Straits Air Freight Express in New Zealand and Aer Lingus.

A steady, dependable, unglamorous earner like the Freighter was in stark contrast to the stainless steel research monoplane Type 188, BAC's first turbojet (other jets had been

Farndon's illustration of the Freighter Merchant Venturer over Sydney Harbour from the 40th anniversary calendar (far left) (Bristol Aero Collection).

A Silver City operated Bristol Freighter loads a Bristol 401 luxury high-speed tourer, 1954 (left) (Airbus).

designed but had not got off the drawing board). This was the last true 'Bristol' aeroplane and one of only three to reach prototype flight after 1945, the others being Brabazon and Britannia.[16] It was designed specifically for supersonic tests in response to government specification ER 134 issued in February 1953. The sound barrier (Mach 1) had been broken by US Air Force pilot Chuck Yeager in the experimental X-1 on 14 December 1947; Type 188 was intended to reach Mach 2 and above. Sustaining high speed in an aircraft subjects the frame to extremely high temperatures – the original government specification had referred to temperatures of 300 degrees centigrade. Stainless steel was the material best able to cope with these conditions at the time and the BAC engineers developed a distinctive form of puddle-welding to work with it.[17] High speed also means that the aircraft is travelling too fast for the pilot to operate manual controls, so hydraulic power controls are needed. The aircraft was powered by the Gyron Junior engine from the de Havilland company, which was acquired by Bristol Siddeley in 1961.

Two fully-equipped prototypes of the Type 188 were built, the first making its maiden flight on 14 April 1962. Some of the aircraft's major components were made by Armstrong Whitworth Aircraft, which had been formed in Newcastle-upon-Tyne in 1912 and merged with Gloster Aircraft in 1961, both being by then members of the Hawker Siddeley group. The Type 188 did provide some useful information about the effects of prolonged kinetic heating on an aircraft but, according to Barnes, had little influence on the development of the supersonic Concorde because full-speed flight tests were of limited duration as fuel consumption was so great.[18] The highest speed it recorded was Mach 1.88, which seems rather apt considering its name.[19]

Type 188 on the apron at Filton, c 1962 (below left) (Rolls-Royce Heritage Trust).

Artist's impression of Type 188 in flight (below right) (Rolls-Royce Heritage Trust).

Photograph taken outside Fedden House in 1937 of the original team from the Cosmos Engineering Company at Fishponds (Rolls-Royce Heritage Trust). Fedden himself is standing front row centre.

Turning to aero-engine technology, other than a tentative attempt by Reid to build a three-cylinder engine for his short-lived Monocar project after World War One, BAC did not start making its own engines until the company acquired the assets of Cosmos Engineering, which owned aero-engine and automobile manufacturing facilities at Fishponds. Cosmos went into voluntary liquidation in March 1920, having overstretched its finances and 'struck a bad bargain in a shipping deal' with White Russia.[20] BAC's acquisition cost £15,000 and entailed 'five Jupiters, parts, drawings, patterns, tools and the services of Roy Fedden and a team of some thirty engineers'.[21] The purchase was encouraged by the Air Ministry, which had been asked for help by Fedden. He was anxious to keep his original team together so it could continue with his Jupiter project (an approach to Armstrong Siddeley had been rejected, as had an initial direct approach to BAC). Air Commodore Robert Brooke-Popham came down to Filton at the behest of the Ministry to push the deal through and the new BAC engine department was formally opened in July.[22] A Cosmos Jupiter and Lucifer were displayed at Olympia on the BAC stand the following month.

There were rumours that BAC intended to end engine production within a year because sales had been disappointing and did not justify the investment made to date. However, Gnome Rhone's decision to acquire a Bristol engine licence after seeing the Jupiter at an exhibition in Paris, along with the receipt of a production order from the British government, helped save the department.[23] In turn, it was the engine department that is now credited with keeping BAC in business during the inter-war slump in aircraft orders. The department provided innovative technology that produced reliable performance and high sales, and within a few years BAC had overtaken Armstrong Siddeley as the UK's main producer of air-cooled engines.[24] By 1921 almost all Bristol aircraft had Bristol engines, making BAC 'the leading airframe and aero-engine manufacturer in the United Kingdom'.[25]

This 1930s picture shows the West Works behind the Bristol Flying School (Rolls-Royce plc).

Port-side view of a Pegasus
Mk I.M.3 engine, 1932
(Rolls-Royce Heritage Trust).

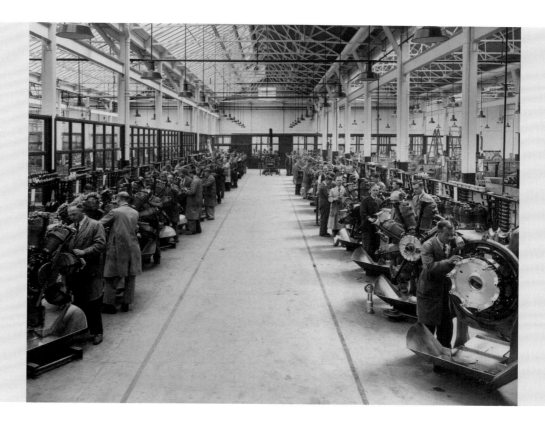

Inside the East Works, April 1937
(Rolls-Royce plc).

The engine department was first housed at the West Works at Filton in hangars that
had been built by Bristol Tramways & Carriage Company at a cost of £5,500. The
workforce rose from around 50 in 1920 to nearly 2,000 in 1930. A major expansion to
the East Works, situated east of Gloucester Road North at Patchway, was completed in
1936 near the start of the rearmament period. The new works had a floor area of over
6,000 square metres (200,000 square feet), along with a separate site for the manufacture
of cowlings and exhaust systems called the Rodney Works. The Gipsy Patch Lane site was
started in 1942.

The department's business was based on producing new engines and overhauling old ones.
The overhaul section was based at Whitchurch aerodrome for many years, having originally
been dispersed there during the war. Engines were stripped down, cleaned and checked,
re-varnished, re-enamelled, re-plated in cadmium, re-assembled and balanced, as necessary,
before being sent for testing. They would then be inhibited (filled with oil) to prevent
corrosion and the cowlings would be fitted around them so that when they reached their
final destination (the Royal Air Force or an airline company, for example), they could be
lifted more or less directly into position on the aircraft with just the mounting bolts to put
in place. The average overhaul life of an aero-engine has improved considerably over the
last 100 years. It can range from up to 20 operating hours for an early Gnome to around
3,500 for a Hercules to 25,000 for a RB211, for example.

Partly through its experience of guided weapons and the early space programme, British Aircraft Corporation at Filton developed expertise in the field of electronics. A centralised Electronics and Space Systems Group was formed to carry forward initiatives and it was this group which developed most of the flight-test instrumentation for the Concorde trials and the revolutionary digital controls for Concorde's Olympus engine intakes. In addition, the Concorde programme led the way in the extensive use of computers to compile, store and share project information. This included the thousands of design drawings that were produced and the diagrams of the complex wiring systems. Having first been used primarily for accounting, aviation drove forward the use of advanced computers in a design and manufacturing role.

View of the Vulcan bomber used as Concorde's Olympus 593 engine test-bed, c 1970 (above) (Rolls-Royce Heritage Trust).

A view showing the air intake arrangement for the Olympus 593 engine, c 1965 (facing page) (Rolls-Royce plc).

University of the West of England
students at the drawing board and in
a lab practical (UWE).

One of the challenges to be met in supersonic flight was how to reduce rapidly the speed of the air entering the engine without losing energy. Only one hundredth of a second is available in which to achieve this reduction before the air reaches the compressor. If energy is being lost from the air, then more fuel is required in compensation to achieve the necessary thrust, and this costs the company money. Not only is fuel expensive to buy, but the more fuel that needs to be on board, the fewer fare-paying passengers who can be carried. In addition, not reducing the speed in time can result in a high-pressure surge, which pilots have likened to the effect of a bomb going off under the wing. A surge can flip an aircraft over or rupture the engine intake. Highly responsive controls are therefore needed to operate the intake ramp which feeds air into the engine. The details of the Concorde intake design are still covered by the Official Secrets Act, but basically the air is slowed down by passing through a series of geometrical surfaces which produce controlled shockwaves.

Highly responsive digital controls were also needed in Concorde to control the flow of fuel between the storage tanks. The position of Concorde's centre of gravity had to be changed depending on whether it was in subsonic or supersonic mode. Balance was largely governed by the weight of the fuel in the tanks positioned in its tail and wings, thereby necessitating a rapid readjustment of the fuel levels in order to keep the aircraft stable. Fuel was transferred to the rear during acceleration past Mach 1 to maintain balance. It was then transferred forward during deceleration from Mach 2 to subsonic speeds. The fuel also absorbed some of the heat generated by air friction on the aircraft skin during supersonic flight.

Other innovative uses of electronics exploited at BAC and its associated companies included the telephone-activated remote start-up controls for Proteus-powered electricity generators in the 1950s, the specialised printed circuit boards that regenerated electricity for satellites in the 1960s and seventies, and the early development of mobile communications.

The high costs of developing such projects and the specialised knowledge required has increasingly led to industry-university collaborations, and the West of England aerospace industry has particularly strong research links with the city-region's university sector. The University of Bristol's aeronautical engineering department was set up at the instigation of BAC, which in June 1945 offered to endow the Sir George White Chair of Aeronautics in the Faculty of Engineering. On New Year's Day 1946 Professor Arthur Collar became the first to take up this post, with the first intake of six students arriving in October. Today, both the University of Bristol and the University of the West of England contribute to a range of aeronautical partnerships and projects, providing research and teaching that benefit students, academics and the industry.

How aeroplanes fly

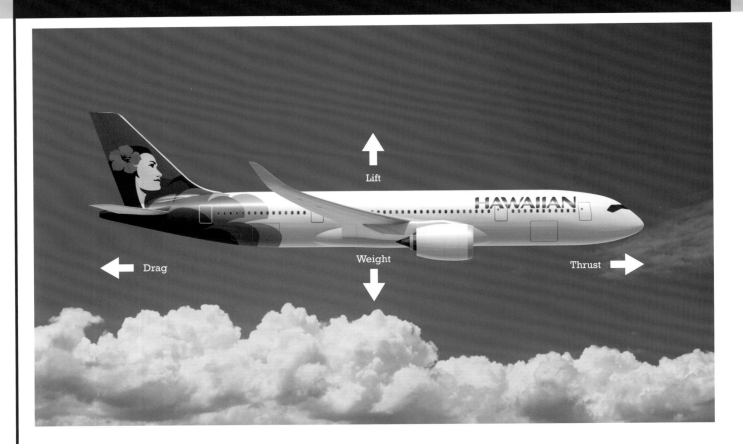

John Cayley defined the problem of mechanical flight by means of heavier-than-air machines as that of making 'a surface support a given weight by the application of power to the resistance of air'.[26]

There are four forces that act on an aeroplane in flight. These are:

- **Lift:** the upward aerodynamic force that comes from air moving over and under the aeroplane's wings.
- **Weight:** the downward force that results from gravity on the aeroplane's mass.
- **Thrust:** the forward force that comes from the aeroplane's engine exhaust or the propeller.
- **Drag:** the backward aerodynamic force that comes from the resistance caused by the aeroplane pushing against the air.

The picture on the facing page shows the four forces acting on the Airbus A350 (Airbus).

The picture below shows where the three axes cross on a Short Sunderland Flying Boat powered by Bristol Pegasus engines (Rolls-Royce plc).

The Wright brothers' achievement in 1903 was important not just because their aircraft got off the ground but because it sustained a controlled flight. Like Cayley, the brothers had begun their experiments with gliders so they could understand control and stability before adding power. Controlled movement is safe and predictable.

The three key words used to describe an aeroplane's controlled movement are:

- **Rolling:** the movement around the axis which runs from the aeroplane's nose to its tail.
- **Yawing:** the movement around the axis which runs from the top of the aeroplane to the bottom.
- **Pitching:** the movement around the axis which runs from one wing tip to the other.

The aeroplane's centre of gravity is located where the three axes intersect.

On most aeroplanes, the pilot can control these movements using special flaps: the ailerons, the rudder and the elevators. When these change position, they change the flow of the air around the aeroplane. By changing the flow of air, the direction in which the aeroplane flies is also changed.

Rolling is controlled by the ailerons on the trailing edge of the wings. When the one on the left wing is up, the right one is down and the aeroplane rolls to the left. When the right one is up, the left one is down and the aeroplane rolls to the right.

The award-winning ailerons designed by Leslie Frise for BAC were first used on the Bristol Brandon in 1924 and continue to be the standard design for aircraft with manual controls.[27] Frise, who was a graduate of the University of Bristol, was encouraged to join British & Colonial by Frank Barnwell in 1916. He was awarded the Sir Charles Wakefield Gold Medal for innovations and service to aviation.

Yawing is controlled by the rudder on the tail fin. When it moves to the left, the nose of the aeroplane goes left and the aeroplane moves left. When it moves to the right, the nose of the aeroplane goes right and the aeroplane moves right.

Pitching is controlled by the elevators on the tail plane. Unlike the ailerons, which move in opposition to each other, the elevators move together. When they are up, the tail of the aeroplane goes down, the nose goes up and it starts to climb. When they are down, the tail goes up, the nose goes down and the aeroplane starts to dive.

Rolling

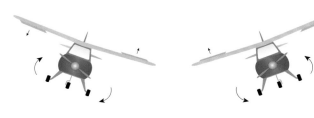

Yawing

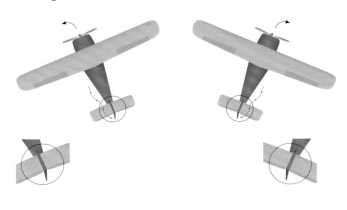

Pitching

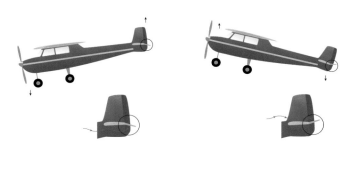

Illustrations above by Vicky Washington.

Arrow indicating the aileron on the M1D monoplane (facing page, top) (Bristol Aero Collection). The photograph was taken when the aircraft won the aerial Derby Handicap at Croydon, August 1922.

Arrow indicating the rudder on the frame of a Bloodhound, c 1923 (facing page, bottom left) (Bristol's Museums, Galleries and Archives).

Arrow indicating elevator on a Bulldog prototype, c 1927 (facing page, bottom right) (Bristol Aero Collection).

Aileron

Rudder

Elevator

& Colonial for the 1911 Gordon Bennett Cup was the company's first monoplane. It led to other variations, but was eventually superseded by Henri Coanda's designs.

Wings

338

Bullfinch with cantilever wing attached below, c 1924 (Rolls-Royce plc).

Production of Frank Barnwell's monoplanes was hampered by the temporary ban introduced by the War Office, but he did have the satisfaction of his M1C making the first flight over the Andes in December 1918. The pilot was Lieutenant Godoy of the Chilean airforce. The M1C's Le Rhône rotary unit was replaced with a Lucifer radial engine when it was modified as a post-war, single-seater sports and racing monoplane, the M1D.

The extra wings on biplanes and triplanes can provide more lift than is achieved by monoplanes. This means that large aeroplanes can fly at lower speeds without stalling, and also take off and land at shorter runways. The struts and wire bracing that keep the wings parallel give a strong, light structure but increase the drag and hence the demand for fuel. The last Bristol biplane was the Type 123 fighter, of which only one prototype was built. This had its flight tests in June 1934.

Hugo Junkers patented his cantilever wing design in 1910 and the Junkers Ju-1 made its maiden flight in 1915. A cantilever wing does not require any external struts or cables – even non-cantilevered monoplanes have some of these – as it is held in place by the strong, single beam or spar that runs through it, end to end. The beam does increase weight but this potential drawback is usually offset by the reduction in drag.

Some of BAC's earliest cantilever wings can be seen on the Bullfinch and the Bagshot, both designed by Barnwell. Two prototype Bullfinch monoplanes and one prototype biplane were ordered by the Air Ministry in April 1921. They were trialled by the Royal Air Force but no production orders were received. One prototype Bagshot monoplane was built in response to specification 4/24, an invitation to design a large, two-seater, twin-engined fighter issued in December 1924. It had an all-metal, semi-cantilever wing and made its first flight in July 1927. Again, it did not go into production. Other innovative cantilever designs from BAC, which could claim to be leading the field in this area, included the Type 133 fighter

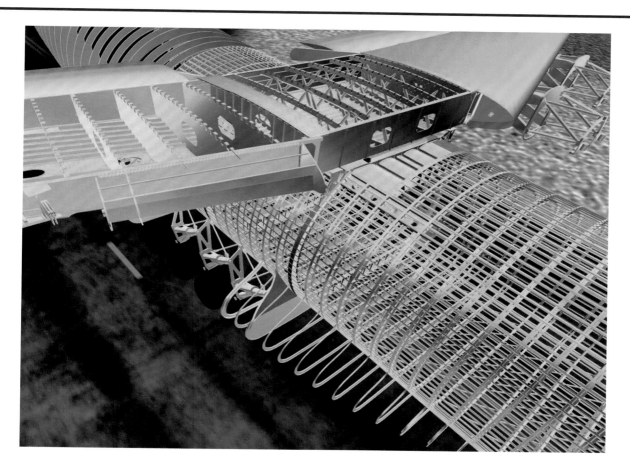

Computer simulation of the structure of the A400M wing, 2007 (above) (Airbus).

Engineer at Filton working on A400M wing, 2008 (facing page) (Airbus).

and Type 142. By the late 1930s, cantilever wings were the norm for almost all large aircraft worldwide as, combined with monocoque construction, they allowed for sleeker bodies and faster speeds.

After World War Two, ideas for flying wings started to be explored, but of more immediate interest was research on delta wings ('delta' means 'triangle'). Delta wings generate less drag at high speeds than straight ones – hence they can achieve supersonic flight more easily – but have the disadvantage of increasing it at low ones, which can lead to instability. The challenge facing designers was therefore not just to reach those high speeds but also to maintain control when flying subsonic. The Bristol Type 221 research aircraft was first flown at

Filton on 1 May 1964 by Godfrey Auty. It was a modified Fairey Delta that was given a so-called ogee (double-curve) wing to test its handling capabilities. Some of the findings from this research project were later used on Concorde.

Today, Filton is one of two UK sites that form the Airbus Centre of Excellence for Wing Design, the other being Broughton in North Wales. The wings of the A320 airliner were the first to be built here for the Airbus consortium, though Filton aerodynamicists had been consulted by Airbus' Hatfield office during the development of the earlier A310 wings. Structural test wings are kept in storage in a hangar at Kemble airfield throughout the lifespan of aircraft for reference in case of failure.

Pistons and propellers

The internal combustion engine was a late nineteenth-century invention but had already been anticipated by Sir George Cayley earlier in the century when he realised the type of power source needed as the prime mover for mechanical flight. William Henson and John Stringfellow's experimental models used specially designed light-weight steam engines that required an external boiler and furnace to work the pistons and drive their rudimentary propellers.

If combustion could be achieved internally, the result would be a more compact engine, reduced weight per unit of power and increased efficiency. Internal combustion engines were first used in cars and motorcycles. Some of the early aeroplane designers tried using these engines in their aircraft, but they were usually underpowered and too heavy to achieve flight. In any case, their primitive ignition systems made them hopelessly unreliable. Engines specially designed for aeroplanes were needed.

The power of a four-stroke internal combustion engine comes from four separate actions taking place consecutively inside each of the engine's cylinders.

1. Suck: the piston is pulled down, and air and fuel are sucked in through the inlet port at the top of the cylinder.
2. Squeeze: the inlet port closes, the piston is pushed up and the air inside the cylinder is compressed.
3. Bang: the fuel is set alight with a spark. This causes an explosion inside the cylinder (the combustion). The piston is pushed down strongly.
4. Blow: the exhaust port opens at the top of the cylinder and hot gas from the explosion is pushed out. The exhaust port closes, the piston is pushed up and the sequence begins again.

All aeroplanes powered by piston engines use propellers. With a four-stroke cylinder engine, the propeller is turned using some of the energy produced by the combustion during the third stroke. The piston is connected to a crankshaft by a connecting rod. The power of the piston turns the crankshaft and the crankshaft turns the propeller. At any moment, one cylinder of a multi-cylinder engine is firing and producing power to turn the propeller so the action is continuous. They fire in an even sequence so the power is delivered smoothly. In a nine-cylinder engine, for example, the sequence of firing would be 1, 3, 5, 7, 9, 2, 4, 6, 8, 1, 3 and so on, rather than 1, 2, 3, 4..., as this equalises the stresses on the crankshaft. The amount of thrust the propeller provides depends on the speed and the angle (pitch) at which the blades cut through the air.

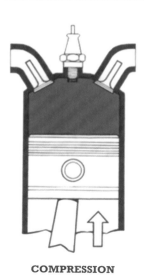 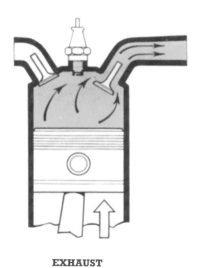 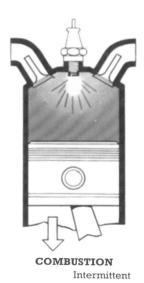

AIR/FUEL INTAKE   **COMPRESSION**   **EXHAUST**
Waste gases   **COMBUSTION**
Intermittent

Diagrams showing the four stages inside the piston engine cylinder
(Rolls-Royce plc).

Twin-bladed propeller powered by a Jupiter engine in a Bullfinch, c 1927
(Rolls-Royce plc) and three-bladed de Havilland propeller powered by a
Hercules engine in a Beaufighter, c 1938 (Rolls-Royce Heritage Trust).

Jupiter VIII fitted in Type 109 long-range prototype aircraft, c 1928 (Rolls-Royce plc).

In the early days of flight there was a danger that aero-engines would overheat and burn out or catch fire. One solution was the rotary engine, which had its cylinders arranged in a ring that rotated at the same time as the propeller turned. This helped prevent overheating as the cylinders were cooled by the cold air through which the engine spun. The Gnome used in the Bristol Boxkite is an example of this type. An alternative solution was an in-line, water-cooled design such as the Rolls-Royce Falcon used in the Bristol Fighter, in which coolant was continuously pumped around the outside of the cylinders. It passed through an external radiator (which extracted the heat generated by contact with the hot cylinders) before going back round again.

BAC became known for its expertise in designing and manufacturing air-cooled radial engines, of which the most famous was probably the nine-cylinder Bristol Jupiter. In September 1921 Jupiter I became the first air-cooled radial to pass the Air Ministry's 50-hour type test. Two years later Jupiter II became the first to complete the 150-hour test. Jupiter ratings ranged from 290hp to 595hp. Horsepower (hp) was traditionally used to indicate the level of thrust produced by an engine. The nineteenth-century inventor James Watt had worked out how much force a horse exerted to turn a wheel in a mill. This became his unit

A Hercules 767 in its clam-shell carrier, 1935 (Rolls-Royce Heritage Trust).

of measure for his steam engines, which he intended would replace horses (for example, 2hp is twice the power produced by the average mill horse).

The Jupiter had poppet valves that moved up and down to open and close the inlet and exhaust ports. In a sleeve-valve piston engine, a sleeve is fitted between the piston and the cylinder wall and rotated or slid back and forth. The sleeve has holes in its side that align with the ports at the appropriate stages in the cycle to let in air or expel exhaust. A sleeve is subject to less wear than a poppet and has fewer component parts. A further advantage is that in a poppet-valve engine, the exhaust gases exit through a narrow gap which can burn and erode the sealing surfaces and deposit carbon more readily than is the case with the larger ports on the sleeve. These factors mean the sleeve-valve engine can generally remain in service for longer between overhauls

than a poppet. The system was patented for use in the automotive industry in the early twentieth century. BAC's nine-cylinder Perseus was the first sleeve-valve engine cleared for flight (1932) and the first such engine to be developed commercially. It made its first flight in October 1933 in a Bulldog. It was rated at over 800hp. The Hercules sleeve-valve engine had its first run in January 1936. It was a 14-cylinder radial, with the cylinders arranged in two rows (a first for BAC). Over 50,000 were built before production ended in 1966 and it was the most successful sleeve-valve in the world. It developed from 1,270hp to 2,300 hp. The Centaurus had its first run in 1938. This was an 18-cylinder, two-row sleeve-valve radial which began at around 2,000hp and eventually reached 3,200hp.

A production run of cylinder liners for sleeve-valve engines, c 1940 (Rolls-Royce plc).

The No 4 Shop where Theseus was assembled, c 1949 (Rolls-Royce plc).

A Perseus Mk XIIc being installed in a de Havilland Flamingo, c 1939
(Rolls-Royce Heritage Trust).

Farndon's illustration of Theseus during 500-hour run
(Bristol's Museums, Galleries and Archives).

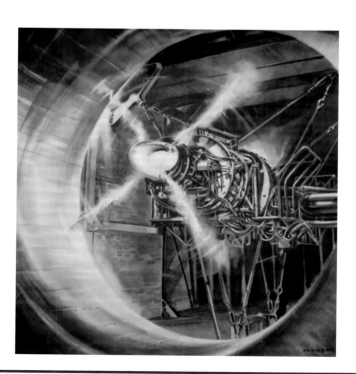

In 1948 the Bristol Theseus became the world's first turboprop engine to pass its type test. This engine retained the use of propellers to produce thrust, but the propeller was driven by means of a gas turbine rather than a piston engine. A new gas turbine test-bed was built at Patchway in 1949. Theseus was designed by Frank Owner, Fedden's successor at BAC. While other companies were looking to jet engines for use in large airliners, BAC preferred the turboprop, using the Bristol Proteus in Britannia. An article in *The 'Bristol' Quarterly* explained the differences and advantages:

> Turboprop and jet engines are essentially similar so far as the power-producing parts are concerned: both are gas turbines. The basic difference is that one does its work by driving a propeller, the other by ejecting a high-velocity stream of hot gas. But it is quite erroneous to believe that the turboprop was a preliminary step to the jet engine – that the jet is more modern and therefore better. The jet came first; the turboprop is a more recent development of the gas turbine aircraft engine and has won its place because it is a more efficient engine for airline requirements.[28]

With Proteus, BAC also pioneered the adaptation of aero gas turbines for marine use and electrical generation.

Roy Fedden

If BAC's reputation in its first decades as a leading manufacturer of airframes was largely down to the designs of Frank Barnwell, then its success as the manufacturer of engines in the inter-war period can be attributed to the work of designer Roy Fedden.[29]

Fedden was born in Stoke Bishop, Bristol on 6 June 1885. His father was a sugar merchant. He was educated at Clifton College and the Merchant Venturers' Technical College in Bristol before taking up a three-year engineering apprenticeship with the Bristol Motor Company of Redcross Street. In 1907 he entered the drawing office of the company Brazil, Straker and Co in Lodge Causeway at Fishponds. He brought with him his design for a motor car, which was developed into the 12/14 Shamrock that was exhibited at the Motor Show at Olympia in November. The following year he became the company's Works Manager and Chief Engineer.

According to Fedden's biographer:

> His interest in motor cars, which in those early days he not only built but raced, never left him, but the First World War changed the course of his engineering career... His factory turned to the manufacture of Rolls-Royce and Renault aircraft engines and during the rest of his life as a professional engineer, aircraft engines were his dominant interest.[30]

Portrait of Roy Fedden by Dorothy Wilding, c 1934 (Rolls-Royce Heritage Trust).

Brazil Straker was approved for Rolls-Royce engine production in 1915 (the only firm to receive such an accolade) providing the company did not design its own liquid-cooled engines in competition. It began production with the six-cylinder Hawk, followed by the Falcon. On 5 April 1917 the Royal Naval Air Service issued a specification for a fixed, air-cooled radial engine. Fedden, by now Brazil Straker's Technical Director, and Leonard 'Bunny' Butler, its Chief Draughtsman, worked together on designs for their 14-cylinder, two-row Mercury and nine-cylinder, single-row Jupiter, submitting them to the Air Ministry the following year. Brazil Straker had recently been taken over by an Anglo-American financial group which

Playing cricket at Clifton College, c 1900 (above) (Clifton College).

The Brazil Straker works at Fishponds before World War One (right)
(Fishponds Local History Society).

had hived off aspects of the business in which it had no
interest, including the Fishponds factory. This was renamed
Cosmos Engineering. Fedden remained Technical Director
and Butler became Chief Designer.

The Cosmos Mercury made its first flight in British &
Colonial's Bristol Scout F on 4 September 1918. The
Cosmos Jupiter had its first flight in the Bristol Badger in
1919 and used the one-off Bristol Bullet as a flying test-
bed. These ventures marked the beginning of a partnership
between Fedden and Barnwell which was strengthened
when Fedden and his team joined BAC in 1920. Fedden
persuaded the company to invest heavily in development.

He also had written into his contract that he would
be paid royalties on his designs, something the directors
later came to regret. After a slow start, by the end of the
decade Fedden could point to an illustrious and profitable
track record as 'between 1920 and 1930 Bristol air-cooled
radial engines were installed in 262 different prototype
aircraft throughout the world, over 70 of which went
into production'.[31]

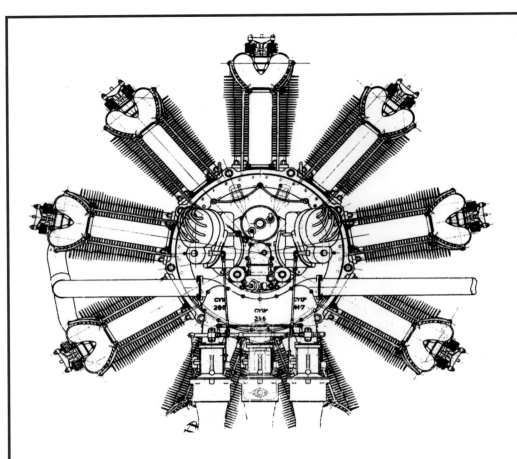

Rear end view of the Cosmos Jupiter I engine, c 1919 (Rolls-Royce Heritage Trust).

Advertisement for Bristol radial engines and Bulldogs, 1931 (facing page) (Bristol Aero Collection).

Fedden's Bristol Mercury, a nine-cylinder, highly supercharged radial, had its first run on 21 September 1926 and its first flight on 4 May 1927. It was designed originally for the Schneider Cup Race and its rating ranged from 500hp to 1,065hp. On 30 January 1931 type tests were completed on the long-stroke Mercury V, which became the Pegasus (the Air Ministry had insisted that the name be changed). On 7 November 1938 a Pegasus-powered Vickers Wellesley set a new world distance record of 11,120 kilometres (7,158 miles), the engine having already achieved considerable success in setting records for altitude. Demand for Pegasus is credited with the introduction of a night shift at Patchway by the end of 1932.

Fedden was described by colleagues as an autocratic man, driven to perfection, who set exceptional standards for himself and others. He fell out with the BAC board in 1942, the year he was knighted, and was forced to resign (he had never been a board member himself). Although the circumstances are unclear, the dispute was possibly over the

board's proposed introduction of a commercial manager to oversee the engine division, something they doubtless realised would annoy him. On leaving BAC, Fedden was appointed Technical Adviser to the Air Ministry and from 1942 to 1945 he was special adviser to the Minister of Aircraft Production, Sir Stafford Cripps. His research into US higher education led to the publication of the Fedden Report in 1944, in which he recommended the setting up of a postgraduate college of aeronautics in the UK. Out of this came Cranfield College, 'the embodiment of his vision', which opened in 1946.[32] The college later became the Cranfield Institute of Technology. Fedden was on its board of governors from its inception until 1969.

Fedden was president of the Royal Aeronautical Society in 1938-40 and 1944-5, aeronautical adviser to the North Atlantic Treaty Organisation from 1951 to 1952 and was associated with the Dowty Group from 1953 until 1960. He died at his home, Buckland Old Mill, on the Usk at Bwlch on 21 November 1973.

Altitude records

During the 1930s BAC's engine department achieved international acclaim through its association with the setting of new altitude records.

The first to be broken by the company during that impressive decade was on 6 September 1932, when Chief Test Pilot Cyril Uwins flew to an altitude of nearly 13,404 metres (43,976 feet) in a modified Vickers Vespa biplane powered by the Pegasus IS3 engine. This was the first time the world's altitude record was held by the UK. Two years later, on 11 April 1934, Renato Donati in a Caproni biplane, also powered by a Pegasus, attained 14,533 metres (47,680 feet), claiming the record for the Italians.

The following month, on 14 May 1934, a Westland Wapiti set a new record for diesel engines using the Bristol Phoenix, an experimental version of the Pegasus. The aircraft, flown by Harald Penrose, attained 8,368 metres (27,453 feet). Westland was based at Yeovil in Somerset and had been manufacturing aircraft since 1915. The Wapiti was a general-purpose military biplane that first entered service for the Royal Air Force in June 1928 in Iraq. On 3 April 1933 Squadron Leader Lord Clydesdale and Flight Lieutenant McIntyre became the first pilots to fly over Mount Everest in two modified Wapitis (the Westland-Houston PV 3) powered by the Pegasus. The private enterprise was financed by the ultra-patriotic Lady Houston, an eccentric former suffragette and adventuress. It was made at a time when the mountain summit had yet to be scaled on foot. The drama of the flight, which was

captured by observer-photographers Colonel Blacker and Sidney Bonnet, was heightened by the knowledge that there would be no place to land if they got into difficulties. BAC could take pride in the fact that the crate of engine spares that had been taken on the expedition returned to Filton with its seals unbroken. Roy Fedden's engines had not required a single replacement part.

On 28 September 1936 Squadron Leader F R D Swain became the first pilot to exceed an altitude of 15,000 metres when he reached 15,230 metres (49,967 feet) in the Bristol Type 138A powered by a specially designed, supercharged, four-bladed Pegasus engine. This was the first time the altitude record had been captured by an aircraft and engine made by the same company. The Type 138A had been built in response to an Air Ministry specification for a high-altitude research aircraft. It was based on an earlier Frank Barnwell design which BAC had been unable to take forward as a private venture because of the prohibitive cost. The detailed work was carried out by Clifford Tinson. The Type 138A was a large, wooden, single-seater, light-weight monocoque monoplane with a fixed undercarriage. Swain had to wear an experimental rubberised suit, made airtight by a metal band around the waist, and a pressure-helmet into which oxygen was pumped. Exhaust gases were pumped around the cockpit to keep him warm. The cockpit also had a unique safety feature – a form of dead-man's handle – in case the suit failed and Swain lost consciousness.

The altitude record was reclaimed by the Italians on 8 May 1937 in another Caproni biplane, but was back in British possession on 30 June 1937 when Flight Lieutenant M J

Renato Donati prepares for his record-breaking flight, 1934
(Bristol Aero Collection).

Adam reached 16,440 metres (53,937 feet) in the modified Type 138A. The aircraft had been made lighter by having smaller, brakeless wheels fitted. The pitch of the engine's propeller had also been altered to improve performance.

Such achievements brought welcome publicity to the company and were exploited in its advertising material. It also potentially had national benefit, as an editorial in *Flight* prompted by Adam's achievement declared:

> Records have both an unseen value and a concrete value. The prestige which the possession of a world's record brings to a country is reflected in a number of ways, one of which is increased value of aeronautical exports. It may even add weight to the word of that country at an international conference. Certainly it makes taxpayers more willing to support the country's Air Force when they are assured that the designers are capable of providing machines of real class.[33]

Farndon's illustration of the Type 138A from the 40th anniversary calendar (facing page) (Bristol Aero Collection).

BAC advertisement promoting the Everest expedition (top) (Rolls-Royce Heritage Trust).

BAC continued to break records. Here is Walter Gibb (in white) after breaking the world altitude record on 20 August 1955 in an English Electric Canberra powered by two Bristol Olympus 102s (left) (private collection).

Jet engines

Like the piston engine, the jet engine has four key actions – sucking, squeezing, banging and blowing. The difference is that these actions take place continuously in different parts of the engine, rather than in separate stages.

- Suck: air is sucked into the engine through the intake at the front by the rotating blades.
- Squeeze: the air is driven through the engine by the compressor blades, which squeeze it into a tighter and tighter space.
- Bang: fuel is sprayed into the compressed air and ignited so it bursts into flames.
- Blow: the hot gases of the flames generate energy to turn the turbine blades. The turbine produces the power to drive the compressor. The gases blow out the exhaust at the back of the engine, thrusting the aeroplane forward.

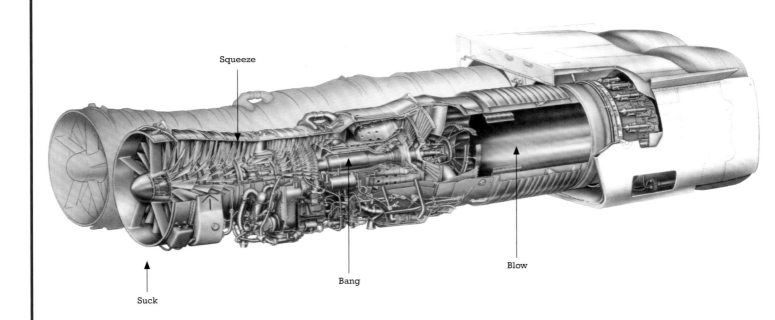

Illustration showing the location for the four stages using a cutaway drawing of the Olympus 593 Mk610-14-28 Concorde engine (Rolls-Royce plc).

The UK's first jet test aircraft was Gloster Aircraft's E28, which was fitted with Frank Whittle's pioneering gas turbine. It made its maiden flight in May 1941. The country's first jet fighter was also built by Gloster Aircraft. This was the Gloster Meteor, which commenced operations in 1944 and set a new world speed record of 606mph on 7 November 1945, 137mph faster than the previous record holder.[34] By this stage the original engine design had been taken over from Power Jets Ltd by Rolls-Royce of Derby. BAC was assigned a post-war contract to oversee modifications to the aircraft, but this was cancelled. The company had not been involved in the early jet research as Roy Fedden believed it would take too much research and development to get a jet engine to perform as well as a piston one; it was an unnecessary distraction. BAC had done some work for Whittle, however, including undertaking material tests on turbine blades and machining compressors at the Spring Quarry underground factory. An office block opened in the early 1960s at BAC's Gipsy Patch Lane site at Patchway was named Whittle House in the designer's honour.

When BAC eventually entered the jet age, it needed to employ new processes at the factory and purchase new machinery. It was now making turbine blades and casings of fabricated steel sheet, which required different welding techniques from those used before. New test-beds were also needed for the different types of jet engines, although some beds that had previously been used for piston engines were able to be converted.

The Bristol Olympus, the company's first pure jet engine, was a two-spool turbojet. In a turbojet all the thrust comes from the hot gas blown out the exhaust at the rear. This is in contrast to a turbofan, like the Rolls-Royce Trent, where the thrust comes from the hot exhaust gas *and also* from the cold air that an additional fan at the front pushes around the sides of the core engine. The two-spool system was pioneered at BAC. Compression takes place in two stages by means of two compressors acting in series, each driven by its own turbine. This results in lower fuel

consumption. Like all engines, the Olympus was developed as a family, so although it retained the name, the Olympus 593, as used in Concorde, had a different capacity and purpose from the original Olympus 100. Individual modifications were also required to suit the different locations into which the engines were installed, for example modifying the fuel system to suit a particular aircraft's type of intake. In the course of development, Olympus' thrust capacity increased from around 40 kiloNewtons/9,000lbs to 178 kiloNewtons/40,000lbs. BAC continued the development of the engine as a private venture for many years in the face of government insistence that the UK should have only one large-scale jet-engine programme, Rolls-Royce's Conway.

Olympus series number B 01-1 had its first fixed test-bed run on 6 May 1950. Flying test-beds are also used in engine development. Where possible, it is preferable to test a new engine on an established aircraft – otherwise, both are untried. English Electric's Canberra was first used as a

Spraying an Olympus 101 engine with a protective layer to prevent moisture seeping in during storage, c late 1950s (Rolls-Royce plc).

The Vulcan runway fire, 1962 (Rolls-Royce Heritage Trust).

flying test-bed for the Olympus on 5 August 1952. Series number 01-1/2B set new altitude records in a Canberra on 4 May 1953 (19,406 metres/63,668 feet) and 29 August 1955 (20,083 metres/65,890 feet). The aircraft was flown by Wing Commander Walter F Gibb, who was BAC's Assistant Chief Test Pilot at that time, having joined the company as an apprentice in 1937. During the war he had supported the Dambusters Squadron as flight commander with 605 Squadron. The company also acquired one of the four-engined Avro Ashton aircraft for test purposes. The Ashton had been built to a specification from the Ministry of Supply for the study of high-altitude flying.

The Avro Vulcan was another aircraft used by BAC as a test-bed, from the Olympus 100 through to the 593. In one particularly memorable incident, on the afternoon of 2 December 1962 a Vulcan used for tests on the Olympus 320 burst into flames on Filton's main east/west runway. The shaft failed and the whole turbine was flung off, cutting the airframe in half and setting the aircraft alight. The Vulcan airframe and Olympus engine contained magnesium alloy and observers recalled that once lit, the aircraft went up like a firework display. When burning oil spilled from a collapsed wing, it ran down the runway to the BAC fire engine that was in attendance. That, too, was consumed by flames and destroyed beyond repair.

Other Bristol jet engines originally developed before the Rolls-Royce merger were the Orpheus, a light-weight, single-spool turbojet, the prototype of which had its first run in December 1954, and the Pegasus, first run in 1959 and used for vertical take-off and landing. Orpheus' main claim to fame is that it powered the Gnat, as used by the Red Arrows in their first displays (they later switched to the Hawk powered by the Patchway-built Adour). Pegasus is associated with the Harrier jump-jet.

Stanley Hooker played an important role in the BAC jet engine programme. In September 1948 Hooker left Rolls-Royce in Derby having fallen out with Ernest Walter Hives, head of the Aero Division. He was invited to join BAC by his friend Reginald Verdon Smith, who was then a company director and would become BAC's Chairman and Joint Managing Director in 1955. Smith, a great-nephew of Sir George White, had joined BAC in 1938 after initially embarking on a career in law. In 1953 he was knighted for services to Bristol, in particular for his contribution to the city as Chairman of the Bristol Local Employment Committee.

Hooker was BAC's Chief Engineer on the engine side from 1951 and later a director of Bristol Aero Engines Ltd. When Rolls-Royce merged with Bristol Siddeley in 1966, Hooker was not appointed to the new board, perhaps because of the ill-feeling dating back to his leaving the company in 1948, and he retired in September 1970. A month later he returned as Technical Director to help the Derby works with its problems with the RB211 engine. He was unable to resolve the situation before Rolls-Royce was forced into insolvency as result of the spiralling development costs. The funding of RB211 was taken over by the government, which acquired the company's aero assets. Hooker, who was knighted in 1974, died on 24 May 1984 in the Chesterfield Hospital, Clifton, Bristol.

The Pegasus 11-61 engine on pre-rig test, c 1990 (top) (Rolls-Royce plc).

Sir Stanley Hooker standing in front of a Britannia, c 1952 (left) (Rolls-Royce Heritage Trust).

Pre-fabrication

The BAC directors, like any responsible business people, were always looking for alternative ways of exploiting their factory's technology, machinery and human resources when there was downturn in demand for its usual product. One area that proved lucrative for a few years was the pre-fabrication of aluminium buildings.

Wartime bomb damage in Palmyra Road, Bedminster, Bristol, photographed by Jim Facey c 1940 (Bristol Record Office).

In February 1944 Sir Stafford Cripps, Minister of Aircraft Production, called a meeting of representatives of the leading UK aircraft manufacturers to discuss how the industry might help to address the housing crisis brought by the war. Thousands of homes had been destroyed or rendered uninhabitable by bombing raids and it was essential that a rebuilding programme be initiated as soon as possible. The government recognised that the aviation industry had both the materials and the skills to achieve this. BAC was represented at the meeting by Captain Kenneth Bartlett, who said that 'the aircraft industry is not a cheap producer' so the priority would not be to produce inexpensive housing but to provide work for redundant labour, to which the Ministry officials 'were quick to retort that speed, low cost and efficiency were all part of the same picture'.[35] It was originally proposed that half a million pre-fabricated temporary homes for UK use would be manufactured, in addition to those that were needed for export to war zones overseas. However, because of the unexpectedly high estimates submitted by the aircraft companies, the government target was rapidly cut. In the event, approximately 13,000 people were employed nationally at the peak of production in 1946 and a total of 54,500 homes were eventually completed.

Work was overseen by the Aircraft Industries Research Organisation on Housing (AIROH), jointly formed by the Ministry of Aircraft Production and the Ministry of Works. The founder-members from industry were BAC, Morrisons Engineering Ltd, J V Rushton (Wolverhampton) Ltd, Prefabricated Constructions Ltd, Aero Engines Ltd, Blackburn Aircraft Ltd, General Aircraft Ltd, Hawker Siddeley Ltd and High Duty Alloys Ltd (five of the nine being in the aircraft business). Similar diversification was also taking place in aviation companies in other countries that had been involved in the war. The advantage of using aluminium for the building programme was that it was strong but light, so the pre-fabricated sections could easily be transported from the factory for speedy assembly on site. It was also in plentiful supply in the aviation industry, having been bought in bulk for the war effort and then no longer needed for aircraft production.

BAC (Housing) Ltd was set up as a subsidiary of the main company and the BAC workforce at Weston-super-Mare was diverted from the building of Beaufighters to this new line of work. According to *The 'Bristol' Quarterly*, 'So rapidly and efficiently was the change-over effected that in mid-1945 the first bungalows were taking shape at one end of the production line as, at the other, the last aircraft reached the final assembly stage'.[36] Wall sections were made in four different heights, all 1.2 metres (four feet) wide, either ready-glazed or solid. The roof sections came with an insulated ceiling. The sections were given an external protective weather-resistant finish in the factory. They were then bolted together on-site onto previously prepared concrete rafts and lined internally with standard-sized sheets of hardboard. BAC also provided the builders with jigs for the bungalows' erection.

In Shirehampton on 30 July 1945 the first tenant moved into a BAC-built AIROH bungalow. Over 11,000 were completed in the first three years of production. In addition to Shirehampton, other pre-fab homes in the area included those at Sea Mills, Little Stoke, Henleaze, along Shellard Road and in Roycroft Avenue in Filton and by Filton Station. Several non-BAC-built pre-fabs are still occupied in Bristol despite being conceived as a temporary stopgap.

When the demand for homes receded, BAC turned to larger buildings with the production of pre-fabricated sections for schools. Local authorities were looking for 'flexibility, economy, and a degree of permanence

The
A·I·R·O·H
HOUSE

THE BRISTOL AEROPLANE COMPANY LIMITED

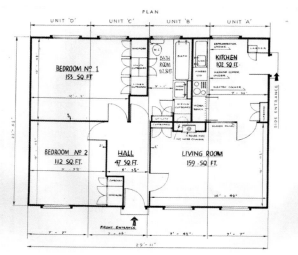

Cover of BAC's AIROH brochure, c 1946 (top) (Bristol Aero Collection).

Floor plan from the AIROH brochure, c 1946 (bottom) (Bristol Aero Collection).

comparable with that of traditional structures'.[37] In 1948 the UK's first permanent pre-fabricated aluminium school was erected at Lockleaze in north Bristol. It had 12 classrooms and could accommodate 480 pupils, with a separate school for infants built next door. The schools were officially opened on 9 March 1949 by the Minister of Education. The buildings are still in use as part of Romney Avenue Junior. Over 450 BAC schools were built in total for 95 different education authorities. Sites included Shield Road in Filton, Trevenson in Cornwall, Packmoor near Stoke, Leyland in Lancashire, Blackpool, Sheffield, Glasgow and Inverness.

The largest BAC Mk I school in Britain was opened at Ballingry, Scotland in September 1950 for 600 children. BAC's Mark II multi-storey system was used to build the thousand-place Green Farm Comprehensive in Coventry. The same system was used for the BAC apprentices' school at Filton. A Mark III system was also developed that was suitable for tropical and sub-tropical countries.

Post-war demand for pre-fabricated buildings soon eased in the UK, so BAC looked to overseas markets. Among such projects was a 50-bed aluminium hospital in Greece. Erection was completed in two months in 1951 by 12 local workmen supervised by a BAC foreman. Pre-fab schools were built under licence in Australia after an initial batch of 26 had been exported in 1950, and in 1952 the first Australian aluminium post office opened. That same year it was announced in *Bristol Review* that the BAC Housing Company was to be renamed The Bristol Aeroplane Company (Weston) Ltd to reflect the fact that activities taking place at the site were not confined to pre-fabs. By the end of the year, for example, the company had taken on extensive subcontracting work for Britannia from BAC's Aircraft Division.

Cover of *Bristol Review* showing crates of pre-fab sections in transit to Australia, 1950 (facing page) (Bristol Aero Collection).

Opening ceremony at Shirehampton AIROH, c 1945 (below) (Bristol Aero Collection).

Brabazon

The Bristol Brabazon, the UK's largest civil transport aircraft, was a commercial failure but could in many ways be regarded as a technological success. Looking back with the hindsight of the 1950s to his conversations with Sir George White, Harry Harper wrote:

> One point I particularly recall raising: an intriguing argument was beginning to crop up in air circles about the practicability of building any very large type of flying machine. Some critics thought the sheer structural weight might preclude it from being a practical load-carrying proposition. I asked Sir George what he thought. After a moment, he said that in his experience, when any seemingly insoluble structural or engineering problem cropped up, new and improved techniques generally came along with the right answer. And so he reckoned that means would be found to take advantage of the greater size of the various components to effect weight reductions impossible in small-scale construction.
>
> When I think of that now, I find myself wondering if Sir George could already see in his mind's eye such future giants as the Brabazon and the Britannia.[38]

The Brabazon committee, chaired by J T C Moore-Brabazon, by then Lord Brabazon of Tara, was formed in December 1942 to plan post-war civil transport on the assumption that the Allies would be victorious. BAC was initially excluded from the group of aircraft manufacturers who were invited to join the consultations but, after protests, Leslie Frise attended the committee's first meeting, which was held in London on 14 January 1943. On 11 March the government announced that BAC would be starting an initial investigation into one of the committee's five recommendations – a large transatlantic airliner – providing this would not have a detrimental effect on the company's war work. The Brabazon Committee Type 1 (Bristol Type 167) was Frise's last project for the company before leaving to work for Percival Aircraft at Luton, where he would later be responsible for the Provost and the Jet Provost, among other aircraft. Several BAC employees left Filton to join the team he gathered there.

Cuneo's painting of the construction of the Brabazon hangar, August 1947 (Airbus).

Naked Brabazon during construction, c 1946
(Special Collections, Bristol Central Library).

Construction of the Brabazon prototype began in October 1945. This was developed from an earlier unrealised design for a 100-ton bomber. When the Brabazon was planned, it was on the lines of the pre-war Imperial Airways flying boats, providing an upmarket service for around 100 upmarket passengers, with an onboard cinema, lounge, cocktail bar and sleeping quarters. It was a liner of the air comparable with *Queen Mary* or *Queen Elizabeth* and its construction was closer to that of shipbuilding than aeroplane manufacture in terms of its scope and the methods used.

Brabazon was 54 metres (177 feet) long with a wingspan of 70 metres (230 feet). Being so large, it required a stronger, longer, wider runway than other aircraft, not just for normal take-offs but also in the case of emergency landings if the brakes failed. The existing Filton runway needed to be enlarged and in March 1946 it was announced that Charlton Village, adjacent to the site, would be demolished to provide the necessary space. Most residents were re-housed in council homes in Patchway, paying a special subsided rent. This was supposed to be a temporary measure while a replacement village was built at St Swithuns, but this promise was not kept and people either stayed on in Patchway or eventually drifted off to other places under their own means, thereby breaking up the original

Aerial view of the Brabazon hangar and east/west main runway at Filton, c 1970 (Rolls-Royce Heritage Trust). Although it got limited use from Brabazon, the new runway was an essential facility for BAC to have as it entered the age of large airliners.

community.[39] Those who had previously been living in dilapidated cottages at Charlton were obviously keener to be relocated than those who had had more substantial homes. The Carpenter's Arms, known as The Chippy and a popular lunch-time haunt for BAC workers, was also among the buildings lost. The runway was said to have caused a shortage of cement in the South West because so much was needed for its construction. Brabazon was so heavy and so big it could only be towed into position on the runway using a 40-tonne Scammel tractor borrowed from the Army, where it had previously been used to tow tanks.

A new hangar covering an area of eight hectares had to be built for the aircraft's assembly. Its curved, cantilevered roof was constructed using methods developed from the manufacture of aircraft wings and it was described as 'one of the most impressive industrial buildings of the century'.[40] During the nearly two years that elapsed between Brabazon's fuselage shell being towed into the hangar on 4 October 1947 and its final assembly, various development tests were conducted, including of the aircraft's hydraulic surface control units in an Avro Lancaster and of its combustion heaters in a Bristol Buckmaster.

Brabazon's maiden flight took place on 4 September 1949. Bill Pegg, who had succeeded Cyril Uwins as Chief Test Pilot in 1947, was at the controls. To observers on the ground the aircraft looked to be flying unusually slowly at take-off, but this was an optical illusion due to its immense size. Powered by eight Bristol Centaurus piston engines driving contra-rotating propellers, it eventually attained 250mph at 7,620 metres (25,000 feet). A 'Brabazon at

Brabazon emerges from its hangar, 1949 (above) (Peter Rushby Archive).

Brabazon at Farnborough airshow, September 1950 (right)
(private collection).

Bristol at Home Day' was held at Filton on June 10 1950 for BAC's employees and five days later the aircraft gave demonstration flights at London airport.

Despite a positive response from the public, the market was not ready for an aircraft built on this scale. Airline companies were moving into the jet age, leaving piston engines behind. In addition, in the US manufacturers were having some success in converting their large bombers for civil use, thereby meeting existing market demand. Unable to find customers willing to buy it, BAC sold the one and only Brabazon at scrap metal value to a London merchant who began cutting it up in October 1953. Designs for a MKII prototype powered by Proteus were completed, and at least half of the aircraft was built including the fuselage and most of the wing.

Brabazon logged less than 400 hours' flying time but, according to C H Barnes, among others, 'the research and manufacturing experience gained from building and flying so large a pressurised prototype established the Company in an unassailable technical position in the field of

structural design'.[41] Experience of Brabazon led Archibald E Russell and his BAC design team to devise new, long-life structures for bigger, faster aircraft and these were applied to the Britannia. Valuable lessons were also learned about the use of pressurised cabins, hydraulic power controls, AC electrical generation on aircraft, electric engine controls and gust load alleviation systems. In addition, the specially built runway and hangar meant BAC was in a position to move into the large airliner business at a later date. Held in affection by those who saw it, Brabazon was likened by Barnes to Isambard Kingdom Brunel's mammoth ss *Great Eastern*, 'a pioneer on the grand scale born a generation too soon for its environment'.[42]

Archibald E Russell

Archibald E Russell led the teams which designed the airframes of Brabazon, the Freighter, Britannia and Concorde, among other aircraft. He was born on 30 May 1904 in Wotton under Edge, Gloucestershire, and claimed his early enthusiasm for engineering was inspired by his childhood Meccano set.[43] He went to East Dean grammar school, Cinderford, where his father was headmaster, and Fairfield secondary school, Bristol before winning a scholarship to the University of Bristol. In 1924 he graduated with a BSc in automotive engineering and started as assistant fitter at Bristol Tramways' bus maintenance depot, helping to keep the Bristol fleet on the road.

A friend recommended him to Frank Barnwell and in May 1925 he became Assistant Stress Calculator at BAC at Filton, being promoted to Chief Stress Calculator a year later. In this role he contributed to the success of the Bristol Bulldog with his research into the still novel use of steel-strip in airframes. He was promoted to Chief Technician, working under Barnwell and Leslie Frise, and helped to develop the use of stressed-skin construction. An early application of this method was the Type 142, Britain First, which formed the basis of the Blenheim bomber. Russell was BAC's Technical Designer from 1938 and succeeded Frise as Chief Designer in 1944, a position he held until 1960 when he became Technical Director. He was later Managing Director and then Chairman of the Filton division of the British Aircraft Corporation, but was described by his biographer as 'the sort of engineer who liked to get his hands dirty' rather than one who would confine himself to his office.[44] He retired in 1969.

Russell served on the Supersonic Transport Aircraft Committee of the Ministry of Transport and Civil Aviation from 1956 to 1959, and the last decade of his working life was dominated by the Concorde programme. He led the British design team and was Deputy Technical Director of the Anglo-French airframe committee. He frequently clashed with Pierre Satre of Sud Aviation, the committee's Technical Director, who felt that they should both confine themselves to policy rather than getting involved in the more hands-on details – something Russell was unwilling to do. Russell also encouraged competition between the British and French teams, believing that 'sharp criticism of each other's work ensured high standards, despite complaints from some quarters that this approach wasted

Archibald E Russell standing in front of Britannia, c 1957 (above)
(Rolls-Royce Heritage Trust).

The pre-production Concorde 01 has a fuselage section lowered into position
while the cabin section awaits position on jigs to one side, 1968 (right) (Airbus).

time and deprived the project of strategic leadership'.[45]
However, notwithstanding the antagonism that the fiery
tempered and opinionated Russell sometimes engendered,
he did become a friend of Sud Aviation's Louis Giusta, with
whom he jointly chaired Concorde's executive committee.

Russell died at his home in Hayle, Cornwall on 29 May
1995. Among the honours he was accorded during his
career were an Honorary Doctorate from the University of
Bristol in 1951, a CBE in 1955 and a knighthood in 1972.

Plastics and composites

Reflecting on changes seen over the previous 50 years of flight, an article in the Spring 1954 edition of *The 'Bristol' Quarterly* said: 'After 20 years wood gave way to steel, which was in turn superseded some 20 years ago by aluminium. Now there are signs that aluminium may soon be challenged by an entirely new group of materials, the reinforced plastics.'[46]

BAC's involvement in plastics came out of its Armament Division which had been set up in the rearmament period of the late 1930s. Plastic was initially only used for specialised components, but it also had the potential for use in basic structures when reinforced with a glass base or asbestos (this was a period when the risks of asbestos poisoning were either unknown or ignored). An early example of a reinforced plastic structure was the radome of the Bristol Brigand. This was the dome-like shell used to house the aircraft's radar antenna. Reinforced plastic was also used in the air ducting for Britannia, which *The 'Bristol' Quarterly* claimed to be 'the most sophisticated cabin atmosphere conditioning system that has yet been devised'.[47] Other plastic features on Britannia included the perspex glazings on the windows, the fibreglass-laminate aerial coverings, the foamed PVC filling in the doors and bulkhead of the cabin, and the isocyanate foam filling of the seats.

Section of plastic ventilation system, c 1957 (above) (Bristol Aero Collection).

Insulating Britannia fuselage with fibreglass, c 1957 (facing page) (Bristol Aero Collection).

Plastic was generally lighter, cheaper and more efficient than metal-based equivalents, and offered better insulation. BAC experimented with its possible use in wings for high-speed (subsonic) aircraft and fuselages in the mid-1950s. This led to work on plastic drop tanks, developed in association with the Aerodynamic Section of the Royal Aircraft Establishment (RAE). A drop tank is an expendable 'external fuel tank on an aircraft which can be jettisoned when empty'.[48] The tank is fitted under the

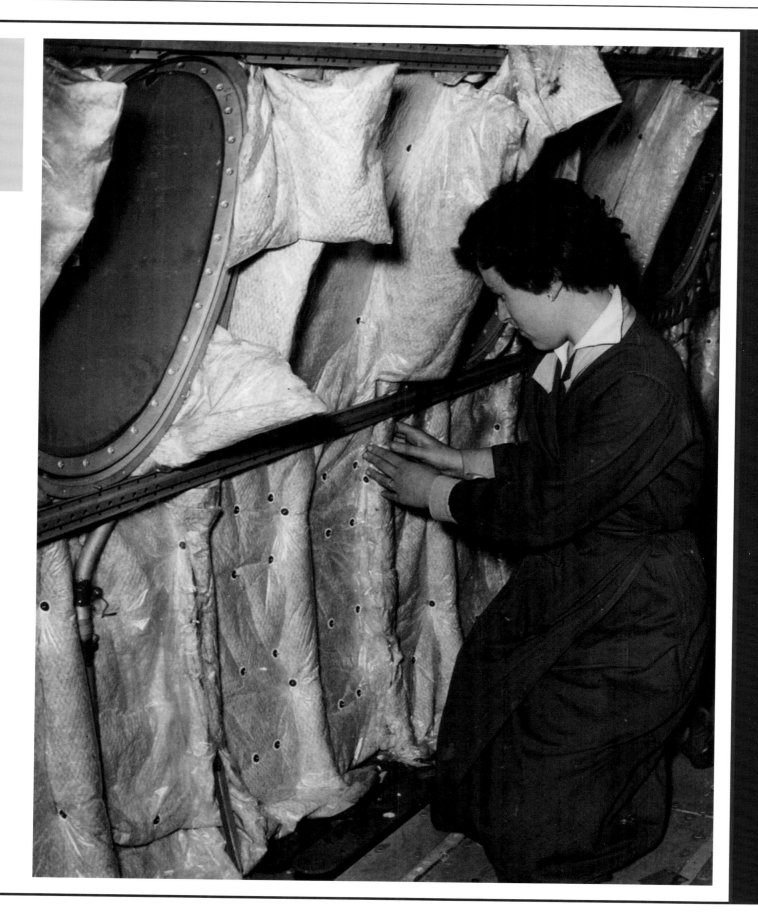

Plastic bubble car, c 1962 (left) (Bristol Aero Collection).

Plastic drop tank, 1954 (above) (Airbus).

wing and falls away from the aircraft horizontally. The RAE designed the tank's shape, while BAC was responsible for its structural design, the manufacturing methods and the cooling processes. The tanks were mainly produced in a range of standard sizes which helped to keep production costs to a minimum, but some were specially manufactured in bespoke sizes for individual aircraft. Each tank had three main shell sections with high-pressure-moulded internal frames that were assembled by hot gluing. Durestos, a plastic-based material impregnated by asbestos, was used to make the shells as it was unaffected by extremes of temperature or humidity. The drop tank cap was made of metal. The two most important selling points for the BAC tanks were that they could be stored easily as the shell sections nested together, and they were easy to assemble in the field, requiring only 15 minutes, two or three unskilled men and a screwdriver.

Other BAC plastic products included slotted tube well pipes exported to Pakistan, where the highly acidic soil caused metal pipes to corrode. The machine for making the pipes was designed, made, tested and delivered by Roland Cross of Cross Manufacturing. There were also various plastic components for the Navy, radar scanner and missile components, and motorcycle fairings. BAC built plastic bodies for a kit-form bubble car, the Lotus Elan and Bristol Aerojet's Elite racing car. In the late 1950s there was a design study for plastic railway coaches. Between 1953 and 1959 glass-fibre-reinforced plastic hulls were produced for the Alpha Dinghy (the world's first production glass-fibre dinghy). They had been designed by a team at Oxford University led by Ian Proctor. At that time, only the aviation industry had the experience to handle this new material. When first displayed at the Earls Court boat show, the dinghy's hull was cut in half and floated in a pool to demonstrate that it was unsinkable thanks to its foam-filled buoyancy, another world first. BAC also built two 9.5 metre (31-foot) glass-fibre cabin cruisers based on an initial, shorter design in wood commissioned by *Yachting World*.

Bristol Aeroplane Plastics Ltd became Rolls-Royce Composite Materials, one of the peripheral 'Bristol'

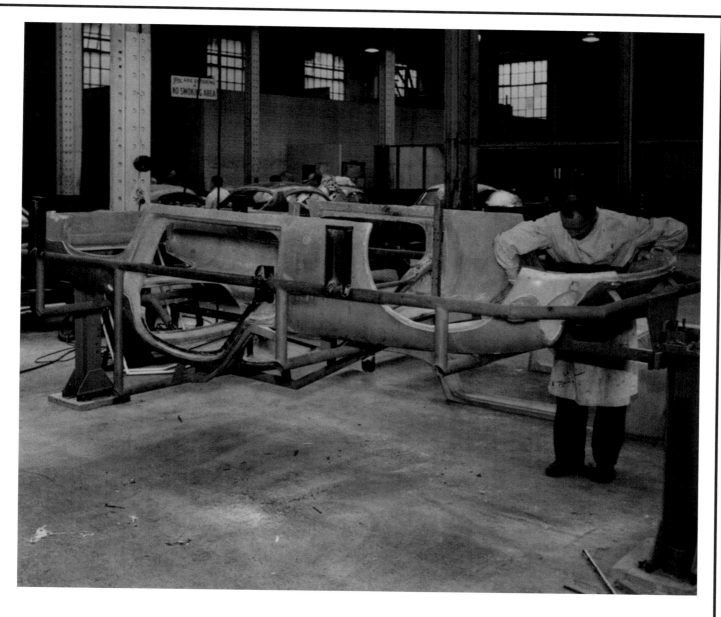

BAC plastic body for the Lotus Elan (photographed for the BAC Car Division by Ted Ashman).

companies acquired in the 1966 merger. Its main job was to service the fan blades of the RB211 engine. When Rolls-Royce was declared bankrupt, Composite Materials became part of British Petroleum.

During the early development of the A400M and A380 wings, the former Composite Materials buildings at Avonmouth were taken over by some of the Airbus subcontractors because of the lack of space at Filton.

Composite materials were first applied on primary structures for Airbus aircraft in 1985 and the use of composites has increased steadily since then. Research into advanced composite materials is an important part of the work at the Filton site, which is home to a £12 million Composites Structures Development Centre. This forms part of the UK's National Composites Network. Composites can be stronger than metal but weigh the same or less. Airline companies are always looking for ways of reducing the non-paying load – cargo and passengers pay their way, but structures and fuel do not.

Space programme

The UK's first space programme was started by the Royal Aircraft Establishment at Farnborough in 1957. As a continuation of this work, British Aircraft Corporation was appointed the prime contractor for the payload assembly (the package of instruments needed for the experiments to be conducted on the mission), overall vehicle procurement and launch of the Skylark sounding rocket. A sounding rocket is a 'small research rocket that ascends to the Earth's upper atmosphere and proceeds in a sub-orbital trajectory, studying the atmosphere, the planet, or outer space'.[49] After its initial launch in 1957 Skylark was regularly used into the 1990s, with occasional launches after that. The 441st and final launch took place from Esrange, Sweden on 2 May 2005.

British Aircraft Corporation's expertise in space technology had partly developed from the work of BAC's Guided Weapons Department. Operations were initially centred in Stevenage at the former facilities of English Electric, but transferred to Filton in 1967. The company had provided the instrumentation for the first Anglo-American research satellites, UK/Ariel 1 (1962) and UK/Ariel 2 (1964), and was the prime contractor for UK/Ariel 4, which was launched by the National Aeronautics and Space Administration from Vandenberg Air Force Base in California on 11 December 1971. British Aircraft Corporation had designed and manufactured Prospero, the first wholly British scientific satellite, which was launched into low orbit at Woomera, Australia on 28 October that same year. Prospero was designed to test basic systems for use in future satellites and was also employed in a one-off experiment to detect micrometeoroids.

The Intelligence Telecommunications Satellite Consortium was set up in 1964 to operate a worldwide system of commercial communications satellites. Its first such satellite, Intelsat 1 (Early Bird), was launched on 6 April 1965. Intelsat 4 was the first of the satellites to be manufactured outside the US. It was built by British Aircraft Corporation for Hughes Aircraft of America and launched into geostationary orbit by Atlas rocket from Cape Canaveral, Florida in 1971. Geostationary means that the satellite 'remains above the same point on a planet's surface because it completes one orbit in the same time it takes that planet to rotate once on its axis'.[50] British

Launch of a Skylark solid-fuel, high-altitude sounding rocket from Woomera in Australia, 1960 (facing page) (Science and Society Picture Library/NASA).

Launch of Britain's first satellite, Ariel 1, 26 April 1962 (top) (Science and Society Picture Library/NASA).

Ariel 1 (above) (Science and Society Picture Library/NASA).

Aircraft Corporation led the STAR consortium for the first European geostationary scientific satellite (GEOS), which was launched by Delta booster from Cape Canaveral in 1978. It was used for geodesy, a branch of mathematics based on the study of the Earth's shape and area.

British Aerospace (Filton) built the Giotto comet interceptor for the European Space Agency, which was launched by Ariane rocket from Kourou, French Guiana in July 1985. This was Europe's first space probe and its launch was timed to coincide with the reappearance of Halley's Comet, last seen in the inner solar system in 1910, the year BAC was founded. Giotto was the first interceptor to perform a close fly-by of two comets (Halley's in March 1986, Grigg-Skjellerup's in July 1992), the first to provide pictures of a comet's nucleus, the first to return from interplanetary space, the first to use Earth for a gravity-assisted manoeuvre and the first spacecraft to be reactivated from hibernation mode. The Giotto project was eventually taken over by Hawker Siddeley.

British Aerospace Space Systems, which later became Matra Marconi Space, was the prime contractor for the European Space Agency's Polar Platform satellite (sometimes called Envisat) from 1990 to its launch in 2002. This is the largest European satellite to date. The full-scale engineering model for this was assembled at the University of Bristol and is currently in storage at the Bristol Aero Collection at Kemble.

In 1956 BAC also set up a rocket manufacturing facility at its former war-time shadow factory in Banwell near Weston-super-Mare. Three years later this became a joint venture with the American company Aerojet General and was known as Bristol Aerojet. It was the main source of rocket motors in the UK until 1991.

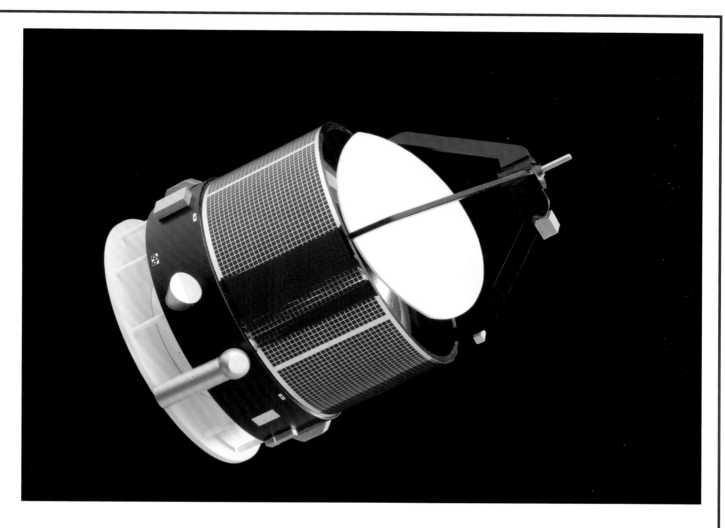

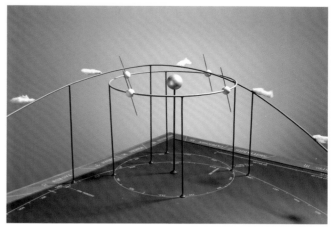

The GEOS development satellite undergoing system tests in the
electromagnetically clean test facility, 1971 (Filton Library).

Scale-model of the orbit of Halley's comet made c 1910
(Science and Society Picture Library/Science Museum).

Detail of Giotto probe, 1985 (top) (Science and Society Picture Library/
Science Museum).

Nora Lang in the Wages and Accounts Department (Office System) in East Works filing away steel plates carrying employees' clock card numbers, names and addresses, December 1951 (Roll-Royce plc).

Section 3:
The Workforce and the Community

Without Sir George White, BAC would never have started. Without Sir Stanley White and his fellow directors, the company would never have stayed in business. Without the likes of Frank Barnwell, Roy Fedden, Stanley Hooker and Archibald E Russell, there would have been no product for the company to sell. Without thousands of people over the last hundred years, most unsung, many overworked and some undoubtedly underpaid, the company's aero-engines and aircraft would never have been built.

For decades BAC was to North Bristol what Wills tobacco was to South Bristol and Fry's chocolate was to the South East of the city – a large-scale employer that had a major impact upon the structure and culture of the local community. Other significant Bristol employers over the last century were the city-centre docks, shipbuilders Charles Hill & Sons Ltd, which launched its last ship in 1977, engineering firms like Strachan and Henshaw, manufacturers of paper-handling and printing equipment, and packaging companies like Robinson. These were the type of industries where generations of families worked together, where young boys would be encouraged to follow in their fathers' footsteps by taking up apprenticeships and where work colleagues were often social ones too, as well as neighbours.

Getting something as large and complicated as an aircraft from the drawing board to the skies involves people working in areas of development, production and sales. In addition there are people needed to manage and provide services for the employees. This entails hundreds of different roles within the factory. Some of these have been in existence for decades, some are more recent additions, some are long lost and forgotten. Among these, in no particular order, are carpenters, stringers, draftspeople, designers, scientists, riveters, setter operators, buyers, crew, data processors, welders, pilots, technicians, fitters, various types of engineer, electricians, cooks, delivery drivers, painters, secretaries, cashiers, security guards, cleaners, chauffeurs, progress chasers, flight support managers, coppersmiths and tinsmiths, trainers, technical authors and illustrators. There are specialists and all-rounders, the unskilled and the skilled, apprentices and old hands. Some roles have been lost as materials, processes and products have changed. For others, it has become cheaper and more practical to use outside subcontractors or to switch from permanent, in-house resources to bought-in, short-term ones.

British & Colonial sheet metal workers at the Brislington works, c 1918 (detail) (Bristol's Museums, Galleries and Archives).

All these people are organised into different sections, departments and divisions within the company. These might include the various shops such as machine, fitting, plating, stripping, balancing, bonding, polishing, heat treatment and trimming. There might be departments for mechanical research, data processing, upholstery, structures, facilities planning, X-rays, maintenance, aerodynamics, translation, communication, estimating and cost control, servicing and spares. Then there are the stores, the design office, the jig and tool rooms, the foundry, the failures laboratory, the grinding section, catering, material control, packing and despatch, the woodmill, procurement, the sparkatron section, the assembly hall, production control and the engineering test lab. Employees could be working in a very noisy environment or an almost silent one, from the dirty to the ultra clean, the gloomy to the brightly lit, experiencing the intense heat of the salt baths in the treatment room or the bone-jarring cold of a hangar on a freezing winter's morning, among hundreds of co-workers or alone.

Everything has to be thoroughly documented during the complex process of building an aircraft – something that is particularly vital when dealing with multi-million pound contracts. At one time, all the paperwork generated by development, production and sales required a multitude of employees to manage it. Offices were filled with the continuous noise of manual typewriters, mechanical calculators and Banda reproduction machines. Projects required project managers and project assistants, administrators, secretaries and clerks and the production of racks upon racks of carefully maintained procedural manuals, partly for internal use to ensure standardisation, partly for external inspectors. The introduction of computing systems has reduced some of the administrative roles and the print output, but it has also created new posts and procedures.

A group of war-time women workers at British & Colonial, c 1918 (left) (private collection).

War-time riveter, c 1940 (facing page, left) (Bristol Aero Collection).

The Chemical Laboratory in the West Works, where experiments are being conducted to determine different compounds for properties of metals, oils or fuels, c 1930 (facing page, right) (Rolls-Royce plc).

The amount of contact that takes place between office staff and those on the shop floor (also referred to by some as 'the works') and between the different factory sections is largely dependent on the nature of the job being done, as is the extent of individual awareness of the bigger picture. Someone in the stress office, for example, might need to know the weight and centre of gravity of everything from the smallest rivet to the entire aircraft, and so has to be involved in each stage of a project. Someone else may only be concerned about one highly specialised and isolated area. The type of job may also result in a different sense of company loyalty, identity or pride.

Traditionally, there was a clear demarcation between different types of work and different grades of employee. Such distinctions still remain, but until the 1960s or beyond there were many more tangible signs of the company hierarchy. There were different places to eat, with separate canteens for the workers and the staff, the senior secretaries, the junior secretaries, management, visitors, the executives and the directors. There were different types of food available: highly calorific self-service bulk for the workforce, who sometimes had to provide their own cutlery, more elegant fare with waitress service for management. There was the tea urn brought round on a trolley for the works, coffee and biscuits for the staff. There were different dress codes, different coloured overalls (with white ones kept for when VIPs were passing through), different cough medicines in the segregated medical centres, and different working hours, pay and conditions. Staff had mirrors in their toilets, shop-floor workers did not. Staff had their titles on their payslips, shop-floor workers just had their names.

Shop-floor workers and staff had different clocking-on machines. The works day-shift usually started at 7.30am, with staff starting an hour later. Until the mid-1950s the normal working week included Saturday mornings for the works, but some apprentices opted to do civil defence training then as the hourly rate was better. Some shop-floor employees worked permanently on nights, others did it in shifts, with a period of high productivity occasionally demanding a 'burster', which meant working from early morning one day right through to lunch the next. Shop-floor workers were generally paid weekly, staff were on a monthly salary. Some former shop-floor workers were given an interest-free loan by the company when they were promoted to staff to tide them over until their first salary payment. During the 1950s and 1960s the engineering unions were working to get parity of conditions of employment for works and staff where it would be of benefit to their members (for example, pensions, sick pay, holiday entitlement), but were generally happy over the disparity that meant shop-floor workers could be paid overtime but staff could not. Overtime could make a substantial difference to the workers' pay packets, and sometimes it was not worthwhile financially to be promoted.

The shop-floor workers were sometimes subjected to what today would seem an excessive level of supervision. For example, toilet breaks were overseen by the Toilet Controller who issued a key to the cubicles and made employees sign in and out, recording their time away from the shop floor. In the tool room at Patchway, shop-floor workers only had access to the washroom to wash their hands five minutes before the end of the day, unless they had special permission (there were no sinks in with the toilets). Coats were hauled up on racks out of reach at the start of the day and not lowered until clocking-off time. There was also little regard for what is now considered basic health and safety: normal practice included working without ear protectors surrounded by noisy machinery, handling asbestos, breathing in toxic fumes and entering the test cell to make manual adjustments when an engine was running on the test-bed.

However, employment conditions and salaries at BAC were generally considered good for the time. There were various bonus schemes, most of which were standard practice in the industry but others which were particular to the firm. Shop-floor workers would be paid extra on top of their basic wage if a job was completed in less time than had been anticipated. All work was checked and signed off by inspectors to avoid corner-cutting on quality, and the allocated time could be renegotiated with a rate-fixer if it was considered unrealistic because it was either too short or too long. By contrast, if no work was available, workers went on to the reduced rate of 'waiting time' and had to remain on standby on the factory premises. There was a range of opportunities for earning individual bonuses and other perks. Most departments, for example, had suggestion committees and the best ideas were awarded a cash prize. Among those reported in the 1953 Christmas issue of *Bristol Review*, for instance, were £5 awarded to I Pitt of SAB Progress in the Aircraft Division for a suggestion relating to helicopter flying controls and £3 to S G Batten of Car Fitters in the Car Division for modification to the Step Member Fixing Flange. Merit awards were also available.

In addition to those who lived in or around the main factory sites at Filton or Patchway, who could walk to work, BAC employees travelled in from across the local area including Horfield, Bishopston, Southmead, Downend, Kingswood, Eastville and Westbury-on-Trym. Many travelled by bus or coach, with vehicles arriving at the factory gates at least every minute during peak periods. For years, women were allowed to leave work five minutes earlier than men so they had more chance of getting a seat for the journey home. During World War Two there were also coaches taking employees to and from Filton and Patchway to work their shifts at the outlying dispersal sites, including Clevedon and Corsham. Some of these continued to be in use after the war had ended, during the months it took to dismantle the temporary workshops. In addition a rail route was available from Filton North via Henbury to the dispersal site at Avonmouth. A new station platform was built behind the BAC factory canteen there and a dedicated service was run especially for the employees. Company coaches and occasionally aircraft would also link up the different sites around the country when the big amalgamations of the 1960s came, carrying post and passengers. Hundreds of employees arrived at work by bike and both of the main sites had rows upon rows of cycle racks. Filton had one of the UK's first dedicated cycle lanes, which ran down the sides of Filton Hill.

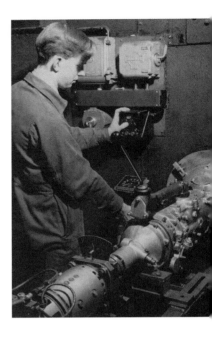

Testing gearbox in the car division, 1950s (above) (Rolls-Royce Heritage Trust).

War-time machine cutter, c 1940 (facing page) (Bristol Aero Collection).

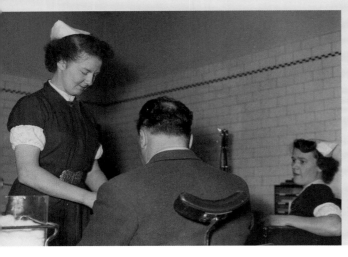

Travel by bus or bike remained the most popular form of transport until the early 1960s, particularly for shop-floor workers who were usually less able to afford private cars than the staff. The peak-time rush was slightly staggered by the late finishers and early starters, but there was always a noticeable surge at the beginning and end of the working day around the factory gates and neighbouring streets. Today, most of the employee traffic at the aerospace companies is car-based and employees tend to live further way. The method of transport and homeward destinations may have changed, but the start and finish of the working day is still a significant event as around 8,000 employees have to get in and out of the main sites.

As well as employment, the presence of BAC and its associated companies has brought physical change to the local area. Filton, a small Gloucestershire farming community when British & Colonial first began operation, rapidly witnessed the expansion of the works and the change of land-use from agricultural to industrial. For local residents the sight of

Typing pool showing women working at Imperial manual typewriters, 1948 (top left) (Rolls-Royce plc).

The Medical Centre, October 1954 (bottom left) (Rolls-Royce plc).

Man working on magnesium casing for Centaurus in the light alloy foundry, c 1947 (above) (Rolls-Royce plc).

aircraft became a familiar one after 1910, with the drone of engines a constant background noise. The noise could be more than just a tolerable drone for those whose homes backed onto the test-bed areas or the sections of the airfield used for outdoor runs. When tests were being made on the Type 188, for example, the aircraft was lined up between specially devised metal cones in the testing area to deflect some of the sound, but complaints were still received from residents about windows rattling and glass breaking. Generally, complaints about the noise, dirt and smell generated by the factory sites were fewer when more of the local population worked for the company and understood that their jobs were dependent on the occasional inconvenience.

When British & Colonial first started its operations, many of the former farmers and farmhands who had worked on the properties that were bought by the company for its building programme went to work in the factory. The two-acre meadow directly in front of Fairlawn Avenue was used as one of the company's airfields, attracting large crowds for flying displays from 1911 onwards. The houses on the avenue served as employee homes and offices, and were gradually incorporated into the factory complex, set behind security barriers, while still being partly occupied as residential housing. The last tenants moved out in 1976, and the buildings were demolished in 1996 to make way for a car park.

Although the factory steadily spread across the surrounding fields, the company retained use of some farm land at least until the 1950s. During World War Two any available pockets of growing space were given over to food supply for the employee canteens as part of the war effort. In 1951 a profile in *Bristol Review* described 180 acres of gardens owned by the company extending over various sites, including a nursery and greenhouses at Fairlawn House, vegetable beds between Works Road and the Assembly Hall, and the home fields of Westwood Farm.[1]

The 1920s saw the start of a mass housing programme at Filton, prompted by the increasing size of the workforce. Developers were enthusiastically buying up the small, scattered farms and demolishing some of the old Victorian properties to create modern housing estates. However, according to *The Aeroplane*, these were also the 'years of consolidation and the evolution of design rather than years of production', so employment at the works could be precarious and there were job losses.[2] Having a large number of people made redundant at one time had a knock-on effect on the viability of local shops and other services, as well as individual home life. Like other UK aviation companies, BAC had to divert some of its resources into other activities because the post-war market was so weak. While coach bodies were being built at BAC, for example, pianos and milk churns were being produced at Westland in Yeovil, and fish friers and car bodies constructed at Gloster Aircraft.[3] BAC did have the advantage of being part of the Air Ministry's protection ring, the Society of British Aircraft Constructors, for both airframe and aero-engine production and received enough official specifications to keep the core business ticking over. However, in 1931 the continuing overall downturn in demand led to further redundancies and BAC's aircraft manufacture and reconditioning 'were almost at a standstill' by 1934.[4] The engine department enjoyed greater security than the airframe side and skilled workers were generally better off than the women and semi-skilled, who were considered more expendable.

In 1935 the BAC workforce doubled in six months as a result of the government's rearmament programme, rising from around 4,200 in June that year to 8,233 by Christmas. By the end of 1938 it had risen to 14,000. It doubled again between June and December 1939, and in 1943 peaked at 52,095, including the shadow factories and dispersal sites, as a result of the mobilisation effort for the Allied invasion of Europe. Rearmament had necessitated a huge building programme, as C H Barnes explained:

> The erecting shop, unaltered since 1916, was doubled in floor area by an extension on the south side, the new bay having full span folding doors opening on to a new internal road leading direct to the airfield. Large extensions were also made to the tool room and machine shop; a new wing assembly shop was built, also new metal stores for Alclad sheets and very extensive anodising and cadmium plating plant, which took the place of the former stove-enamelling baths. The floor space required for fabric work and doping was much reduced, but a new spraying shop had to be built for cellulose painting of components and later for applying camouflage to the complete aircraft.[5]

During the course of the expansion programme, the last of the old farms west of the A38 were bought out and built on. Hayes Lane, which linked Charlton Village to Gipsy Patch Lane, was closed, as were several public footpaths – the source of a long-running dispute between the company and the parish council. By 1939 BAC had 'the largest single aircraft manufacturing unit in the world', occupying 732 acres.[6] The increase in the number of employees needed to operate the expanded facilities had a wide-ranging impact, for example internally on the management of payroll procedures and catering, and externally on the demand for local housing and social services. There could no longer be any doubt that Filton was now a company town, for better or worse.

During rearmament, BAC recruitment managers had been scouring the country for suitable personnel, not necessarily those experienced in aircraft manufacturing but those with appropriate engineering skills gained, for example, in the shipyards of Belfast, Southampton, Tyneside and the Clyde. More new people moved into the area at the start of the war to take up temporary positions, including staff seconded from the Royal Air Force and a large contingent brought in from Wales. Hot-bedding took place, with shift workers sharing beds in rented lodgings around the clock. Redundancies were made

Man using the technique of lost wax process to make jet engine component parts, c 1957 (Rolls-Royce Heritage Trust).

across the UK industry at the end of the 1943 production peak with the exception of de Havilland, Vickers and A V Roe, which continued to get preferential treatment in the awarding of military contracts. There was still demand for Bristol engines at this time but, other than the Beaufighter, the Bristol aircraft were by now largely obsolete and the company was excluded from this elite group. Further redundancies and redeployment were inevitable at the end of the war.

Employment picked up at BAC with the later stages of individual projects like Brabazon and Britannia. Around this time there was also concern about shortages of manpower and materials in the industry generally, and a lack of investment. An editorial in *Bristol Review* in 1951 stated:

> Recent official statistics confirm what we know from our own experience – that the engineering industries are not getting the men they need to tackle rearmament as well as exports. More than that, the key industries actually seem to be losing ground to luxury trades such as perfumery...

At present public opinion seems still quite unaware of the gravity of the hour. It is indeed because, ostrich-like, the public prefers lipsticks and other personal luxuries to arms, exports and other essentials, that more men are going to make the former and fewer the latter...

If all do not pull together, all will assuredly go down together. And – it is later than we think.[7]

Some would argue today that the situation has remained unchanged. This was in a period when the post-war housing shortage, partly caused by German bomber raids, was forcing local people to move away from Filton, Patchway and the surrounding areas, but also when skilled workers were having to be brought down from northern England to fill places at BAC.

At the turn of the 1960s, the UK government was keen to reduce the number of airframe and aero-engine companies in line with a reduction in funding available for research and development. At the same time, the companies that remained were encouraged or forced to amalgamate as it was thought there was strength in numbers when competing in the world market. The enforced Bristol Siddeley alliance of 1959 formed from Bristol Aero

Looking through a mask into the bright light of a furnace spyhole, c 1960 (left) (Rolls-Royce plc).

Office full of IBM punch-card machines, 12 February 1960 (facing page) (Rolls-Royce plc).

Engines Ltd and Armstrong Siddeley Motors Ltd created a combined workforce of 27,500 split across sites in and round Patchway and Coventry, bringing the new company closer in scale to the giant concerns operating in the US. Similarly, Bristol Aircraft Ltd joined Vickers and English Electric to form British Aircraft Corporation. This policy carried on into the mid-1960s under George Brown's Industrial Reorganisation Corporation 'which assisted industrial mergers in an attempt to create larger, more efficient units which could compete with industry in the USA and elsewhere'.[8] Brown was Secretary of State for Economic Affairs from 1964 to 1966. His Ministry of Technology's short-lived programme of getting military suppliers to explore alternative peacetime technologies allowed British Aircraft Corporation at Filton to become briefly involved in ocean engineering projects relating to oil and gas fields in the North Sea.

At Filton and Patchway there were recruitment drives for the Concorde programme after the post-Britannia lull. Some of the employees taken on during this period were formerly at Gloster Aircraft, which had become part of the Avro Whitworth Division of Hawker Siddeley Aviation. People were also recruited from the former Blackburn Aircraft in Hull, Shorts of Belfast and, from 1970, Handley Page, the last of the old aviation independents to hold out against nationalisation. The employment boost brought to the area because of Concorde was, however, offset by cuts in the government's military budget, which led to the cancellation of the TSR2 project and further redundancies. The industry generally was also becoming less labour intensive as manual labour made way for mechanised and then computerised production methods. At one time in the Bristol area, as engineering work temporarily dried up at one local company it had been possible to move to another that did have work, thereby keeping highly prized skills within the local area and minimising unemployment. For example, someone might go from BAC to Dennis Fire Engines to Douglas Motorcyles and back to BAC when they got another contract. This became less feasible as company structures, manufacturing methods and the economy changed.

In 1971 there was a period of considerable uncertainty caused by the Rolls-Royce bankruptcy that had resulted from Derby's problems with the protracted RB211 project, which would eventually be saved by Bristol engine expertise. The company was nationalised as Rolls-Royce (1971) Ltd in a government-backed deal that kept the core workforce intact. The 1970s generally were a difficult time in which to be involved in manufacturing industry. For example, the three-day weeks introduced in early 1973 to limit the use of electricity during the miners' work-to-rule meant that companies were trying to do a week's work in the few days when power was available. This was particularly difficult to manage with processes that required a set curing or drying time, like those used in reinforced plastics. By 1975 the Concorde programme was winding down, leading to yet another round of mass redundancies. A quarter of the Aerodynamics team at Filton was lost, for example.

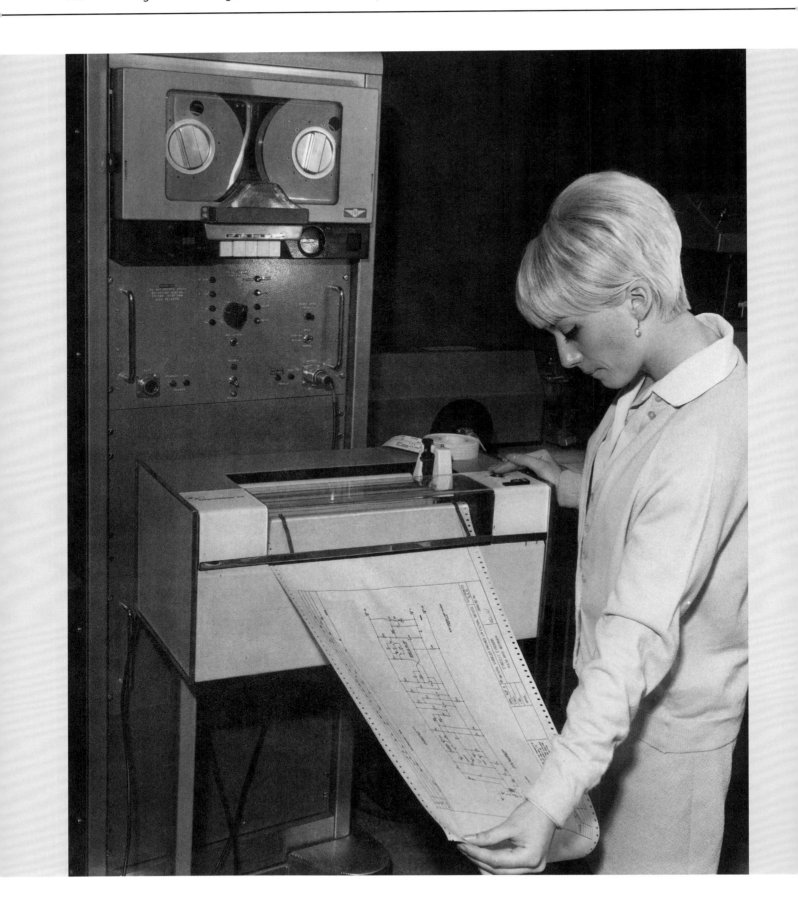

Man with his protective mask resting on his head about to begin welding pipes at Bristol Siddeley (above) (Rolls-Royce plc).

Woman collecting a plan of a circuit diagram of a pulse rate recorder of a Bristol Siddley engine, June 1966 (facing page) (Rolls-Royce plc).

Further redundancies followed the British Aerospace strike of the early 1980s when the employers chose to switch to contracting-out for some skills and services to save money. In the 1990s British Aerospace closed entire departments at Filton. Thousands lost their jobs, including the whole of central IT. This coincided with redundancies at Rolls-Royce, which had previously also had cutbacks following the short-lived build-up to the Falklands War. However, whenever possible, skilled workers would be redeployed within a company in expectation of future contracts. Over the years there were also a number of lucrative projects that did not originate in Filton or Patchway but kept some of the workforce in employment, including converting old VC10 civil aircraft into air refuelling tankers for the Royal Air Force, providing an F-111 fighter bomber maintenance base for the US Air Force, performance testing for the Jetstream trainer and converting of passenger A300s and A310s into freighters for the Airbus consortium.

For decades, aviation has been an industry of peaks and troughs, with increasingly long lead-times on projects before starting production. This has had an impact on the infrastructure of the local community in which the companies have been based. Throughout the war years and into the 1950s and 1960s, the shops opposite the main BAC gate at Filton were vibrant. This was the main shopping street for the town and included a bakery, tobacconist, bank, greengrocer, butcher's shop, chippie, café and barber. Even if BAC employees used the company canteens or brought their own lunch to eat, they would still use some of the local facilities, sitting on the wall outside the bank to soak up the sunshine during their lunch break. When the break was reduced from an hour to 45 minutes and the main gate was moved to the other side of the complex, most of the shops quickly went out of business. However, when the big redundancies of the late 1980s and 1990s occurred, the repercussions for the local area were less dramatic as the majority of employees were no longer locally based and it had been years since they had used local services. It was not like the devastation to a local economy and culture that was caused by the closing of the pits in Welsh mining villages, for example.

With the enforced mergers and nationalisation came a change in the company ethos. The White family's personal investment and involvement in the company meant BAC retained a culture of generally benevolent paternalism for decades. This was common across many factory-based businesses during the early period of industrialisation. Paternalism is defined as:

> a style of management that involves looking after employees in a 'fatherly' manner. It is an approach that assumes managers know best and that they have the welfare of their employees at heart... Paternalism is often associated with small firms where there are close personal interdependencies.[9]

Generations of families in the work-force also inevitably contributed to the family feeling at BAC: fathers, mothers, cousins, uncles, aunts, grandparents, siblings, children shared a common experience and work became an extension of home. By the 1960s the paternalistic attitude of directors in what had once been BAC had gradually faded and a more modern corporate leadership style came in with a new wave of younger managers. The work-place ethos became both more and less formal. On the one hand, procedures set by head office were followed for promotion and discipline, which meant decisions were more impersonal and clear-cut, while on the other, in at least some departments, managers, staff and workers were now on first-name terms and had more democratic access to facilities and services.

Until recently it was still possible to make internal calls between Rolls-Royce at Patchway and Airbus at Filton on office telephones and to use the internal mail service across the two companies, but the split of the original BAC identity had begun decades earlier. The White family interest had gradually receded with the reorganisation of the late 1950s and the 'Bristol' name had first been lost from the airframe side with the forming of the British Aircraft Corporation and then from the engine side with the Rolls-Royce merger in 1966. However, the BAC still acted as a holding company owning a percentage share in both of the new concerns.[10] British Aircraft Corporation's corporate office in Pall Mall, London was made responsible for integrating the training of the different companies and that of the overseas subsidiaries, from apprentices to managers, as part of the creation of a new, unified company culture. It became harder to retain a distinctive identity at Filton. Similarly, at Patchway, decisions were increasingly being made company-wide in Derby and some of the previous autonomy and identity was lost.

Nationalisation was also seen by many employees as an imposition from a central government that, having largely abandoned the UK aviation industry, was now allowing faceless civil servants rather than work-place engineers set the company agenda. In addition, there was growing influence from Europe. The Concorde programme had captured the hearts of local people but it also marked the further breakdown of the traditional system through the partnership with the French. Only global companies can afford the high costs that are now associated with aircraft design, and this can mean a loss of local connection and influence.

Some long-term employees welcomed the various changes to the company culture brought by the mergers, restructuring and inevitable passage of time. They found it stimulating to be employed by three or more companies during the course of their careers while staying in the same place physically, for example, Bristol Aeroplane Company, British Aircraft Corporation, British Aerospace and Airbus. Each company brought a fresh outlook, a new way of doing things and the dismantling of some of the old hierarchies. Others

Tool room workers shortly to be made redundant check the list of jobs on display in the British Aircraft Corporation canteen, 1976 (top).

Manufacturing Systems Engineer using gap-gun laser metrology equipment to measure the inboard engine attachment point on A400M wing at Filton, c 2007 (bottom) (Airbus).

liked feeling part of an identifiable, smaller-scale family concern, and preferred the old paternalism to a large-scale bureaucracy where filling in the correct paperwork sometimes seemed more important than creative thinking.

Those who joined either Rolls-Royce or the various incarnations of the airframe side after the changes were made would have started with a different set of reference points for their culture and community, having their own source of pride in their work. In addition, the company changes have been paralleled by wider changes that have affected the nature of community both within and outside the factory gates. These have included changes in the means of communication, now that more is being conducted remotely rather than face-to-face; in travel, with employees now used to commuting longer distances to and from work; in the concept of a career path, with people moving job more frequently rather than having a job for life; and in spending power, with most grades of employees able to afford to live outside the Filton and Patchway catchment area in satellite estates like Yate or Thornbury and beyond to Portishead, Weston-super-Mare, South Wales and the Midlands. A sense of community may not necessarily have been lost over the last hundred years in the West of England aviation industry, as some older people may fear; it may just be different from what it once was. Corporate responsibility initiatives, such as volunteering, school liaison and charitable work, and support for employees wishing to become Justices of the Peace, governors or councillors, for example, have helped to root the companies in the local community now there is no longer an automatic buy-in through mass local employment.

Apprenticeships

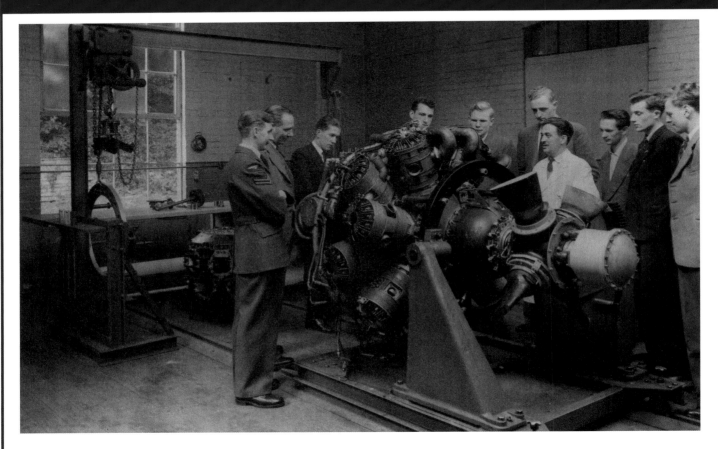

It was a frequent claim that someone with a BAC apprenticeship could get a job anywhere in the world, it was so highly valued. It was a reputation that could perhaps only be rivalled in the UK industry by de Havilland at Hatfield.

The company produced thousands of thoroughly trained, well-rounded, high-quality aviation workers. It was not unknown for an employee to work his way up through the company from apprentice to improver to skilled to management, having joined at age 16.

BAC apprentices came from all walks of life and from all over the country as well as overseas. The apprenticeship the company offered was thought to be particularly beneficial for those who had received minimal formal schooling. It was described by some as polishing diamonds in the rough and giving them a chance to shine.

In the period immediately leading up to World War Two, technical apprenticeships generally lasted five years. This included day release to the Merchant Venturers Technical College in Bristol, which was accredited for engineering by the University of Bristol, and a six-month rotation through the different departments. The rotation should have happened automatically, but occasionally the system broke down and apprentices had to push to get moved on or they would find themselves stranded in the same place for a year or more. The apprentices usually gained experience by being partnered as assistants to skilled workers, a system sometimes referred to as duckboard engineering. This led to fewer mistakes being made at a crucial period of production than if they were left to muddle through a job by themselves. One of the things the apprentices might be taught was how to work accurately to a small scale in order to make the intricate, precision parts that were fitted together into larger airframe or aero-engine sections. Graduate Apprentices, who had degrees in engineering, usually went straight into the design or technical departments rather than working their way around the shops.

In war time the company preferred, if possible, to get people quickly onto the production line rather than having the usual apprenticeship period. This meant that some of the war-time apprenticeships were reduced to about four years at most and there were no indenture papers issued at the end as they were not officially recognised by the trade. Some of those on the truncated apprenticeships did no classroom work at all, while others only received enough basic schooling to enable them to produce test pieces before going into the work place. Some therefore attended evening classes or enrolled on correspondence courses to boost their qualifications. The war-time apprentices were also expected to do their share of fire-watching and to join the Local Defence Volunteers, later the 13th Gloucesters Home Guard.

In the early 1950s there were concerns generally within BAC about the lack of skills and brain power available to the industry. This led the company to increase its investment in training in all departments. The training programme was overseen by the Training and Education Policy Committee chaired by Sir Reginald Verdon Smith and was primarily administered through the education committee of each division. In addition to the apprenticeships, there was clerical and secretarial training, undergraduate vacation training, supervisory development, management training and adult technical training. Every member of the work force – shop floor, staff and executive – had opportunities to develop their potential through a continuous training process. The company also supported a self-study scheme, financially rewarding those who gained qualifications by this method. In addition, there was a certain amount of what might be termed life-skills training. Trainee secretaries, for example, were taught to change plugs and ball cocks, and there were opportunities for young employees to take part in Voluntary Services Overseas projects, go on outward bound courses and attend a range of cultural lectures.

Young engineers grouped around a Bristol sleeve-valve engine in the Royal Air Force training building to the north of the main east/west runway, August 1950 (facing page) (Rolls-Royce plc).

Queen Mary being shown around one of the apprentice training rooms at BAC, 1939 (left) (Airbus).

The three standard British Aircraft Industry apprenticeships were classified as Trade, Engineering and Student. There were also Graduate Apprenticeships for those coming direct from university, which entailed a two-year course on industrial practice (graduates not taking the apprentice route went straight into a job). Hundreds of apprentices at a time were taken on at BAC for each three-monthly intake when the scheme was at its peak, and there were often three or four applicants for every place available. The assessment procedure for school leavers usually included a headmaster's report, skills tests, Moresby aptitude tests and one-to-one or board-style interviews. The company saw an apprenticeship as an investment for the future and needed to be sure that its money would be well spent. The assessment panel was looking for evidence of persistence and dedication in the applicant, and not necessarily academic brilliance (although different areas of work needed different qualities). The average apprenticeship lasted between four and six years, with a minimum starting age of 16, usually followed by a two-year journeymanship. National Service could be deferred until the apprenticeship was completed. There were also some early, pre-apprenticeship employment opportunities with the company for school leavers of 14 or 15, such as being a junior office clerk or working as an engraver.

From 1961 those apprentices who were living away from home could spend at least their first year in residence at Barnwell Hall (after their first year, most apprentices went into lodgings). The hall was operated through the YMCA and was located on the Filton airfield in a building formerly occupied by the 501 squadron mess; residents had to cross the north runway to reach it. Peter Parfitt was its warden from its opening until its closure in 1976. The number of occupants rose from 97 in its first year to 140, but there were only a handful of apprentices living there in the final years because of a general reduction in apprentice recruitment and a policy of giving priority to those who lived locally. Some of the craft apprentices, who were on the lowest pay scale, were able to claim subsidies from the Youth Employment Office to cover their board at the hall. Apprentice wages were generally low, and many had to supplement them by taking on bar work and other casual labour or being subsidised by their parents; however, there was the promise of good money once the apprentice had qualified. Apprenticeships in other aviation companies had to be paid for, but BAC's were free – another incentive for applying there.

During the apprenticeship, on-the-job training was supplemented by specialist courses, usually starting with six months' basic training in the training workshop, learning to use different types of machinery – milling machines, grinders, shapers, lathes – and producing appropriate specimen items. Apprentices then rotated through different departments (shop floor and/or office) under the supervision of a qualified employee, gaining overall experience. Each was then asked which section he or she wanted to work in when their apprenticeship was completed. The company would do its best to place them, or would advise them to consider something more appropriate to their skills. The apprentices all made a master piece for their guild award. This might be a scribing block or a tool box made from scratch. The piece demonstrated that the apprentice had learnt different techniques of handling raw metal – shaping, cutting, bending, welding, brazing – to produce something accurately to a standard specification. This was particularly relevant if the apprentice was going to work in one of the tool rooms where skilled employees had to be capable of producing a variety of tools, fixtures and equipment on different types of machine, of which the most highly prized was the Genevoise jig borer imported from Switzerland. Also, for many years apprentices would collectively make a presentation piece to give to the person who awarded that year's prizes.

Technical courses were provided on a day-release or one-week-a-month basis, or as a sandwich course in six-month blocks. Many apprentices also attended evening classes. Increasingly they were acquiring academic qualifications, including Ordinary National Certificates, Higher National

Certificates, Higher National Diplomas, DipTechs and City & Guilds, as well as learning practical skills. BAC, like de Havilland, operated its own technical school which in 1955 transferred into new premises on the site of the former Saunders Farm at the end of Filton Avenue opposite the Rodney Works. The school was housed in a 'Bristol' pre-fabricated building. Additional buildings were soon added to what was now recognised as a college rather than a school, and up to 600 apprentices might be on site at any one time. Learning together in a BAC-run college meant that the apprentices were gaining not only skills but also a sense of family spirit, company loyalty and high morale.

The training workshop grew to 17 sections, each with its own dedicated instructors, and had over 200 machines. It was partly run as a factory, producing items on request for the tool rooms in the advanced machinery area (where the university vacation or gap year students were usually located). There was a roughly 50:50 split between those destined for the top works (the airframe side) and those heading for the bottom works (the engines). They would all mix together until the time came to prepare for joining the workshops and offices on the factory sites. Here their training would continue under the auspices of the Central

Apprentices engaged in various tasks overseen by instructors in a BAC training session, c 1960 (Rolls-Royce plc).

Education Committee and the Training Department. In addition to the training workshop, the college had specialist sections for fittings, electrical, tinsmiths, welding and drilling, laboratories and lecture rooms. There was a BAC Secretarial Training Centre upstairs, from which students went on day-release into the factory. The male apprentices and the female secretaries were kept strictly segregated during the day and the ACES (Arts, Culture, Education and Science) club in the college cellar became a popular social venue to mix in. The building later formed the basis of Filton College, which celebrated its 50th anniversary in 2010.

The numbers of apprentices taken on in the industry today have inevitably fallen in accordance with the number of vacancies available for them to fill on completion of their training. Many of the positions that apprentices were once prepared for have gone. One setter operator, for example,

can set up computer-controlled machines to do work that once required dozens of apprenticed employees. Another change in recent years has been the significant increase in graduate recruitment, with a university or college degree an essential requirement for many appointments. Degrees are also often needed to secure promotion. The 16-year-old rising to be a senior executive is now a less likely prospect, but not impossible. The numbers may have fallen but craft and technician apprenticeships are still supported by the industry using the time-honoured method of learning on the job from those with the experience, skills and technical knowledge to pass on to the next generation.

Bristol Siddeley workers at the training college opposite Rodney Works, July 1960, the year the site became part of the new Filton College (below) (Bristol Aero Collection).

Apprentice fitter at Rolls-Royce working on a Pegasus engine during its rebuild for the Royal Navy Historic Flight Swordfish, c 1993 (facing page) (Rolls-Royce plc).

New Filton House

The original Filton House is a three-storey, eighteenth-century farmhouse. In July 1911 it was bought by Western Wagon & Property Company (WWP) from Samuel Shield, whose family had owned the Filton Laundry since 1869. Sir George White was WWP's Chairman.

Old Filton House and New Filton House with a Bristol car on the driveway, 1952 (Airbus).

The house was leased to British & Colonial the following month for use as the company's general offices. British & Colonial bought the house in 1917. In April 1936 New Filton House was opened adjacent to it. The opening coincided with the production boom of the rearmament period, and the stylish Art Deco building reflected the new confidence and standing of the company. Painted white after the war, it became a striking local landmark that could be seen for miles.

New Filton House was built by the Bristol construction company Cowlins and designed by the London-based architect Herbert Austen Hall (of Whinney, Son and Austen Hall), whose other commissions include the Town Hall at Lambeth and the Gas Board headquarters in Bristol. Hall sought to harmonise visually the old and new headquarters, which were built at right angles to each other and linked by a single-storey extension. He used a similar window arrangement in New Filton House to that of the earlier building and stepped the top floor back so it did not overwhelm the old farmhouse. Materials used in the façade included traditional red and blue brick, and York and Bath stone. In July 1936 a 14-page article on New Filton House was printed in *Architecture Illustrated* and September's issue of *Architecture and Building News* that year included a seven-page feature, demonstrating the interest generated nationally by the design. The gardens were laid out by landscape designer Mary Anderson and a Mr P H Franklin was the residential architectural assistant.

Art Deco, the most fashionable design style of the inter-war years, was characterised by its sleek lines and stylised, geometric forms. External decorative details at New Filton House included a rampant Pegasus, an allusion to one of the company's most successful engines, on the north-east tower. There was also a bas-relief Mercury roundel over the main entrance in Portland stone and references to the Bristol Jupiter, the Bristol Taurus and the Type 142

New Filton House, 1953, in its post-war white paint (Airbus).

Aerial view of British Aircraft Corporation at Filton with New Filton House in foreground, 1963 (Airbus).

(Britain First). These features inspired by machinery and industry confirmed that the building had been designed for a modern, forward-thinking age. The sculptor was Denis Dunlop.

The marble entrance hall had a brass inlaid zodiac design, which ordinary employees were not permitted to walk across to limit wear. A large, five-panel, sepia-toned window spanning three floors shed natural light upon the main staircase from an internal courtyard. The window, which celebrated the first 25 years of the company, was designed by Jan Juta, the South African painter and muralist. His portrait of a young D H Lawrence hangs in the National Portrait Gallery in London and he was President of the National Society of Mural Painters from 1949 to 1952. For the New Filton House glass, he used an innovative combination of etching, sand-blasting and acid-embossing.

New Filton House has a footprint of 6,400 square metres (21,000 square feet), providing extensive office space arranged over five floors and a basement. As it was a steel-frame structure, the internal subdivisions could be made from non-load-bearing metal screens that could be repositioned if the office layout needed to be changed, making the interior more adaptable than in traditional buildings. Cork was used to insulate the building's external walls and flat roofs. The cork and the rubberised floors absorbed some of the noises generated by the modern, mechanised office, which were exacerbated when they echoed off the expanses of glass and metal.

Like the original Filton House, New Filton House is Grade II listed. Both buildings are currently unoccupied, derelict and subject to vandalism, though it is hoped they will eventually be restored.

Filton housing

In 1904 the Western Wagon & Property Company (WWP) acquired the 69-acre property of the bankrupted Edwin Shellard, which formed part of the Trymhead Estate at Filton. White had briefly lived on the estate in Fairlawn House in the early 1880s.

The directors of WWP were interested in the Arts-and-Crafts-inspired garden suburb movement and initially had ambitious plans to develop their new acquisition along the lines of a small-scale Letchworth. However, a much more conventional development scheme eventually materialised. Similar garden suburb schemes were being proposed for Shirehampton, Sea Mills and Keynsham but also failed to fulfil their architectural and planning promise, in part because of the outbreak of World War One.

In 1908 WWP built two sheds on part of the old Shellard property and leased these to Bristol Tramways for the building and maintenance of its fleet of motor buses. These formed the basis of the British & Colonial aviation company works in 1910. WWP also began developing Fairlawn Avenue, which later came under the management of the new company. The first of the three- and four bed-room terrace-homes here were available for rent from 1908. In addition to the acquisition of the old Filton House property in 1911, another large parcel of land, Westwood Farm, was acquired in 1923. This was taken over by BAC when WWP ceased trading in 1935.

The district of Filton Park, which lies directly on the Bristol - South Gloucestershire border, was planned by Sir George and his brother Samuel, Managing Director of WWP, on their company's share of the Trymhead Estate. The houses were available to all, but were particularly convenient for workers employed at the Bristol Tramways depot and later the aviation works. They were also convenient for catching the tram into Bristol city centre and connections to the wider service. Roads and drainage were completed between 1909 and 1911, and in 1912 WWP reported that 20 small, model residences had been built and were all now occupied by tenants. Further development was curtailed by the coming of the war and was not resumed until 1926. By the following year the number of houses had increased to 38, of which 14 were sold as leasehold; the rest were rented out.

In his address to the 1931 WWP Ordinary General Meeting, the houses were described by Chairman William Verdon Smith as being especially attractive to buyers because of their appearance and their convenience. He reassured his audience that the estate's desirability would be maintained throughout its development. The estate now had 98 houses, of which 92 were owner-occupied. However, in 1932 it was reported that building work was to be temporarily suspended as extensive council estates had been built in the vicinity, which meant there were sufficient houses available to meet the present local demand. The 1933 WWP's annual report said that development had resumed but was still sluggish, the estate by now comprising 112 houses and 37

Newly-built houses on Braemar Avenue, Filton Park Estate, constructed by William Britton and Son, March 1927 (Bristol Record Office). Later that year the directors of WWP announced that the cost of some of the houses on the avenue had been reduced; their slow sale was mainly attributed to the smallness of their gardens.

undeveloped acres. In 1934 an additional 15 houses and six shops were built on land within the estate that had been sold on ground-rent terms to individual builders. WWP was wound up the following year.

The resident population of Filton increased nearly five-fold in the first 20 years after the aircraft works opened, rising from the 658 reported in the 1911 census to 3,041 in 1931. By 1939, with the start of the war, it had reached 10,000. Over the years, fields and parcels of farms had gradually been sold to small local builders like Jennings and Prosser for further housing development.

Drawers, tracers and illustrators

Among the many skills required in the design, manufacture and operation of aircraft is that of being able to express technical ideas visually on paper.

Traditionally, a draftsperson would make a detailed drawing with pencil, paper and tracing paper based upon a designer's specifications. The drawing could be a plan of a complete aeroplane captured from three different view-points (above, side on and from the front) or details of a small component part. It could be drawn the exact same size as the finished product, or accurately scaled up or down. It could be of factory equipment, tools and fixtures made in-house, such as trolleys or jigs (custom-made structures designed to hold specific components or sections in place during assembly or machining to ensure uniformity).

A tracer, usually a woman, would then trace this drawing by hand in Indian ink onto linen to make a fair copy. The paper version was considered the master and too valuable for everyday use; the tracing was more durable as linen was stronger and it could be cleaned. This meant it was a more practical resource in the workshop. If the design was scrapped completely, the ink from the tracing could be soaked off and the linen re-used for handkerchiefs. For years the tracers formed an enclave protected by their supervisor, Monsieur Lavrille, that escaped Roy Fedden's edict forbidding the recruitment of female employees on the engine side of the company. In addition to tracings, drawings were needed for what was called 'full-scale layout' where they formed the basis of metal templates that were used as patterns for the cutting-out of structural parts.

BAC engine department drawing office, c 1928 (below left) (Rolls-Royce plc).

Production Drawing Office No 3, known as New Office Block, based in the back of Whittle House, 1967 (below right) (Rolls-Royce Heritage Trust).

Large Drawing Office, Rodney Hall, c October 1932 (Mrs Jackie Owen collection). The woman on the right-hand side, second from the bottom of the picture, is Jackie Owen's mother, Clara, the daughter of 'Bunny' Butler. It is thought that the debonair man standing at the rear on the right is Monsieur Lavrille.

The value of having a picture is that it could be passed to someone on the shop floor and that person would probably be able to work out quite quickly what was required with minimal additional instructions. Pictures could also be modified fairly easily if their meaning was unclear or the finished product did not work as expected.

In the latter stages of World War Two, technical illustrations came in to use, which made following instructions even easier for those not able to understand the two-dimensional elevations used in plan drawings. The illustration, unlike the drawing, replicated a three-dimensional perspective. The illustrators needed to work out a suitable angle from which to view the object so essential detail was not lost. They worked from the original drawings and also drew from life. The illustrations were used in maintenance, repair, operation and overhaul manuals that were not only needed in the workshops but also required by the aircraft's operators. The text of the manuals was usually written by technical authors working with the draftspeople, engineers and workshops. The authors then provided guidance to the illustrators, while a chief illustrator planned the layout. Most of the work for modern-day manuals, including the illustrations, is done on computer, which possibly results in clearer instructions but means the artwork has lost some of its individual character.

Illustrators have also played an important role in company advertising material. Although photographs and, now, computer-generated images are used, so too are hand-drawn illustrations. Advertising artwork produced by BAC tended to be linked to copy that extolled the technical capabilities of the company's products. By contrast, its airline customers, like Imperial Airways, British Overseas Airways Corporation and British Airways, were keener to emphasise the experience of passenger travel. Their artwork was selling a life style. It is perhaps no coincidence that some of the most visually sophisticated and alluring artwork was produced during the golden age of passenger flight in the inter-war and immediate post-war period, when flying had a glamour and mystique it has largely lost today.

Installation diagram number
FB35270 of a Mercury V.S2 engine,
1933 (Rolls-Royce Heritage Trust).

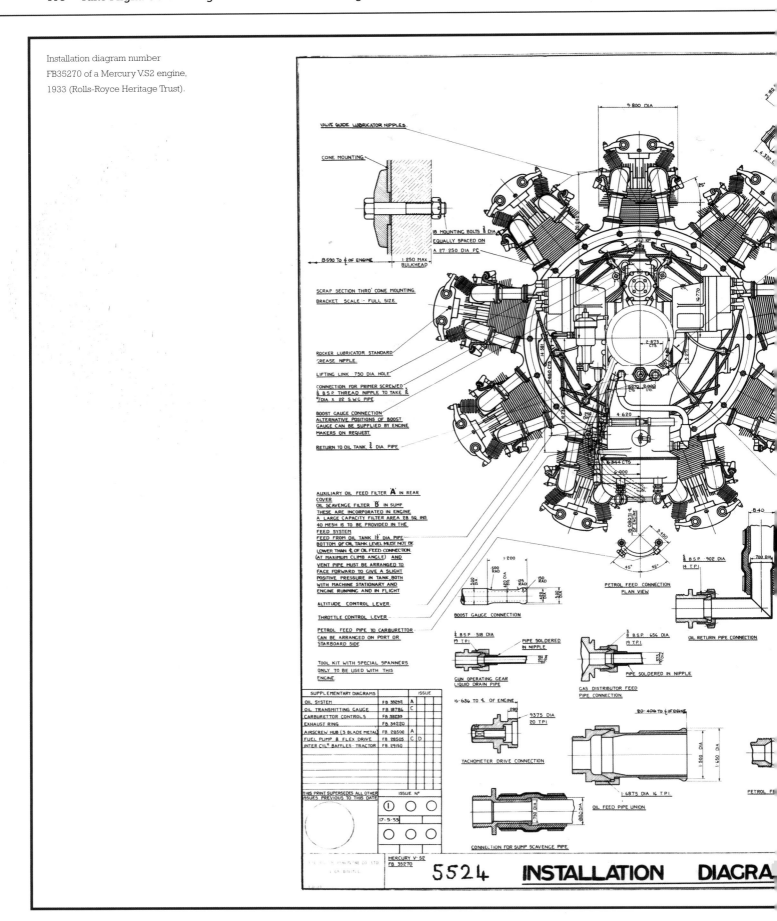

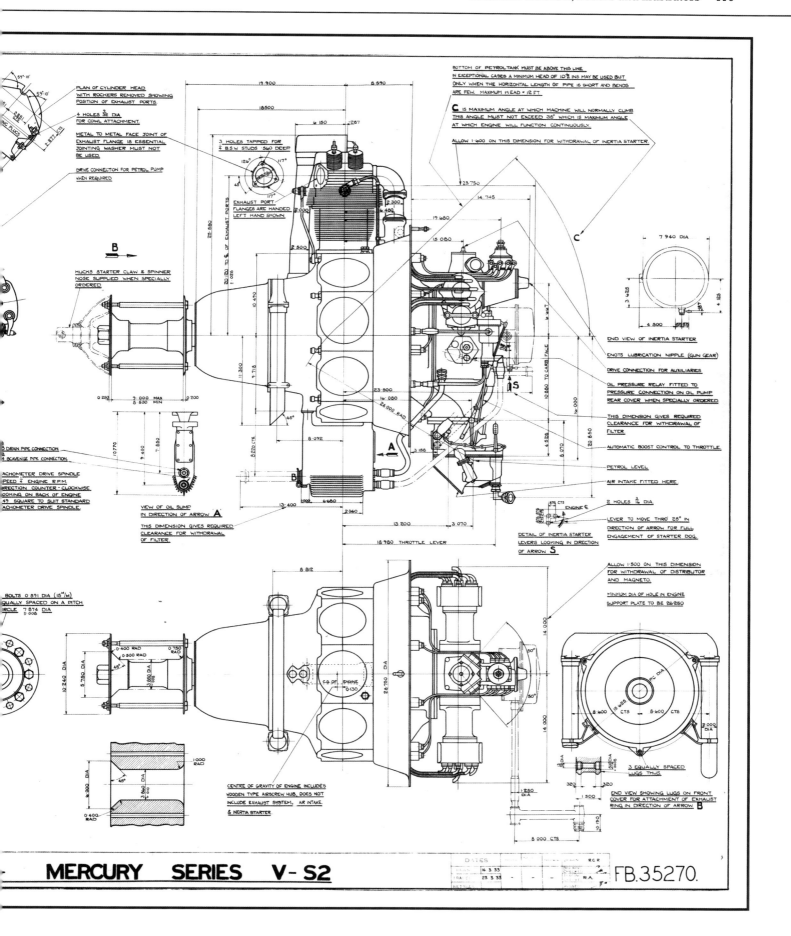

MERCURY   SERIES   V- S2

FB.35270.

The Welfare Association

The original sports pavilion just prior to demolition, 1993 (BAWA).

The Bristol Aeroplane Company Welfare Association (BAWA) was founded 1942 'to provide a centralised service for sickness pay and sports and social activities' for BAC employees.[11]

BAWA had offices within the factory site and also took over BAC's club house on the playing fields at Southmead Road. The club house had been built in 1938 during the works' expansion. When BAC was split and engines and airframes went their separate ways, the land the pavilion was on remained with Bristol Siddeley. It is still owned by Rolls-Royce, which receives a peppercorn rent. In 1973 BAWA was subtly renamed the Bristol Aerospace Welfare Association to reflect the changes that had taken place in the local aviation industry while retaining the same initials. It moved into new, purpose-built facilities in the early 1990s (the old club house was demolished in 1993) and in 1992 became BAWA Healthcare and Leisure.

BAWA was originally a combined sports and social club, sick club and benevolent fund. Around 90 per cent of BAC employees were members. By the 1980s membership still stood at around 80 per cent of those working at Rolls-Royce and British Aerospace. Today it has about 6,000 members. For the standard individual monthly membership rate, they still receive insurance benefits, including coverage of spectacles, dental treatment and medical fees, but there is also a cheaper, sports-only package. In addition to Rolls-Royce and Airbus, current company members include Bristol Cars and MBDA. Although some of the old family identity has gone with the increasing recruitment of graduates on placements rather than generations of long-term employees, BAWA is still one of the few company-oriented organisations in the UK offering sports, social and welfare facilities to members.

At its peak there was an elected BAWA representative for roughly every 300 members. Their job was to collect dues, sick-notes and other claims, distribute benefits and deal with individual problems among their constituents. BAWA provided the only kind of sick-pay that most company employees were able to claim at that time. Members contributed 6d a week to receive this. Some of the support offered by the Association was gradually taken over by statutory provision through the National Health Service, but members still had the benefit of a strong sick-visiting team up until the 1980s, as well as access to convalescent homes. The main BAWA office was situated by the Medical Centre on the Filton site. This was also where the representatives held their monthly meetings. 1993 saw the end of the provision of dedicated office space at Rolls-Royce and British Aerospace, and of representatives being allowed to 'clock-on' when attending BAWA committees during the working day.

Nearly 40 different sports and social clubs were affiliated to BAWA during the 1940s and 1950s. There were clubs for chess, athletics, swimming, hockey, tennis, badminton, rugby, darts, small-bore shooting, football, bowls, skittles, archery, cricket, table tennis, golf, billiards and snooker,

Cover of War Relief leaflet (BAWA). This provision was inaugurated in January 1940 to assist dependents called to service. A National Savings Group was formed the same year.

squash, fencing, sailing, bowling, boxing and sub-aqua. Hobbyists could join the Camera Club, the Esperanto Club, the Radio Society, the Canine Society, the Aeromodelling Club, the Aquarists Club, the Gramophone Club, the Chrysanthemum Society, the Astronomical Society, the Drama Club and Documentary Film Group. For musicians there was the Light Orchestra and the Works Band.

The Bristol Aeroplane Company Motor Sports Club was formed in 1944 and membership had reached 200 by the following year. Meetings were held at the Anchor Hotel on Filton Hill. The club was wound up in May 1946 and replaced by the 500 Club for owners of cars under 500cc. It became the BAC Motor Club in 1955 and was absorbed into the ACES (Arts, Culture, Education and Science) Motor Club in 1967, when it became affiliated to BAWA. It was re-launched in 2001 as the Bristol Pegasus Motor Club.

A departmental dinner in the 1950s (Bristol Aero Collection).

ACES provided a social outlet specifically for the apprentices. Members sometimes linked up with activities run for the residents at Barnwell Hall, which had its own social programme: an annual sports day, an annual 25-mile walk, darts, rugby, snooker, model-making and flying, film shows, football, cricket and table tennis teams, and monthly dances, when women would be brought in by bus from nurses' residences in the city to dance to the music of the resident band, The Blue Diamonds. Barnwell Hall residents were not allowed alcohol on the premises, but for the first few years of operation were able to join the Royal Air Force's Officers' Mess, which was nearby. The apprentices also built pedal cars for the annual 24-hour rally organised by the University of Bristol around College Green and later Whitchurch airport, working on the vehicles in the factory workshops after hours over many months, using off-cuts provided by the company stores.

Other sports and social activities at the company pre-dated the founding of BAWA. The BAC Rugby Football Club was established in 1921, for example, as a works team which played external fixtures. Many employees were also encouraged to join flying clubs and learn to fly, with their lessons subsidised by the company. There were dances, outings, social and welfare clubs, and retirement clubs organised within individual departments, and impromptu Christmas parties that spilled from lunch time into the afternoon. There were interdepartmental challenges in skittles, bowls and other sports. The trophy cabinet at BAWA Healthcare and Leisure includes one for the annual cricket challenge, for example, which in 1925 was won by the Saw Mill. When the company split into two divisions, airframes would challenge engines. The Foreman's Association organised fact-finding trips to factories around the country, which also soon turned into social occasions.

The West of England Annual Sports Day was held at the BAWA playing fields for many years. In addition to the usual athletics meetings, there would be other events for the employees and their families to enjoy including fancy dress competitions, a flower show, competitive exhibitions of tropical fish, cookery competitions and band concerts. There would be an evening dance in the clubhouse ballroom where bands such as Ambrose and his Orchestra might be heard playing.

Cycling race, c 1960s (Stan Sims).

The BAC staff rugby team, April 1931 (Bristol Aero Collection). Among the players is Leslie Frise, third from right in middle row.

Union activity

In 1901 Sir George White resisted attempts by the National Union of Gasworkers and General Labourers (motto 'Love, Unity, Fidelity') to unionise the Bristol Tramways workforce, leading to 450 men walking out on strike.[12]

Even though White remained wary of unions, which he felt could restrict an individual employee's potential, a union shop was established at British & Colonial in 1915, as reported in the April minutes of the Bristol Cooperative Tin and Iron Plate, Sheet Metal Workers and Braziers.[13] Generally, trade union co-operation with the war effort across the country led employers to become less hostile to union membership at this time. However, by 1917 war weariness, overwork and food shortages led to some industrial unrest – despite the Munitions of War Act (1915), which prohibited strike action. In 1918 2,000 British & Colonial aircraft woodworkers went on strike for a war bonus and wage increase, but by the end of the war the company had only lost about 13 days of work through industrial disputes, so had fared better than others.

Trade union membership in the aviation industry increased from 1935, coinciding with the production boom of rearmament. Unions were particularly concerned about the dilution of skills resulting from the employers' increasing use of trainees and semi-skilled labour. The rearmament programme had consolidated and advanced the process begun in World War One of breaking down complex products like aircraft into 'their constituent operations [so that] semi-skilled "handy-men", boys and women could take over the skilled man's work'.[14] This was monotonous, machine-paced work designed to increase the rate of production and cut labour costs. It led to the decline of traditional apprenticeships in favour of taking on trainees, which in turn led to a skills shortage by the late 1930s. The Amalgamated Society of Woodworkers boycotted BAC during the rearmament period as it was opposed to any form of piecework, but the impact of this on the ability of the company to recruit employees was lessened by the fact that airframes were no longer primarily made from wood.[15] Other craft unions were able to take advantage of rearmament by strengthening their position where their skills were essential; increased employment meant increased union membership and increased influence.

After the war a typical aircraft factory would have representatives of a variety of unions because the industry had developed through the use of so many different crafts and trades. At BAC, for example, in addition to the Amalgamated Engineering Union (AEU), the Transport and General Workers Union (TGWU) and the Association of Supervisory Staff, Executives and Technicians, there were various woodworking unions, the pattern-makers' union, the tinsmiths' union, the coppersmiths' union and a lone member of the piano-tuners' union (a left-over from the days of piano wire in airframe construction). This could occasionally lead to demarcation disputes.

Picket at gates of British Aerospace, Filton, August 1984 (facing page).

Police breaking down the workers' blockade at British Aerospace, August 1984.

for bonuses. Wages were negotiated nationally for the work-force grades, so this was not the responsibility of the shop stewards at company level – except if there was a local dispute for the payment of a rate over and above the national agreement. A long-running area of contention taken up by the unions was that of pensions, whereby staff received a contributory pension and shop-floor workers did not. This was resolved in the 1970s. There was similar discontent over the fact that only staff were paid sick leave.

The Joint Shop Stewards Committee comprised the leading shop steward of each union within the company. At BAC the AEU and TGWU had more than one representative because they had so many members. In the 1950s the Treasurer of the committee was the lone shop steward from the piano-tuners' union. The committee elected a chairman who was allowed by the company to work full time on union matters. On the airframe, side shop stewards had to clock onto a 'shop steward card' if they were doing union business, but on the engine side some shop stewards had always been able to work full time on union business. The committee was only supposed to meet in the evenings, but if a particularly urgent problem arose they would say they were 'convening in the Carpenter's Arms', which meant the gents' toilets in the carpentry shop.

Shop stewards would accompany members to disciplinary meetings, collect subs on pay day (before bank accounts and direct debits), be involved in demarcation disputes, and be consulted in the event of industrial injuries. They also helped with negotiations with the rate-fixer over the bonus scheme, which could be as much as two-thirds of a shop-floor worker's pay packet. By the 1960s fixing was abandoned and performance bonuses had become part of the general salary negotiations. This was a fairer system for those working in areas such as the detail shops, where they were making lots of small components, and it was easier for the rate-fixer to calculate the length of time needed to produce them, thereby reducing the opportunity

The committee would try to reach a settlement within the company where possible. If the dispute went beyond the company, union officials would negotiate on the members' behalf with the Employers Federation in a local conference at Engineer's House in Clifton Down. If discussions reached the national level, they would take place between the Confederation of Engineering Unions and the Employers Federation in York. From 1975 the Advisory, Conciliation and Arbitration Service (ACAS) added another possible layer of negotiation. A dispute was only officially recognised if it had been discussed nationally. Occasionally, guerrilla tactics would be used. In 1975, for example, the British Aircraft Corporation buildings were occupied by shop-floor workers and staff were locked out for half a day during local pay negotiations.

Voting for the ending of the nine-week dispute, October 1984.

In 1957 a national rolling strike that started in the West Country was called by the AEU. Following a membership drive, union membership among the workforce in the assembly hall at Filton rose from 50 per cent to 100 per cent in the week before the strike was due to take place. One of the advantages of being a union member was that you could claim strike pay. Although the majority of employees joined the AEU, some joined the TGWU and other unions. The work force was out for ten days.

In 1970 there was a sympathy strike by British Aircraft Corporation workers who refused to handle supplies from Fine Tubes Ltd of Plymouth, which produced precision metal tubing and tube components used by the aviation industry. This meant an alternative source of supply had to be found for the Concorde programme. In 1971 Rolls-Royce resumed purchasing supplies from Fine Tubes, where the long-running industrial dispute continued, and the management threatened workers with dismissal if they refused to handle them. This led to the walk-out of 2,000 employees and the intervention of Tony Benn before a compromise agreement was reached. Margaret Thatcher's Employment Acts of 1980 and 1982 made sympathy strikes and secondary picketing illegal.

In the summer of 1984 a British Aerospace shop-floor pay and overtime dispute at Filton resulted in nine weeks of industrial action, picket lines at the gates and the occupation of the premises. It was unusual as it involved both the airframe and the dynamics sides of the company. The management had to obtain a court injunction, backed by the presence of 60 police officers, to evict the strikers from the site. Staff operated from temporary offices set up in local hotels, people's homes, village halls, schools and other sites during the stoppage. Some of those involved in this dispute thought one of the reasons it escalated was that managers at Filton were making decisions and giving promises to the union officials that were not sanctioned by the company head offices at Stevenage and so could not be followed through.

Bristol Cars

The BAC post-war diversification programme aimed to retain as much of the workforce as possible. It included the establishment of a luxury-car manufacturing division which began production in 1946.

There had been an earlier attempt by BAC to enter the field of car design as well as production after World War One. A prototype single-seat light vehicle named the Monocar had been planned by Wilfred T Reid, but the project was abandoned after only two were built. One was bought by Herbert Thomas, the other was given to Reid.

Type 400 (photographed for the BAC Car Division by Ted Ashman).

Type 401 with Brabazon (photographed for the BAC Car Division by
Ted Ashman).

BAC began its new venture by acquiring a controlling
interest in AFN Ltd, makers of Frazer-Nash cars. H J
Aldington of AFN was Managing Director, with Reginald
Verdon Smith of BAC appointed Chairman. Sir Stanley
White's son, George, also joined the board of directors.
Aldington used his military connections to acquire plans,
drawings and some development engines from the BMW
factory at Munich, which was in the American zone of
occupied Germany. These assets were transported to Filton
against US wishes and later negotiated as part of the
German war reparations to the UK. It was rumoured that
the company had the opportunity to obtain Volkswagen's
business instead of BMW's, but chose a limited-edition,
upmarket model over a mass-produced family car. This
makes sense when it is remembered that the company's
expertise lay in high-cost, top-end engineering rather than

mass-production. BMW's former chief engineer, Fritz
Fiedler, joined AFN where he continued to develop the
BMW 328 engine. By mid-1947 it had become apparent
that BAC and AFN had differing interests and intentions
and the link was severed. The name Bristol Cars Ltd had
already been registered, but the operation continued under
the BAC umbrella for the next few years.

One of the key selling points of the Bristol cars today is
that they continue to be hand-built, high-performance
vehicles. They are aimed at the discriminating purchaser
who recognises the subtleties of character in a car made by
skilled workers. One example of the attention to detail,
as described in *The Bristol Quarterly* in 1956, is that 'the
pleats of the seat cushions... are laid outwards from the
centre of the car' to facilitate the movement of sliding
across to exit.[16] There was an element of transferability of
skills, procedures, equipment and tools from BAC's main
business but, *'Bristol' Quarterly* pointed out:

[the] affinity with aviation... goes rather deeper than in the standards of workmanship, inspection and material quality. There are two elements which colour all thinking in aviation design, namely, efficiency and lightness, and it is but natural that Bristol cars should reflect these qualities of their parentage.[17]

During the development stage of the early designs, scale models were tested in the University of Bristol wind tunnel to assess drag, pitch and yawing (BAC later built a dedicated wind tunnel of its own) and the full-size prototypes were tested on the Filton runway. The company still boasts that its staff is 'drawn from an aviation background to ensure that they are steeped in the traditions of superior engineering, unimpeachable quality and a total devotion to safety'.[18] Design and production matters which are characteristically those of the motor car industry include 'the niceties of transmission, weight distribution, pedal loads, seating comfort, electrics', all of which are highly specialised areas of engineering.[19]

The first Bristol car was the two-litre Type 400, a two-door, four-seater sports saloon (1946-1950). This was followed by the five-seater Type 401 saloon (1948-1953), Type 402 drophead coupé (1949-1950), Type 403 saloon (1953-1955) and Type 404 fixed head coupé (1953-1955). The Type 405 (1954-1958) was the company's first – and as yet only – four-door saloon. A two-door drophead version of this vehicle was built in collaboration with Abbott of Farnham.

In 1951 BAC acquired the premises of the former Filton Laundry and this became the home of the car division's racing team. Among many racing triumphs, in 1955 Bristol 450 road racers won the Le Mans 24-hour rally in the newly established team prize, coming first, second and third in Class E. The final Bristol car with a BAC-designed and built engine was the Type 406 (1958-1961). Each engine was built exclusively by one fully qualified mechanic. The same principle of using dedicated, skilled labour was employed for the building of gearboxes, steering gears, the front suspension unit and rear axles.

In 1956 BAC became the holding company of Bristol Aircraft Ltd, Bristol Aero Engines Ltd, Bristol Helicopters Ltd and Bristol Cars Ltd, all operating as separate, wholly owned subsidiaries. This facilitated mergers with other companies for the production of engines and aircraft, the selling of the helicopter business and, in 1960, the purchase of Bristol Cars by George White, who was joined by Anthony Crook, a former RAF pilot and racing driver, as a junior partner. In the 1990s Bristol car production moved from the old Filton premises to Concorde Road in Patchway.

Type 405 drophead outside the Brabazon hangar (facing page) (photographed for the BAC Car Division, from the collection of Shawn Thomas).

Type 406 alongside Britannia (above) (photographed for the BAC Car Division, from the collection of Shawn Thomas).

Cooper Bristol racing car (right) (photographed for the BAC Car Division by Ted Ashman).

An animated discussion at BAC in front of a map of the world, 1953 (Rolls-Royce plc).

Section 4:
Worldwide Connections

As early as 1910 British & Colonial was making commercial contacts abroad, developing these up until the beginning of World War One. BAC and its associated companies continued this development, setting the foundations that today make the West of England's aviation industry of international significance in terms of conducting business (sales, licensing, subcontracting, maintenance and the provision of training services) and opening up world travel.

Cover of *Bristol Review* publicising the global market for Bristol engines, 1931 (Bristol Aero Collection).

Table 1 lists some of BAC's overseas subsidiaries, associated companies, agents, concessionaries, representatives and distributors in 1956, the year BAC was reorganised as a holding company. Although still firmly embedded in the local community by its Filton roots, BAC was a truly international company.

Table 1 BAC's Overseas Interests in 1956

Subsidiaries	Locations of Agents, Concessionaries, Representatives and Distributors
Bristol Aeroplane Company of Canada Limited (Montreal) Bristol Aero Engines Limited (Montreal) Bristol Aero Engines (Western) Limited (Vancouver) Bristol Aircraft (Western) Limited (Winnipeg) The Bristol Aeroplane Company (Australia) Pty Limited (Melbourne) Bristol Aviation Services Pty Ltd (Sydney) The Bristol Aeroplane Company (New Zealand) Limited (Wellington) Bristol de Mexico SA DE CV (Mexico City Airport) **Associated Companies** Aeronautical Supply Company Pty Limited (Melbourne) Societe d'Exploitation et de Constructions Aeronautiques (Paris) Talleres Aeronauticos de Barajas SA (Madrid)	*Europe:* Ankara, Athens, Bromma, Brussels, Cologne, Copenhagen, Dublin, Dusseldorf, Geneva, The Hague, Helsinki, Lisbon, Madrid, Milan, Oslo, Paris, Prague, Stockholm, Vienna, Zurich *Middle East and Africa*: Bulawayo, Beirut, Cairo, Damascus, Jeddah, Johannesburg, Nairobi, Tangier, Tel Aviv *Indian Subcontinent, Far East and Australasia*: Adelaide, Auckland, Bombay, Colombo, Hong Kong, Karachi, Melbourne, New Delhi, Rangoon, Sydney, Tokyo, Wellington *Caribbean and South America*: Bogata, Buenos Aires, Caracas, Georgetown, Kingston, Montevideo, Rio de Janeiro, Santiago *North America*: Chicago, Indiana, Long Island, Montreal

When Sir George White first tried to sell his Boxkites to the War Office, he offered to 'abstain from all business with foreign powers', presumably thinking the government would not want advanced British technology falling into the hands of future competitors or enemies. However, the Secretary of State for War, Richard Burdon Haldane (later Viscount Haldane and the second

Chancellor of the University of Bristol), 'preferred the Company to develop business abroad without restriction'.[1] The first overseas sales were to Russia; the order for eight Boxkites was negotiated with the Russian Attaché in Paris by Émile Stern in November 1910. In April the following year, the aircraft was displayed on the British & Colonial stand at the St Petersburg Russian Aeronautical Exhibition, where it was awarded a gold medal and certificate of merit. The company's Russian connection continued into the 1920s, when a large number of three-cylinder Lucifer engines were specially produced for the Soviet market.

In December 1910 British & Colonial organised an overseas sales mission and demonstration tour for the Boxkite, with two each of the biplanes being transported to India and Australia. The Indian mission was led by Farnall Thurstan accompanied by Henri Jullerot as Chief Pilot and two mechanics, Mr Bendall and Mr Webb. The tour began in Calcutta, West Bengal and received favourable reports from *The Times of India*, the city's largest newspaper, which was owned by a Bristolian. While the biplanes were being reassembled after their journey and prepared for demonstration flights, Jullerot was invited by the Commander in Chief of the Indian Army, Sir Moore O'Creagh, to give a talk at Fort William to several hundred officers on the subject 'Aviation in its Military Aspects'. By 6 January 1911 the aircraft were ready for public displays, the first of which was given at Maidan racecourse in front of an estimated crowd of 700,000. Jullerot recalled:

> Passing over the fort I continued my flight in the direction of the cathedral, and then went back to the grand stand of the racecourse, and after a few laps round the course gave an exhibition of more tricky flying such as spiral *vol planes* and the like, much to the delight of the crowd. It was the first absolutely successful flight they had ever seen, and at first they seemed to regard me as a kind of incarnated air-god. Later on, however, they became less overawed, and would come out and look at the machine and sit hour after hour in the hope of seeing me fly.[2]

A few days later the aircraft were transported by train to the Deccan plateau, where the tour team had been invited to take part in the military manoeuvres. Captain W Sefton Brancker, who was later knighted for his work in setting up the UK's Air Ministry, had his first experience of flying when he accompanied Jullerot on a series of reconnaissance flights, resting his map on the pilot's back and keeping a tight hold on his compass and sketch pad. Their flight on 16 January lasted 45 minutes, setting a British record for cross-country flying with a passenger. Jullerot later took part in the Northern Manoeuvres at Karghpur. However, although O'Creagh recognised its potential, the Indian army could not afford to become involved in aviation at that time.

The Australian mission was led by Sydney Ernest Smith, accompanied by the pilots Leslie Macdonald and Joseph Hammond who gave demonstrations using Boxkite No 10. On 23

Boxkite in India (right)
(Bristol Aero Collection).

This certificate, presented to British
& Colonial at the 1st International
Air Exhibition in St Petersburg,
1911, says: 'To the company
for construction of aeroplanes
'Bristol' (England), for a beautiful
performance of the aircraft system
and for its broad organisation of
production' (facing page) (Bristol's
Museums, Galleries and Archives).

February 1911 mechanic Frank Coles became Australia's first aircraft passenger when he flew
with Hammond in a demonstration at Geelong, Victoria. A businessman from Melbourne,
M H Baillieu, became Australia's first paying passenger the following month when he took a
19km (nearly 12 miles) flight with Hammond. In September William Ewart Hart, a dentist
from Parramatta, bought Boxkite No 11, along with some spare parts, for £1,333. He was
taught to fly by Hammond's mechanic, making his first solo flight on 3 November 1911.
He was Australia's first qualified pilot and was awarded his licence by the Aerial League of
Australia on 5 December 1911. He had previously been awarded a special plaque when, on
18 November, he flew 76km (47 miles) from Penrith to Sydney to complete the first cross-
country flight in New South Wales. In 1914 the Bristol Boxkite was adopted by the flying
school at Point Cook, Victoria for training Australia's first wartime pilots.

During 1911 and 1912 Thurstan also arranged various demonstrations for overseas
customers for the Prier monoplane, with Hammond as the pilot. In all, one-third of
British & Colonial's aircraft built between 1910 and 1914 were exported.[3] In addition to
Russia, sales were made to France, Spain, Italy, Sweden, Turkey, Romania and Bulgaria
to government and private customers. After World War One the company reinstated
its overseas sales agents and set up its first New York office in the hope of developing
American sales from the Bristol Tourer (a variation on the Fighter) and M1C monoplane.
This office closed at the end of 1920 as a result of Congress raising import tariffs which
made it unprofitable to do business there. Most of the aircraft that had been ordered
before the tariff was raised were sold in the UK, with a few going to Canada, Spain and
Australia. BAC never did succeed in breaking into the American market as there was too
much home-grown competition, though the company did try to accommodate potential
customer needs by building and buying components to American standards.

Cultivating foreign markets helped keep BAC in business in the inter-war years, according to *The Aeroplane*: 'This lean period would have been leaner still without the foreign sales. Business overseas augmented the annual output, and it was maintained by continued attention to the needs of foreign buyers, until the home market suddenly expanded in 1935.'[4] During World War Two the company strove to maintain its level of exports wherever possible, knowing it would be difficult to regain trade links once they were lost. It also needed to continue providing after-sales service to its customers, which required overseas representatives and overhaul facilities.

Lieutenant George Pinnock Merz climbing aboard a Bristol Boxkite aircraft, 1914 (facing page, left) (Australian War Memorial A03918). Merz was the first Australian pilot to be killed in action when his aeroplane was forced down and attacked in Mesopotamia on 30 July 1915.

Portrait of an officer shaking the hand of a pilot in a Bristol Boxkite aircraft at Point Cook Aviation School, August 1915 (facing page, right) (Australian War Memorial DAD0034).

In addition to sales, overseas licensing and subcontracting agreements proved lucrative. Before World War One such contracts included the granting of a licence in 1912 to Caproni to build Coanda monoplanes in Italy and to Breguet in 1913 to make Coanda TB8 biplanes in France. Bulldogs were built under licence in Japan in the 1920s. There were Beaufort Division factories established in Australia in 1939 with personnel trained at Filton and BAC employees sent out as supervisors. Blenheim IVs were built under licence in Canada, where they were called by the original name of Bolingbroke. A lengthened version of the Britannia 253 was developed by Canadair under licence as the CL44 followed by the CL44D, which had a swing tail to give unimpeded access to the cargo bay.

On the engine side, thousands of Jupiters were built under licence in Belgium, Canada, Czechoslovakia, France, Germany, Hungary, Italy, Japan, Poland, Portugal, Spain, Switzerland, USA, USSR and Yugoslavia. Other licensing agreements included Lucifers built by ATDK, Japan; Titans built by SABCA, Brussels and OGMA, Portugal; Mercurys built by Tarmmerfors Linne-Och Jern-Manufactur AB, Finland; Neptunes built by E W Bliss, New York; Pegasuses built by Societe Piaggio, Italy; Perseuses built by Polish Skoda; Aquilas built by Sigma, France; Hercules built by SNECMA, Paris; and Orpheuses built by Hindustan Aircraft Ltd in India. Tauruses were licensed for production in Sweden, Poland and France but none were built there.

The company's training facilities also established international links. The early pupils at the Bristol Flying Schools included several private individuals from overseas. The first schools set up abroad on the Bristol model were at Madrid and Halberstadt, which were both established in February 1912. The Spanish school was supplied with British & Colonial aircraft, while the one in Germany was licensed to manufacture the aircraft themselves through the Deutsche Bristol-Werke (half of its capital came from the British & Colonial directors). This agreement was cancelled on 23 June 1914. In August 1912 a Bristol school was set up at Mirafiore in Italy.

Back in Filton during the 1950s, the Bristol Aircraft Servicing School at Filton designed courses for civil and military aircrews so they could prepare for the Air Registration Board. The intake also included aircrews from around the world that were flying BAC-built aircraft. The school was housed in the Britannia Assembly Hall. At Patchway the Engine Servicing School was a self-contained educational unit, which was expanded following worldwide demand for turboprop courses. It was based in the Rodney Demonstration Hall. There were also overseas apprentices at the BAC school on Filton Avenue, and the company set up special schools in Mexico, Cuba and other countries for the training of crews for airlines operating the Britannia.

From the 1960s onwards the scale, cost and complexity of aviation projects meant international collaboration became increasingly necessary and it is rare today for a company to be able to develop an aero-engine or airframe alone. Among the early collaborative projects at Filton and Patchway that involved overseas partners were Concorde and the Olympus 593 engine, as well as the missile and space programmes.

The development of the international aviation market coincided with major changes in passenger flight. The world's first scheduled air passenger service was provided by Deutsche Luftschiffahrts-Aktiengesellschaft on Zeppelin airships in 1910. By the time World War One had broken out, 34,000 passengers had been carried on over 1,500 flights by the company. The number of passengers that could be carried on the early aeroplanes was limited because aero-engines were not yet powerful enough to carry heavy loads. By the beginning of the 1920s bigger aeroplanes were being built as engine capacity increased, but it could be an uncomfortable ride. The passengers would usually have been packed together on hard seats, unable to hear each other speak because of the noise of the engines. As the cabins were not yet pressurised, the pilot either had to subject his passengers to the giddiness and nausea of altitude sickness and freezing temperatures when flying at high altitude, or keep the aircraft low, increasing the risk of being buffeted by thermals and storms.

By the late 1920s some of these problems had been resolved and a privileged few came to enjoy the magic, excitement and romance of airline passenger flight as long-haul routes were developed in the wake of those carrying international airmail. However, it was not until the 1960s, with the coming of the large airliners and the introduction of tourist and economy class seating, that world-wide travel began to be available to more than just a wealthy elite who had the money and time to make leisurely, expensive flights. The first modern passenger airliner was the Boeing 247 of the 1930s. This was a sleek, state-of-the-art, all-metal, twin-engined monoplane and one of the first aircraft to have an automatic pilot facility. It also had a sound-proofed, heated cabin, an onboard toilet, upholstered seats, and individual reading lights and air vents for each of its ten passengers. It could fly 50 per cent faster than any other airliner of its day and in May 1933 set a new record by flying from New York to San Francisco in less than 20 hours. Of more lasting impact, perhaps, was Douglas' DC3 which had its maiden flight on 17 December 1935, the anniversary of the Wright brothers' breakthrough at Kitty Hawk.

The post-World War Two period saw a more concerted effort on the part of UK manufacturers to exploit the civil market. The de Havilland Comet was the world's first jet to provide regular passenger services. It was built in response to the Brabazon Committee's Type IV recommendation for a jet-powered, 100-seater aircraft. Later versions were powered by Rolls-Royce Avon 525 turbojet engines. Its maiden flight took place on 27 July

Boeing 247 built 1933 (facing page) (Science and Society Picture Library/Science Museum). This became the oldest aircraft to have flown the Atlantic when it flew from Florida to Wroughton in Wiltshire on 3 August 1983.

1949 and it came into service on 2 May 1952 when it flew from London to Johannesburg for British Overseas Airways Corporation (BOAC).

A series of fatal crashes led to the grounding of the Comet fleet in 1954 while the problem was identified and solved. The accidents were discovered to have primarily resulted from fatigue around the aircraft's square windows and escape hatch. What was learnt about the fatigue life of airframes from this experience was later used in tests for future airliners. Until the Comet investigation it had not been appreciated that if an airframe is repeatedly stretched as the result of stress brought by changing air pressure, there is a limit to how many times it can return to its original condition without damage. Some materials, like polythene, can be stretched without lasting effect; others, like elastic, show they have been overstretched through fraying. In metal, overstretching is indicated by cracks which will eventually fracture, causing the structure to fail. The fatigue life indicates how many cycles of stretching a material can stand before the cracks appear. After the Comet crashes, square corners were no longer used in aircraft to avoid what was termed 'stress concentration'; a curved edge prolongs the metal's ability to withstand stretching (its ductility).

From 4 October 1958 Comet 4 was used for the first scheduled jet passenger service – BOAC's London to New York route with a stop-over at Gander in Newfoundland. However, by this time de Havilland had lost much of its commercial advantage to the US. During World War Two the Americans had concentrated on military transporters while the UK focused on the production of fighters, bombers and reconnaissance aircraft. The conversion of transporters for the burgeoning civil market in the US gave the Americans a head start in the post-war period.

BAC's earliest contribution to passenger travel was the 14-seater Pullman of 1920, the company's first airliner. This was a conversion of the third Braemar bomber and was probably the first British aircraft to have an enclosed cabin for both passengers and crew. Only one was built. The aircraft was held at Martlesham Heath for extensive and inconclusive government tests, so BAC was unable to exploit its commercial potential. By the time there was a demand from airline companies for passenger aircraft, the Pullman was already obsolete. Plans were drawn up for a 40-seater version but this was never built.

Comet on cover of *The Aeroplane*, March 21 1958 (above) (Bristol Aero Collection).

Staged photoshoot for the interior of the Pullman, showing the wicker passenger chairs and ornate décor, 1920 (left) (Bristol's Museums, Galleries and Archives).

Artist's impression of the Type 200, c 1956 (Rolls-Royce Heritage Trust).

After the Pullman and the similarly short-lived Type 75 Ten Seater, BAC largely withdrew from the airliner business. A far more significant contribution by the company in those early decades of passenger travel came through the provision of aero-engines for other manufacturers. These include Imperial Airways' fleet of Short Empire flying boats (Pegasus) and Handley Page HP42s (Jupiter) in the 1930s and, after the war, Airspeed Ambassadors (Centaurus).

On the airframe side, the Brabazon project could be seen as a false dawn. Various 'paper aeroplanes' were schemed at Filton, but never came to fruition, including the Bristol Type 200, a three-engined subsonic airliner designed for a government specification that was eventually filled by the Hawker Siddeley Trident. However, the Wayfarer, the passenger version of the Freighter, was popular with customers and although there were fewer sales than anticipated for Britannia, it carried thousands of passengers around the world and was unquestionably successful in terms of its technological advancements.

BAC One-Eleven, 1962
(Bristol Aero Collection).

In the 1960s the Filton factory secured work building the rear fuselage for British Aircraft Corporation's 79-seater One-Eleven short-range jet airliner and was also involved in the aircraft's marketing and test procedures. The design office and production line were based at the Vickers-Armstrong factory at Hurn near Bournemouth, with a second production line at Weybridge. Over 240 of the aircraft were produced, in various configurations, in the UK and Romania, the last of the British-built aircraft being completed in 1982. For many years it was the highest export-earning airliner for the UK, with overseas operators including American Airlines, Aer Lingus, Air Pacific, Germanair, Gulf Air, Quebecair and Zambia Airways. Powered by Rolls-Royce of Derby's Spey engine, it was gradually withdrawn from service in Europe, in part because it exceeded new permitted noise limits. For a brief period, separate British Aerospace sales teams were in competition with one another trying to persuade airline companies to buy either the One-Eleven or the BAe 146 airliner (originally a Hawker Siddeley project), which had sections of its fuselage built at the Filton factory.

The first ever A320 Airbus wings manufactured at Filton being loaded into a Super-Guppy for transportation to Toulouse (George Rollo).

With the Airbus fleet of airliners, Filton's contribution has mainly related to the specialist design and manufacture of wings. This connection was first established when British Aerospace was given responsibility for the design and final assembly of the wings of the Airbus A320, an all-new, short- to medium-range, single-aisle, twin-engined aircraft. On 30 April 1986 the first set of Filton-built wings was transported to Toulouse on board an Airbus Super-Guppy to be fitted to the A320's fuselage, and the first airline deliveries of the completed A320 were made in the Spring of 1988. GKN is now responsible for the manufacture of civil Airbus wings at the Filton facility, with Airbus continuing to manufacture the wings of the A400M military transporter.

Imperial Airways

The West of England has provided the expertise, workmanship and financial backing for centuries of long-distance travel, dating back from the time of sail and steam to Britannia and Concorde and continuing today with the Airbus fleet.

Among the first people to travel westwards across the Atlantic were Bristol fishermen searching for new waters in which to cast their nets in the fourteenth and fifteenth centuries. Bristol was the starting-point of many voyages of discovery backed by its influential merchants, including John Cabot's inadvertent discovery of Newfoundland on board the *Matthew* in 1497 (he thought he was heading for the riches of Asia). Merchant ships were engaged for centuries in the highly profitable triangular route between Bristol, Africa and the Caribbean and American colonies in which trinkets, cloth and other domestic goods were traded for enslaved African people who were traded in turn for rum, sugar and tobacco. Isambard Kingdom Brunel's first two maritime projects, PS *Great Western* and ss *Great Britain*, were built in Bristol's docks. The region's first major association with long-range aviation came through the provision of aero-engines to the fleet of Imperial Airways.

Imperial Airways was formed on 31 March 1924 in a merger of Instone Airline Ltd, Daimler Airway, Handley Page Transport Limited and British Marine Air Navigation Co Ltd. The new company was subsidised by the government to the tune of £1m spread over ten years, on the understanding that it would revitalise the British-European routes that had become moribund with the war and develop new, long-distance services between the UK and the countries of the Empire. By the outbreak of World War Two it had 'surveyed, opened and developed a series of trunk routes stretching to Australia, Hongkong, South, East and West Africa and a regular mail service to North America'.[5] It had also established a number of overseas aerodromes and protective forts.

Mr Granville, inventor of this airborne version of the Charleston dance routine, takes a pupil through her paces on board an Imperial Airways London-Paris flight, c 1926 (Science and Society Picture Library/Science Museum).

Still from the 1925 film version of *The Lost World* (private collection). This became the world's first in-flight-movie when it was shown on the Imperial Airways London-Paris route.

The British Empire had spread across the world in the wake of trading activity, with raw materials such as cotton, tea and rubber being imported into the UK and manufactured goods exported out. By 1901, the year of her death, Queen Victoria ruled nearly a quarter of the world's population. Nineteenth-century advances in technology dramatically reduced the time it took to transport trading goods, raw materials, mail, civil servants, military personnel and supplies around the Empire through the introduction of steamships and steam railways. Aviation effectively shrank the world still further, reducing the time it took to cover great distances, while simultaneously opening the world up by extending people's horizons and the possibilities of travel.

On 26 April 1924 Imperial Airways flew its first service when a de Havilland 34 biplane piloted by Captain H S Robertson took off from London for Paris. Although this aircraft was powered by a Napier Lion engine, Imperial Airways soon came to rely largely on Bristol engines, and Filton and Patchway engineers were sent around the world to service them. In December 1926 the first consignment of Jupiter VIs was delivered to Imperial Airways to be installed in the de Havilland Hercules airliner for use on the Egypt-India route. Earlier that year the engine had been given a 25,000-mile endurance test in a Bristol Bloodhound flown by Imperial Airways' pilots Colonel F F

Minchin and Captain Frank Barnard. On 11 June 1931 the first of the Jupiter-powered Handley Page HP42s (Hannibal) began operating on the London to Paris service, ushering in a new era of passenger comfort and service. On 29 June 1935 Bristol's sleeve-valve Perseus had its first use in civil aviation on an Imperial Airways' Short L17 airliner.

Imperial Airways is perhaps best remembered for its glamorous long-distance flying boats. On 30 November 1929 a Short Calcutta flying boat powered by three Jupiters flew from London to Karachi, marking the start of the airline company's through air route from the UK to India. The service was extended to Jodphur and Delhi in December. One of the main advantages of using flying boats in the far-flung corners of the Empire was that they did not require runways. Henri Fabre is credited with making the first successful floatplane flight on 28 March 1910. A floatplane is kept buoyant by pontoons attached under the aircraft's fuselage. In contrast, a flying boat is kept buoyant by the fuselage itself, which acts like a ship's hull, usually with additional support from floats attached under the wings. The first successful flying boat flight was made in 1912 by Glenn Hammond Curtiss. The largest flying boat, carrying 169 passengers, was Dornier of Germany's Do X, which first flew in October 1929. It was originally powered by 12 Bristol Jupiters, which were later replaced by Curtiss Conqueror engines. Six engines were pushing, six were

The Dornier Do X, 1929 (Rolls-Royce Heritage Trust).

pulling. Less gargantuan flying boats had accommodation for around 20 passengers in day-time layout, fewer for night-time flights when sleeping berths were used.

The first of Imperial Airways' long-range, four-engined C Class Empire flying boats to go into service was the Pegasus-powered Canopus built by Shorts, which on 30 October 1936 made its first scheduled flight on the trans-Mediterranean route. A total of 42 Empires were constructed for Imperial Airways and Quantas, Australia. The two airlines jointly operated a UK-Australia service which carried its first passengers in April 1935 between Brisbane and London, using a variety of different aircraft for each leg of the journey. They increasingly depended on the reliability, comfort and capacity of flying boats.

From 5 March 1937 all Imperial Airways' flying boats operated out of the Hythe Base at Southampton. This was a busy year for the company. On 2 June landplanes were taken off the UK to South Africa route and replaced by flying boats throughout. Landing stages along the

Nile were used for part of the journey. On 16 June the Perseus-powered Cavalier inaugurated the first British Atlantic air service between Bermuda and New York in partnership with Pan American Airways. The Empire Air Mail Programme was inaugurated on 29 June when the Centurion left Southampton for the Sudan and East and South Africa. On 6 July the Caledonia completed the first of a series of commercial survey flights across the Atlantic. By 1938 Empire flying boats were flying over 113,000 miles a week. A transatlantic mail service using scheduled flights was started on 5 August 1939 on a Southampton-Foynes-Botwood-Montreal-New York route using the Caribou and Cabot. The aircraft were refuelled in the air by Handley Page Harrow tanker aircraft stationed at Ireland and Newfoundland.

Imperial Airways merged with British Airways Ltd to become British Overseas Airways Corporation (BOAC) on 24 November 1939. Part of the company branched off to form British European Airways in 1946, with the remainder becoming British Airways on 31 March 1974. During World War Two BOAC's headquarters were in the Grand Spa Hotel in Bristol (now the Avon Gorge Hotel). Land aircraft were based at the start of the war at Whitchurch airport, which had been requisitioned by the Air Ministry. In the early 1950s BOAC leased the western bay of the Brabazon hangar on the BAC site at Filton while it waited for a delayed hangar of its own to become available at Heathrow. This was used for the servicing of Boeing Stratocruisers and Lockheed Constellations.

Britannia

In December 1946 BOAC issued a requirement for a medium-range airliner to serve on the Empire routes, prompted by the Brabazon Committee's Type III recommendation. Originally, BOAC was looking for a 32-seater aircraft but the company was persuaded to aim bigger.

Their initial thinking had allegedly been determined by how many people would fit on an airport coach that ferried passengers between the terminal and the runway. BOAC's requirements were incorporated into Specification 2/47 from the Ministry of Supply, which received eight designs from five companies. BAC's Bristol Type 175 was thought the most promising. This eventually became Britannia, the world's first long-range turboprop, described by *Bristol Review* as 'surely one of the most beautiful things in the air'.[6] The aircraft was nicknamed 'The Whispering Giant' as passengers experienced less noise and vibration than in piston-powered or jet airliners. Extolling its virtues, *The 'Bristol' Quarterly* said the reduction in noise 'combined with the roominess and comfort of its cabin, make long distance travelling at high speed no more tiring than relaxing in an armchair'.[7]

The proposed Britannia family was designed to provide suitable aircraft for short-, medium- and long-haul flights. The Britannia 100 series provided accommodation for 90 tourist or 61 first-class passengers. The Britannia 250 series came in mixed cargo/passenger versions. The all-cargo version, used by the Royal Air Force, had a large, heavy-duty freight door at the front and a strengthened floor, which required specially devised structural tests during the development stage of the aircraft. It was later sold off by the Royal Air Force Transport Command to Monarch Airlines and converted for civilian use as a passenger carrier. The Britannia 300 series comprised long-bodied, short-, medium- and long-range aircraft with extra cabin capacity. In a tourist-class layout the aircraft could carry 139 passengers, thereby bringing 'flying within the reach, for the first time, of smaller purses'.[8]

Originally, BAC planned to use the Centaurus sleeve-valve engine in Britannia but the company turned instead to the Proteus, which, after initial delays, was making good progress by 1950. This was a free-turbine turboprop engine, with two independent turbine wheels, one to drive the compressor, the other to drive the propeller. Stanley Hooker explained: 'This means that each turbine can be designed

Close up of Proteus engine in Britannia 101 in Brabazon hangar at Filton, c 1952 (facing page) (Rolls-Royce plc). The propellers are by Rotol.

Pre-flight checks on the windscreen and nose undercarriage prior to further hot weather tests during Britannia's tour to the Middle East, c 1954 (above) (Peter Rushby Archive). Engines taking in hotter, less dense air than normal have less oxygen from which to create the 'bang' of combustion and therefore produce less power.

to do its own particular job best, without reference to how it affects the other turbine, and both turbines can run (as indeed they do) at the speeds which suit them best.'[9] BAC was looking to develop engines that needed less fuel, thereby reducing costs and increasing space available for revenue-producing loads. The turboprop was considered preferable to the jet because 'a large slow-turning propeller is a better propulsive medium than a narrow high speed jet of gas, unless the aircraft is flying very fast'.[10]

Cold weather trials for Britannia held at Stevenson Field, Winnipeg where refuelling and de-fuelling checks were made in the open, c 1955 (Bristol Aero Collection).

The maiden flight of the first Britannia prototype took place on 16 August 1952 and BAC looked to make delivery of the first instalment of BOAC's initial order of 15 by May 1954, though this deadline was not met. According to an article in *Bristol Review*, 'No other civil aircraft has ever had such intensive pre-flight development' as Britannia.[11] This included tests on a full-scale model wing, a half-scale fuselage and a near-complete functional mock-up. Initial tropical-climate testing began at RAF Idris in Libya in October 1954, with further extensive trials taking place in Johannesburg and Khartoum in March the following year. Route-proving trials for the Air Registration Board, BAC and BOAC took place from September to November 1955 using the third production Britannia 102 (G-ANBC).

The aircraft was formally handed over to BOAC on 30 December 1955, having just received its Certificate of Airworthiness. According to BAC historian Derek James, 'the occasion had been rather up-staged two days earlier, when a de Havilland Comet 3 in BOAC livery arrived back in Heathrow to become the world's first jet-liner to have encircled the globe'.[12] The fleet was due to go into public service in October 1956 but 'an obscure icing problem' on the Proteus, first encountered in March 1956 during a flight to Nairobi, led to further delay.[13] Ice crystals accumulated in the B-skin (which ducted air into the engine) when flying in particular, localised atmospheric conditions, most notably in certain cloud formations over South Africa. The crystals broke off in lumps that passed into the engine, causing the flame to be extinguished in one or more of the chambers (known as a flame-out). It required the combined efforts of BAC, the Royal Aircraft Establishment at Farnborough, the National Gas Turbine Establishment and other research facilities of the Ministry of Supply to solve the problem and get Proteus and Britannia cleared for flight again. The test programme was overseen by Walter Gibb, who had succeeded Bill Pegg as Chief Test Pilot that year. The solution was to introduce jets into the B-skin to keep the air warm and the means to relight the flame quickly if it blew out.

Advertisement in *The Montreal Star* for El Al Israel Airline's Britannia service playing on the fact it flew non-stop without the usual refuelling stages at Goose Bay and Gander, Newfoundland, 1959 (Bristol Aero Collection).

On 1 February 1957 BOAC's Britannia service began when the London to Johannesburg route was inaugurated using a mixed-class configuration of 48 tourist and 19 first-class passengers. On 2 March 1957 BOAC's Sydney service was started; one of the airliners used on the route was completely first-class. On 29 June 1957 a Britannia made the first non-stop airliner flight from London to Vancouver, taking 14 hours 40 minutes. By August that year BOAC's initial order was completed. The aircraft was by now also operating on the airline's Hong Kong, Singapore and Japanese routes. A 24,000-mile demonstration tour of North America was made in August 1957 using G-ANBJ, a Britannia 102 with a modified internal layout. The London

Pictures from promotional brochure for Britannia produced by BOAC, c 1956 (Bristol Aero Collection).

to Montreal leg was the first non-stop Atlantic flight by a turboprop. The Idlewild to San Diego leg made Britannia the first British aircraft to complete a non-stop, coast-to-coast flight.

A second Britannia production line was set up at Short Brothers and Harland Limited in Belfast, which also carried out furnishing and fitting work. BAC had purchased a significant share interest in the company by this stage, giving it partner status. The aircraft had been designed so its structure could be broken down into a series of independent components which could be rapidly produced by subcontractors, leaving BAC 'free to concentrate, to a degree otherwise impossible, on accelerating the process of final assembly'.[14] At Filton, assembly started in the erection shop then moved to the assembly hall where, at the rear of the centre bay, the wings were joined to the fuselage. The work progressed to the front of the bay for the adding of the engines, undercarriage, fins, tailplane, outer wings and control surfaces. BAC could still claim its aircraft were hand-built at this time because of the high level of personal craftsmanship.

The interior design was overseen by BAC's Furnishing Department, guided by the specific requirements of BOAC. The designers were working in a more confined space than would be found on a passenger train or ship and in an environment where weight was a crucial consideration. The design was a combination of aesthetics and engineering, and the department's Design Section included specialists in cabin layout, noise reduction, new materials, vibration, amenities, seating, galleys and décor. The 'Bristol' Quarterly boasted:

> With their design and manufacturing skill and with the cooperation and experience of the airline operators whom they serve, Bristol Aircraft's furnishing team are able to create a standard of artistry in comfort equal to any in contemporary aviation.[15]

There was a tight schedule for putting in the necessary hours for flight approval, which meant that some of the fitters from subcontractors Parnall had to be on board installing the furnishings while airborne.

A major set back to the Britannia programme came on Wednesday 6 November 1957 when a Britannia 301 (G-ANCA) crashed at Downend at 11:57am, killing all 15 crew and technicians on board. The crash took place during a flight to gain US safety accreditation. The fault, possibly in the autopilot's wiring, developed at 457 metres (1,500 feet) and sent the aircraft into a sudden, steep bank to the right, with a rapid loss of control and height. The aircraft was too low to recover and, to avoid the risk of landing in a built-up area, Hugh Statham, an experienced pilot, steered it towards nearby allotments before it exploded on impact in what is now called Britannia Wood. Ten houses were seriously damaged on Overndale Road, but there were no fatalities on the ground.[16] There were other fatal accidents, at Hurn on 24 December 1958 during a check flight for a Britannia 312 and on 22 July 1962 when a Britannia 314 crashed at Honolulu killing 27 people on board. Despite these tragedies, the aircraft generally had an excellent safety record.

The protracted icing problem, dithering by BOAC, the cancellations of orders and other set backs, including a major fire on the roof of the Filton hangar, meant Britannia was not as successful as it could have been. BAC could claim that 'No airframe has ever been so thoroughly tested as that of the Britannia and no manufacturer in Europe is better equipped for the purpose', but such thoroughness came at the cost of losing commercial ground to Boeing and the jet age.[17]

Eighty-five production Britannias were built across the different variants. These were sold to national flag-carriers including BOAC, Aeronaves de Mexico, Cubana, Ghana Airways, El Al Israel Airlines and Canadian Pacific Airlines. The aircraft started to be phased out after 1964 by the fleet airlines, but continued to be used by charter operators,

G-ALRX on the mud of the River Severn following the crash, 1954
(Rolls-Royce Heritage Trust).

some of which either leased or bought the aircraft from the airline companies. There was a licensing agreement with Canadair Limited for the manufacture of maritime reconnaissance and transport versions for the Royal Canadian Air Force.

XM496, based at Kemble Airfield, is the most complete surviving Britannia and was the last example to fly anywhere in the world. It was one of the 253s built in Belfast by Shorts. The Bristol Aero Collection also has on display the nose of G-ALRX, the second prototype Britannia 101. On 4 February 1954, during a demonstration flight for KLM representatives and company VIPs, including Archibald E Russell, the aircraft developed engine trouble. When the engine was restarted it caught fire, setting light to a wing and knocking out the hydraulics system for the landing gear. Pilot Bill Pegg was unable to return to Filton as belly-landing on the runway would have increased the risk of the wings breaking off, igniting the fuel bags contained inside them. Pegg decided to land instead in the mud of Littleton on Severn at low tide. He had made a similar emergency landing there during the war. He calculated that there was less risk of the wings breaking up on the damp mud and that the mud would also put out the fire. The aircraft slid down the bank after its initial landing and was caught by the rising salt-water tide, hampering the exit of the passengers and crew and the eventual recovery efforts, but no-one was injured.

Concorde

The supersonic Concorde programme, 'the largest single technological project in the country and the first to be developed on a joint basis with another country', renewed West of England commercial links with France that had first been established through the trading of the medieval period.[18]

Concorde in British Airways livery takes off to the west from Filton with the Aircraft Assembly Halls (the Brabazon hangar) behind, 1999 (Airbus).

In the late 1950s the UK government was investing heavily in supersonic transport research. Archibald E Russell led the team that designed the six-Olympus-engined Bristol Type 198, which Russell predicted would reach at least Mach 2.2. This aircraft, which was designed but never built, struck the government as too noisy and expensive for development as an airliner and BAC was advised to concentrate on something smaller (the construction number was eventually reallocated to Concorde). The Russell team's next design was the four-engined, 100-seater Type 223. The company, by now amalgamated with British Aircraft Corporation, was offered a government study contract on the understanding that the aircraft would be developed in partnership with another country. The Type 223 was similar to Sud Aviation's Super Caravelle, so a partnership between the two companies seemed advisable. Accordingly, on 29 November 1962 the UK and French governments agreed to finance a joint supersonic civil airliner project by British Aircraft Corporation (represented by Bill Strang, Chief Engineer) and Sud Aviation (represented by Lucien Servanty, Technical Director). The agreement, which formed the basis of the Concorde programme, had been drawn up by the British Minister of Aviation, Julian Amery, and was framed in such a way that, despite repeated attempts to back out, the UK government had to continue working with the French on the project. France seemed to take pride in Concorde nationally, whereas in the UK pride was more localised to the West of England during the development stage. The name 'Concord' was suggested for the new aircraft by the son of a British Aircraft Corporation Public Relations Officer at Filton, with the French spelling adopted by both countries in December 1967.

Russell wanted the joint project to be a large, intercontinental airliner; Pierre Satre of Sud Aviation wanted it be a small transcontinental. The resulting 100-seater intercontinental was a compromise and Russell never ceased to point out that his Type 223 design should have been adopted in the first place, adding to the acrimonious relationship between the two men. The division of responsibility between the UK and France was set at 40:60 on the airframe side and 60:40 on the engine side. Each partner was responsible for obtaining the necessary airworthiness certification from its country's officials. The language barrier was partly overcome by the universal language of engineering drawings and diagrams. In the UK the government payments to the contractors were administered by the Ministry of Defence, even though it was a civil aircraft, because the contract was formulated on a cost-plus rather than fixed-price basis, similar to that of military contracts.

Two production lines were established, one at Filton, the other at Toulouse, with each responsible for the design of the components produced by subcontractors and supplied to them for assembly. The forward and rear fuselages were built at Weybridge, the centre fuselage and wings at sites across France. Filton built the nacelles (engine casings), air intake and engine bay. The Olympus 593 engine was jointly developed by SNECMA and Bristol Siddeley, soon to be Rolls-Royce. As with many aircraft projects, the weight grew between the prototype and production versions of the aircraft during the course of development, leading to the need for increased engine thrust.

The designers and engineers did not want to go much beyond Mach 2.2 as this would have required completely new structural materials because of the intense heat generated, but they still needed to devise innovative components and construction methods to cope with the unusually high temperatures reached. These included new types of engine seal and the installation of flexible mounts for most of the equipment to allow for the expansion of the

Concorde scale model undergoing tests at British Aircraft Corporation's Electronic & Space Systems Anechoic Chamber, c 1969 (Filton Library). Some of the lessons learnt about aerodynamics from BAC's guided missiles programme informed the development of Concorde.

The engineers Archibald E Russell, Sir George Edwards and George Gedge at the Concorde prototype roll-out at Filton, 1968 (Airbus).

aluminium alloy airframe at top speeds. A facility was built at Farnborough for fatigue tests on the airframe, testing that it could cope not only with the heat but also with the rapid cooling that would take place as the speed dropped to subsonic levels while the aircraft was still at a high altitude. Another problem with supersonic flight is that the airframe needs to be an exceptionally smooth surface to minimise air friction. Aerials and lights have to be submerged, for example, and door handles have to be covered, adding to the expense of construction. Analytical tests were needed to assess the likely impact of any protrusions on performance. These crucial details were too small to assess in scale-model form in the wind tunnel.

Much of the design and development work at Filton was centred on the newly built No 8 Drawing Office, with the Concorde Directorate housed in the newly refurbished front of No 7 Drawing Office. Wind tunnel models and various wooden mock-ups were built. One of the mock-ups was used to check the balance as fuel was dispersed through the collector, main and trim tanks. A full-scale cabin mock-up was used for evacuation tests and for showing different configurations of seating to potential customers.

Invaluable lessons were learnt from the highly advanced Filton computer flight simulator (all British Airways flight crew were eventually trained on this). As a rule, delta-winged aircraft need to keep their nose up on landing, but the simulator showed that on Concorde, because of the nose's unusual elongated design, this would have obscured

Chief Test Pilot Brian Trubshaw and Co-Pilot John Cochrane prepare for Concorde 002's maiden flight, 9 April 1969 (facing page) (Filton Library).

Concorde seen from below front showing characteristic wing and engine detail (above) (iStockphoto).

the pilot's vision. It was suggested that a television monitor could be positioned in the cockpit on which the runaway could be viewed, but this was unpopular with pilots. Instead it was decided the nose and visor would be lowered using hydraulic controls, with the pilot looking through a secondary window to view the approach. The flight simulator was also used for conducting incremental tests before putting them into practice on actual aircraft, for example, decelerated approaches and a noise-abatement procedure.

On 2 March 1968 the first French prototype (Concorde 001) had its maiden flight, followed on 9 April 1969 by the first UK one (Concorde 002, referred to by the Filton team as Sierra Tango after its registration letters). The UK prototype was flown from Filton by British Aircraft Corporation's Chief Test Pilot, Brian Trubshaw, to RAF Fairford in Gloucestershire for further tests. The Soviets had achieved their first supersonic airliner flight with Tupolev Tu-144 on 31 December 1968, but this did not enter full commercial service. The US abandoned its supersonic project, Boeing 2707, before it got to the flight stage. Boeing had tried to reach Mach 3, which meant conventional metals could not be used for the airframe, thereby adding to the production costs, the risks and the length of the development process.

Covers of the Concorde partnership's *Supersonic Age* magazine, 1970s
(Bristol Aero Collection).

In creating the British Aircraft Corporation flight
team, Trubshaw mainly used test pilots from Vickers at
Weybridge, who operated from Wisley airfield. Most of
the original BAC test pilots had long-since been made
redundant as no major civil aircraft project had taken place
at Filton since Britannia in the 1950s. Fairford's facilities
were used because the Brabazon runway at Filton was not
long enough. As was standard, Concorde's flight-test period
included an endurance flying programme, simulating
airline operation over a set number of hours. The Concorde
destined for British Airways was flown to the Middle East,
Ghana, India, the Far East and Australia, among other
countries. Overseas test flights were also made in various
weather and heat conditions. The engineers were having
to establish new procedures and regulations in writing the
aircraft's flight manual and in preparing its performance
certification for approval by the Civil Aviation Authority
because they were breaking with convention in terms
of shape and aerodynamic principles. Concorde set the
benchmark for supersonic transport regulations.

For the first time, a portable computer was used to
monitor results during the flights. This was the Elliott 905
developed from the Elliott 903 that had been used for
pioneering flight tests at Weybridge. It was portable in the
sense that it could be transported to the test-flight sites by
sea and overland in a bespoke, large furniture van. It was
therefore not comparable to a modern-day laptop in terms
of bulk, and it also had less computing capacity than the
average modern mobile telephone. However, it was state-
of-the-art for its day.

The Concorde partners and their governments were continually having to justify the project, leading to the Campaign for Action on Supersonic Engineering in the UK. Because of the undercurrent of hostility and scepticism, a question regularly asked at employment interviews for those wanting to join British Aircraft Corporation at this time was 'Do you believe in Concorde?'. The case made for passengers flying by this aircraft rather than conventional jet airliners included shorter flight times, reduced fatigue, quicker check-in times (there were fewer passengers), on-time performance (there was a quicker turn-around), convenient schedules and value for money. An important additional advantage for airlines was the possibility of greater profit.

At Filton it was reported that students had broken into the hangar at the prototype stage and hung up a banner protesting about the project's high costs, leading to increased on-site security. There were also environmental protests about the noise and potential damage caused by the sonic boom. Attempts were made to reduce this impact by adding silencers to the engine, but this reduced performance so the aircraft climbed more slowly at take-off, resulting in a longer-lasting nuisance problem at a lower altitude.

In 1976 a tip-off to the unions from Tony Benn about the possibility of Concorde being scrapped led to a protest gathering of 25,000 employees from Rolls-Royce and British Aircraft Corporation at Filton. The unions were supported by the employers in arranging the hire of around 20 coaches for a march and rally in London, and the union convenors met with Harold Wilson and Tony Benn to discuss the future of the project. This common cause brought shop floor and staff closer together, as well as the UK and French unions. There was some talk that the UK government continued to back Concorde funding at the expense of another British Aircraft Corporation civilian project, the BAC3-11, which was being developed at Weybridge in an international programme competing with the Airbus consortium. However, others felt there was never a market for this rival aircraft and the project would have fizzled out anyway.

Concorde first entered service on 21 January 1976 with simultaneous flights by British Airways from London to Bahrain and by Air France from Paris to Rio via Dakar. The transatlantic service, potentially the biggest money-maker and the most prestigious route, was delayed because of US opposition to supersonic aircraft. Concorde first flew to Washington Dulles Airport in May 1976 and to JFK in New York in 1977.

Covers of Concorde partnership reports on flight (c 1970) and testing (1968) (Bristol Aero Collection).

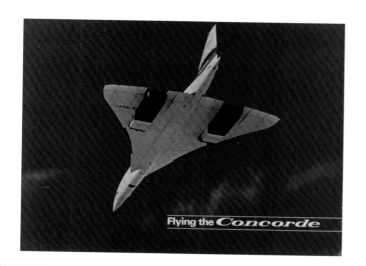

British Aircraft Corporation canteen workers on one of the convoy of coaches that travelled from Filton to London to protest against the threatened cancellation, March 1976.

Concorde was not the first civil airliner to fly faster than Mach 1 – that was a Douglas DC8 which broke the sound barrier in a controlled dive as part of a test programme in August 1961 – but it was the first to carry passengers and was an engineering triumph. It cruised at 1,350mph, reducing the flying time between London and New York to less than four hours. Travelling westwards, the five-hour time difference meant Concorde effectively arrived in the US before it left the UK. Its passengers were said to be more aware of its unusually high speed at take-off and landing than when they were cruising in level flight. The internal sound-proofing meant the noise of the engines was not particularly intrusive in the cabin. Everyone travelled first-class, as had happened in the early days of passenger flight, paying high fares in a small niche market aimed at people who needed to travel places quickly, whatever the cost. This tended to be high-level business directors and media celebrities. In addition to scheduled transatlantic flights, there were exclusive charters with an outward journey by QE2 and return by Concorde, or vice versa. On 8 November 1986 a Concorde circled the world in 29 hours 59 minutes and on 7 February 1996 one set a new record with an Atlantic crossing of 2 hours 52 minutes 59 seconds.

Once any aircraft is in service it requires continual monitoring, overhauling, modifications, repairs and customer support. Where possible, prediction techniques are used to decide in advance which spare parts need to be produced, and in what quantities, for replacement. Rolls-Royce had a Concorde Engine Support Organisation to oversee this work with regard to the Olympus engines and held a biannual Propulsion Unit Review. When Braniff decided to lease Concordes for its Washington Dulles to Dallas service, the aircraft had to undergo further performance-testing to meet certification requirements of the Federal Aviation Administration.

Despite its prestige and aesthetic appeal, the Concorde programme never enjoyed long-term financial security. The development costs had spiralled from a projected £95 million to around £2 billion, partly as a result of the inflation of the 1970s. This was what some termed 'gold-plated' manufacturing in which every element had to be at the top of its range for it to succeed, and this came at a high price. The death knell for the project came with the increase in oil prices and the escalating maintenance costs, which made supersonic flight uneconomic for the airline companies. In addition, symptomatic of continuing American resistance to supersonic travel after the termination of its Boeing project, Pan-Am cancelled its Concorde orders.

Only sixteen production Concordes were ever built (fourteen of which were sold to British Airways and Air France), along with two prototypes and two pre-production versions. In his autobiography, Russell remarked that every new aeroplane amounted to a commercial act of faith on the part of the partner companies because of the high risk involved. The catastrophic crash at Paris on 25 July 2000 shook what confidence remained in the aircraft. The Concorde fleet returned to the air after a £17m refit in 2001, but its time had passed. With 9/11, the transatlantic market had shrunk dramatically and airline companies were also now more concerned about the environment, prioritising aircraft size, quietness and fuel efficiency over

luxury and speed. For many employees at Filton and Patchway who had grown to love the aircraft, it came as a shock to realise that what had once been a symbol of aviation's future was now a symbol of aviation's past.

The last commercial Concorde service operated by British Airways was on 24 October 2003. Concorde 216, which in 1979 had become the last complete aircraft to be assembled at Filton, returned on its final flight on 26 November 2003 and is now a visitor attraction. Most of the Concordes had their hydraulics, leads and other fittings ripped out once decommissioned, but one of the French aircraft is reportedly serviced regularly so it could conceivably fly again at short notice.

A close-up of the cockpit with the nose in full droop position as Concorde G-BOAF, serial number 216, taxies toward the awaiting dignitaries who will accept the handover from Captain Les Brodie, the senior Concorde Fleet training Captain, on its final flight, 26 November 2003 (South Gloucestershire Council).

A380

The Airbus A300 twin-engined, wide-bodied jet airliner family debuted in 1974 when it entered the service of Air France. According to *Flight*: 'Through developing a family concept, covering a wide range of capacities, Airbus threw down the gauntlet to Boeing, eventually matching and then surpassing the US manufacturer in output three decades after the A300's debut.'[19]

The A380 double-decker, wide-bodied jet was announced in 2000 as the most spacious and efficient family yet conceived. The aircraft, which have a capacity of 525 passengers (a mix of first, business and economy classes), have broader seats, more personal storage space and headroom, quieter cabins, more efficient air filters, more natural light, shorter turn-around times and wider stairs than standard large airliners. Optional onboard business centres and social areas are offered to airline companies wishing to customise their fleet.

In accordance with the company's aim of reducing the environmental impact of the industry without sacrificing performance, the A380's emissions from its Rolls-Royce Trent engines are said to be well below current international limits. The unique wing design and the use of composite materials, which account for 25 per cent of the aircraft's structural weight, improve total engine efficiency and reduce fuel consumption (thinner, more aerodynamic wings reduce drag and composites are lighter than conventional materials). The average CO_2 (carbon dioxide) emissions per passenger per kilometre of travel have also been improved and are said to be comparable to that of an economical family car.[20] In addition, the Airbus A380 is the first commercial aeroplane to trial gas-to-liquid (GTL) fuel derived from natural gas, a cleaner alternative to kerosene derived from crude oil.

After an 18-month delay, largely caused by an internal wiring problem, the Airbus A380 first entered service in October 2007 with Singapore Airlines. By February 2010 Airbus had received orders for 202 aircraft, of which 26 had been delivered and were in operation. Airbus in Filton is responsible for the design, engineering and customer support of the aircraft's wings, which are manufactured by GKN, also in Filton. They are then transported for final assembly to Airbus' site in Broughton, North Wales prior to being exported to the aircraft's final assembly sites in France or Germany.

Some of the new technology introduced in the A380 is being developed further for the forthcoming A350 XWB (Xtra Wide-Body), a medium-capacity, long-range aircraft family designed to meet the demands of the next decade and beyond, particularly with regard to fuel economy.

Current international airport rulings limit the footprint of aircraft, so it is unlikely that an airliner will be built

A380

that is bigger than the A380. To do so would create major infrastructure problems at airports. As it is, airports have had to revise the means by which passengers enter the aircraft to accommodate the double decks, and to increase the number of carousels in operation at baggage claim to avoid bottlenecks. The advantage of the A380 is that it reduces the number of long-range airliners required to convey passengers around the world.

Airbus A380 in flight over Clifton Suspension Bridge on its first trip to the UK, 18 May 2006 (Airbus).

Lithographed sheet music cover by Frank M Barton depicting two aeroplanes engaged in a violent aerial dogfight, 1914 (Science and Society Picture Library/Science Museum Pictorial).

Section 5:
War in the Air

Gathering of aeronauts at Bannerdown, Bath, 1902 to see display of war kites by Samuel Cody (private collection). Cody, who was Chief Instructor of Kiting at the Balloon Factory, is reclining on the far right of the photograph taken during the tour arranged by Patrick Alexander.

Few would deny that war accelerated the development of military aircraft, leading to an appalling increase in humankind's capacity for killing, maiming and destruction. Nor would many deny that the technological leaps and bounds required to keep at least one step ahead of the enemy were of benefit to civil air travel.

According to historian Glyn Stone:

> Without the pressure and experience of two world wars, in particular the Second World War and the period of rearmament which preceded it, it is likely that the development of the aircraft industry everywhere would have been severely retarded.[1]

Accordingly, the West of England aviation industry has benefited, in terms of increasing innovation and profit, in times of war, as well as during those interim periods when nations are on the alert for potential attacks.

In the 1950s Harry Harper recalled how Sir George White anticipated British & Colonial getting into civil aviation on the back of initial military contracts:

> As he foresaw it, the future of any commercial air enterprise lay first in persuading Governments to buy machines as scouts and later, as larger and more powerful aircraft were developed, as offensive and defensive weapons. With financial sinews provided by Government orders, it ought to be possible to develop purely commercial types, first for rapid carriage of mails and then, as comfort and reliability grew, for the transport of passengers.[2]

With the coming of full-scale war four years after White founded his company, the opportunity to develop a civil market was set back for some considerable time.

Military interest in flight in the UK began with Lieutenant G E Grover and Captain F Beaumont's 1863 paper to the Ordnance Select Committee at Chatham, in which it was stated that the balloon could provide the means of carrying an elevated observation point for the army. Captain James Lethbridge Brooke Templer of the King's Royal Rifle Corps and the Royal Engineers constructed the army's first balloon in 1878 and balloons were used at the military manoeuvres at Aldershot in 1880 and 1882. As well as balloons, Captain Baden Baden-Powell, member of the Aeronautical Society and brother of the scouting pioneer, also tried to get the War Office interested in large-scale, man-lifting kites for observation purposes. He demonstrated his unwieldy rig at Queen Victoria's Volunteer Review at Dover in 1887.

Baden-Powell had some success because the Army's School of Ballooning was established at Chatham in Kent the following year, although later he was forbidden to take his kites to South Africa for use in the Boer War. The school was joined by the Balloon Equipment Store, which had previously been at Woolwich, and, from 1891, by the Royal Engineers' Balloon Section. The school, store and section transferred to Aldershot in 1897 with the design and production side being known as the Balloon Factory. In 1911 the Balloon Factory, by now based at Farnborough, became the Army Aircraft Factory (later to become the Royal Aircraft Establishment) and went on to become a world-leading centre for aeronautical research. The school formed the basis of the Air Battalion Royal Engineers, which was organised into the No 1 Airship Company and No 2 Aeroplane Company.

Individual members of the military started being trained at the Bristol Flying Schools on a private basis from 1910, and from March 1911 Admiralty Naval officers were being officially instructed in Short biplanes at Eastchurch in Kent. On 14 March 1911 the War Office announced the purchase of four military Bristol Boxkites for the Air Battalion, which were received in May. Earlier that year it had purchased Geoffrey de Havilland's No 2 biplane, renaming it the Farman Experimental 1 (FE1) because of its similarity to Henri Farman's aircraft. In October 1911 British & Colonial offered to train 250 naval and 250 army officers over a six-month period at favourable rates, but the offer was rejected. The War Office did, however, provide 'the meagre sum of £75' to volunteers thought suitable for entry into the Air Battalion who had gained their flight qualifications at their own expense.[3]

At this time the German government was investing heavily in the aviation industry, as became apparent when British aircraft came up against the superior Fokkers when war broke out. In the UK, aviation was largely a private enterprise, but there was some government support. Winston Churchill was the first MP to pilot his own aeroplane and he encouraged Prime Minister Herbert Asquith to request that the Imperial Defence Committee put together proposals for an efficient British airforce as part of the pre-war mobilization plans. In 1912 Colonel John Seely became Secretary of State for War and on 13 April he expanded the Air Battalion to form the Royal Flying Corps (RFC). This had three wings: Naval, Military and the Central Flying School, which opened at Upavon, Wiltshire in June 1912. The RFC was commanded by Colonel Sir Alexander Bannerman, who had learnt to fly at a Bristol Flying School, as had 50 of the RFC's 81 certificated pilots.[4] On 1 July 1914 the Naval Wing of the RFC became the Royal Naval Air Service.

Photograph of a biplane flying over Salisbury Plain, with three army staff officers on horseback in the foreground, c 1912 (Science and Society Picture Library/Science Museum Pictorial).

The War Office trials held at Larkhill in August 1912 to determine which aircraft should be bought by the Army was the first military aero competition in the UK, attracting competitors from home and abroad. Thirty-one designs were on display. These were tested for speed and ease of assembly, suitability for road transport, ability to take off and land in rough country, climbing and altitude performance. The outright winner was a Cody biplane, though the best performance was considered by many to be the ineligible BE2 biplane from Farnborough designed by de Havilland.

'Then came the war in August, 1914,' as Charles G Grey, the founder of *The Aeroplane*, reflected in 1953, 'and as usual we were not ready for it. But, as usual, we muddled through, though I doubt whether, after our 1939 muddle, "our long-suffering star", as Kipling called it, will stand for us again, unless we wake up.'[5] The First World War was the last imperial war and the first modern one, a war seemingly without logic or justification, which has come to symbolise the madness of all wars. It brought home the damage that could be inflicted upon human flesh by technology with the machine-gunning, strafing and shelling of ranks of hopelessly exposed infantry and cavalry. The horror of aerial warfare had been anticipated in H G Wells' *War in the Air* (1908), one of his semi-realistic fantasies in which he depicted 'mass destruction as the apocalyptic prelude to a new, more rational world order'.[6] The first Zeppelin raid took place on 25 August 1914 with an attack on Antwerp. At Friedrichshafen on 21 November 1914, Avro 504s made the first British air attack. In January 1915 the first Zeppelin bombs fell on British soil. In total, around 1,400 British civilians were killed in enemy air raids during the war and one of the realities of modern warfare became painfully apparent: the front line was whereever bombs could be flown and dropped and, despite talk of military targets, death was indiscriminate.

Aircraft were needed by the military for reconnaissance and fighting roles. The Scout C was British & Colonial's first aeroplane designed and manufactured specifically for the war effort, though pre-existing Bristol aircraft had been used as RFC trainers. The Scout was also the first mass-produced, single-seater military aeroplane. Earlier scouting aircraft included the Royal Aircraft Factory's BS1/ SE2 and Sopwith's Tabloid. The de Havilland BE2 two-seater reconnaissance biplane gradually acquired armaments until it took up the role of light bomber. It had the advantage of being particularly stable in flight, but lacked manoeuvrability and had an inconvenient layout with the pilot in the rear and the observer in the front. Before the war, on 12 August 1912, a BE2 broke the British altitude record and was described as being 'the best all-round aeroplane in the world at the time'.[7] BE2 No 218 broke the British non-stop flight record in February 1913 and a BE2 is believed to have been the first British aeroplane to land on the European continent after war was declared. Lieutenant William B Rhodes Moorhouse was the first person to be awarded a Victoria Cross for aerial combat when he was fatally injured having dropped his only bomb on a railway line from his BE2B at Cortrai, Belgium on 26 April 1915.

British & Colonial was among 22 firms instructed by the government to concentrate solely on producing BE2Cs at the start of war. The company had previously needed BE2 business to fill an unexpected gap in production of its own aircraft as a result of the military monoplane ban. It had built over 1,200 BEs in seven variants by the end of war at its Filton and Brislington Tramways works, despite the frustrations that came from discrepancies in the drawings that were supplied, and being caught up in disputes between the War Office and the Admiralty over contracts.[8]

Filton airfield was used by the RFC from December 1915 for preparing air squadrons prior to departure for France, and the No 5 (South Western) Aircraft Acceptance Park was established to process aircraft built by British & Colonial and Westland Aircraft Company. At the factory, Works Manager Herbert Thomas was finding it difficult to replace skilled employees who had enlisted as volunteers, causing severe difficulties in meeting the increasing production demand. A bonus scheme introduced in June 1915 retained some employees until the crisis of 1916 when, following severe losses on the Western Front in the Battle of the Somme, the government could no longer rely on volunteers and introduced general conscription. However, aircraft factories were at the same time designated as 'controlled' establishments to maintain production levels, which meant that people were directed by local labour exchanges to work in them.

In addition to Scouts and BE2s, British & Colonial produced the Bristol M1C monoplane, which served in the Middle East but was not used on the Western Front, a decision described by *The Aeroplane* as 'one of the tragedies of official blundering which Wars can produce'.[9] By 1917 the company was producing the Bristol Fighter, which equipped 17 squadrons on the Western Front and 'was possibly the most out-standing aeroplane of the whole War... used for every purpose except Artillery Observation'.[10]

The Bristol Braemer, a large triplane bomber which made its maiden flight on 13 August 1918, had originally been planned in the autumn of 1917 by Frank Barnwell in anticipation of conducting retaliatory bombing raids on Germany following Gotha attacks on London. The aircraft had two nacelles situated above the middle wing. Each nacelle housed two engines mounted back-to-back, one engine pulling and one pushing. The aircraft was capable of carrying a load of six 114kg (250lb) bombs. The company received an initial order for three prototypes, the first of which was flown to Martlesham Heath for acceptance trials. The second prototype had its maiden flight on 18 February 1919, but by now the Braemar was obviously too late for the war and it was considered too big for peacetime operations by the Royal Air Force (RAF). The RAF had been formed on 1 April 1918 from the merger of the RFC and Royal Naval Air Service. Other prototype military aircraft of this period designed by British & Colonial that did not enter production included the Bloodhound, Berkeley and Boarhound. However, the company managed

RFC mechanic inside the Aircraft Acceptance Park sheds with Bristol Fighters waiting for their engines, c 1917 (Rolls-Royce Heritage Trust).

Braemar Bomber, winter 1919 (facing page) (Bristol Aero Collection).

to keep some of the workforce employed by building Whitworth Siskin IIIA fighters under subcontract.

The Bulldog was Barnwell's response to a specification for a day- and night- fighter to re-equip RAF squadrons in the 1920s. It was of a high-tensile, stove-enamelled, steel-strip construction with dope-sprayed canvas on its main fuselage and wings and aluminium panelling at the front. Bulldog I made its maiden flight on 17 May 1927, with Bulldog II making its first flight on 21 January 1928. The Bulldog was in competition with the two-bay Hawker Hawfinch for the RAF contract. It was a close-run, drawn-out competition but the Bulldog was eventually selected and a production order for 25 was placed in August 1928, with the first deliveries being made in May 1929.

The Bulldog eventually equipped ten squadrons and, because it was developed as a private venture, it was also sold to eight overseas air forces including Denmark, Sweden, Australia, Siam, Latvia and Estonia. The only Bulldogs to see action were those of the Finnish Air Force which were used in the Winter War against the Soviets (1939-1940). The aircraft continued in production until 1934, with the final delivery made the following year. It

was declared obsolete by the RAF in 1937. Over 440 were built, of which the most prolific was Bulldog IIA. It was the last single-engined Bristol aircraft to go into military service; the majority were powered by the Jupiter VII or VIIF. Thanks to its agility, it performed particularly well in aerial displays at air shows. The legendary World War Two Spitfire ace, Douglas Bader, was flying a Bulldog on 14 December 1931 when he crashed on Woodley Airfield near Reading during a demonstration of low flying. He sustained the injuries that resulted in both his legs being amputated, but this did not curtail his flying career.

In the 1920s governments had little interest in rearmament but, according to historian Richard Croucher, 'the changing international situation forced [them] to intervene more actively in the 1930s'.[11] They also needed to keep their countries' heavy engineering plants active and aviation was ideal for this because of its demand for 'large amounts of electrical equipment and components'.[12] In the UK the authorisation for RAF expansion and modernisation was announced on 22 May 1935. Hermann Goering had previously announced the re-formation of the German airforce in contravention of the Versailles treaty. As a result of the rearmament programme, aviation mushroomed from 'a small and unimportant group of luxury concerns into *the* arms industry of the Second World War'.[13] According to C H Barnes:

Bulldog in Japan, c 1930 (Bristol Aero Collection).

Bulldogs depicted on the first aircraft issue of *Bristol Review*, December 1931 (facing page) (Bristol Aero Collection).

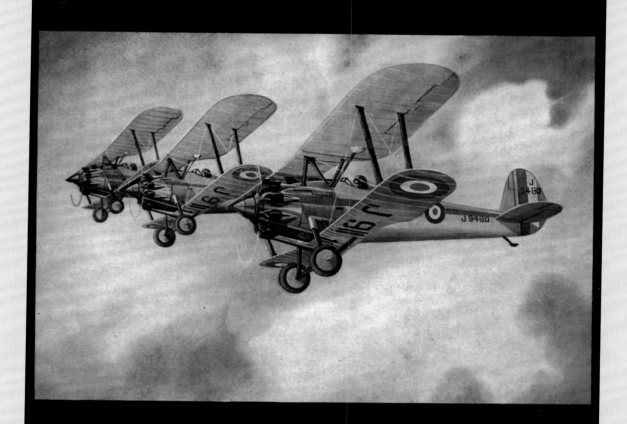

AIRCRAFT ISSUE Nº1

THE
"Bristol"
REVIEW

THE BRISTOL AEROPLANE Cº LTP FILTON BRISTOL

To some extent the delay in re-arming was fortunate, for 1935 was a critical year technically as well as politically; it marked the emergence of a new race of aeroplanes – clean, efficient monoplanes, with cantilever wings, retractable undercarriages and metal monocoque bodies, powered by supercharged engines driving variable pitch airscrews and giving enormously increased power by virtue of high-octane fuel, which was available in quantity for the first time. Had rearmament begun two years earlier, the RAF might well have been equipped with large numbers of biplanes and braced monoplanes, which indeed proved a handicap to the French and Italian air forces when war eventually broke out.[14]

A searing indication of the horrors to come from aerial bombardment was seen in the attack on the Basque town of Guernica in Spain on 27 April 1937, when 45,000 kilos (100,000 pounds) of high-explosive and incendiary bombs were dropped by the German Luftwaffe and Italian Corpo Truppe Volontarie. This was an early example of a new military tactic of blanket bombing a largely civilian target to demoralise the enemy. It was a tactic used by both sides during the Second World War.

The UK government committed over £220 million 'to aircraft, aero-engine buildings and plant' between 1936 and September 1945.[15] Vickers and Beardmore had been the main UK aircraft manufacturers of World War One. They were succeeded in the inter-war years by Hawker and A V Roe (later Avro). Like BAC, these companies were members of the Society of British Aircraft Constructors and therefore received official government contracts. The Society had been formed as a defensive measure in World War One against the monopoly of the Royal Aircraft Factory. Henry White Smith from British & Colonial was its first President.

BAC's relationship with the Air Ministry was sometimes difficult. In a memo to Viscount Swinton, Secretary of State for Air, in March 1936, Sir Stanley White wrote:

> the Company consider that any further expansion of their business, necessarily involving increasing effort and organisation, should be adequately rewarded and that the remuneration to be received for the work which they are to undertake should be fixed on a fair and reasonable basis.[16]

In other words, while willing to do its patriotic duty, the company was not prepared to jeopardise its financial stability.[17] Between 1935 and 1944 the capital employed by BAC rose from £1.977 million to £14.818 million, peaking at £15.177 million in 1943.[18] However, the rise in net profits was restricted by the Finance Act of 1940 and the Ministry of Aircraft Production's insistence that pre-tax profits be reduced.

At the beginning of the rearmament period, prior to starting production of the Blenheim, BAC had the opportunity to expand and train its workforce. It could extend and retool the factory site because it was awarded an Air Ministry contract to produce a consignment of Hawker Audax biplanes. The Ministry sanctioned additional expenditure on buildings, plant and equipment in June 1938, with £400,000 being spent on the airframe works and £966,000 on the engine side.[19] During a slackening of demand in the summer of 1938 and in January 1939, BAC was also allowed stop-gap production of additional Blenheims on top of the original orders it had received. This enabled the company to keep the workforce on in anticipation of increased demand at a later date. To avoid repetition of the problem encountered in World War One when skilled employees had been recruited to the forces

BAC works in camouflage paint at the start of World War Two (Airbus).

Type 142M Blenheim showing engine configuration, c 1935 (right) (Rolls-Royce plc). The aircraft was fitted with two Mercury engines.

South view of construction of No 2 Shadow Factory, May 1937 (Rolls-Royce Heritage Trust).

Standards room at Rootes Shadow Factory, March 1945 (Rolls-Royce Heritage Trust).

without regard for the country's industrial needs, the government introduced a Schedule of Reserved Occupations in 1938, of which the largest number were in the engineering field. From November 1939, employers could apply for deferment for those employed in the occupations and age groups listed, which covered around five million people in the UK. When BAC employees were later inadvertently called up for active service, they could be retrieved by the Manpower Commission and returned to the factory. Those who did choose to go into the service were guaranteed re-employment on their return.

On 13 March 1936 Swinton requested BAC's co-operation in stepping up shadow-factory production in anticipation of war. He said the company would be performing a national service in 'a very dangerous and difficult situation'.[20] The government would bear the cost of setting up the new production units, with BAC providing its technical expertise. Initial attention focused on the engine side of the business. The BAC directors agreed to the proposals provided its own interests were protected – there was a risk that new rival firms would be developed on the back of the shadow factories and that competitors would benefit from BAC's years of development work. They were assured by Swinton that the shadow factories would not be offered any commercial opportunities at BAC's expense and that the scheme would be terminated at the end of the rearmament period unless the country was on a war footing.

The companies approached to become shadow factories were all in the automotive industry: Austin, Rootes, Rover, Singer, Standard, Daimler and Wolseley. Sir Stanley White had suggested it would be preferable to disperse the building of specialised components rather than having shadow companies constructing complete engines.[21] The Air Ministry advised against this but the factories themselves chose to break up the functions, with the engines being assembled and tested at Austin and at BAC. Both Wolseley and Singer had pulled out at this stage. In July 1936 the Air Ministry said it was necessary to include Alvis Car and Engineering Company Ltd in the scheme because of the urgent need to increase production.[22] A second shadow factory group was set up in the spring of 1939 comprising Rootes, Daimler, Rover and Standard, with BAC still as the parent company. BAC also reluctantly conceded to having a separate, Air Ministry-owned assembly and testing factory on land purchased by the government inside the East Works.[23] This was known as the No 2 Shadow Factory and was built by local building firm Robert Watson's, which also constructed some of the Patchway test-beds. In addition, an agency factory under BAC management control was established at Accrington in Lancashire.

The shadow system was extended to cover airframes in 1937. One of the first completed aircraft to be built under this new scheme was the Bristol Bombay. This troop carrier was an Alclad stressed-skin cantilever monoplane. The prototype was first flown on 23 June 1935. The first of these aircraft to come off the production line at Short and Harland

Ltd in Belfast had its maiden flight in March 1939 and the first delivery of Bombays was made to No 216 Squadron in Egypt in September that year. The aircraft's wartime exploits included assisting with the evacuation of Greek refugees in May 1941 and dropping the first Allied parachutists into Southern Italy in November that same year.

Shadow factories were owned and equipped by the government and managed on a day-to-day basis by the shadow companies with direction from BAC, with the exception of Accrington and No 2 Shadow Factory which were also managed by BAC. By contrast, dispersal sites were taken over by the government and BAC was told to run them, or they were leased direct by BAC. In August 1939 the aviation industry received government instructions to take measures to increase production, including taking over a range of local sites to expand the available workspace. At this time, Bristol was classified as a safe zone – the city received hundreds of children evacuated from London until France fell to the Germans and the threat of aerial attack drew nearer. Therefore the initial incentive for BAC to disperse was not, as might be supposed, to escape enemy bombing but to increase the company's ability to produce components, assemble aircraft and engines, carry out repairs and service parts.

Facing page, second row, from left to right:

Firemen dealing with bomb damage in Colston Avenue with view of BAC's Colston Works in the background complete with nets for camouflage and shelters built on the pavement (original photograph by Jim Facey). Although central Bristol was subjected to several raids, the war damage claim for Colston Works was only £91/6/10.

Engine-erecting operations at the dispersal site on Winterstoke Road (Rolls-Royce Heritage Trust). There are frequent comments in the directors' minutes about attempts to improve ventilation in the bonds.

Banwell workers with a Centaurus-powered Hawker Tempest II, 17 August 1945. The man in uniform is possibly an ATA ferry pilot (Rolls-Royce Heritage Trust).

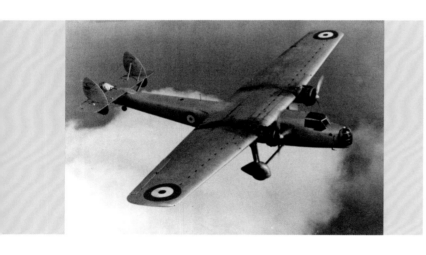

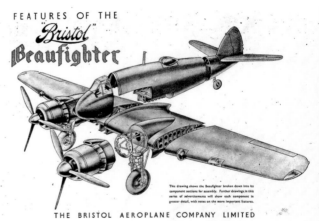

More specific instructions were received by BAC in August 1940 to disperse into the centre of Bristol. For example, part of the Hercules production effort, as well as the Engine Service and Technical Publications Departments, were housed in Colston Avenue, and some of the old tobacco bonds at Canons Marsh and Winterstoke were taken over for engine repairs. There were some night-time attacks on the main factory site that disrupted production in the early days of the war, but it was not until after the big daylight raid of 25 September 1940 that all departments that could operate away from Filton were dispersed. Some of the departments that had previously moved into central Bristol were also now re-dispersed to safer locations. There were over 100 sites used during the course of the war, including Bristol Zoo, Frys at Somerdale, Carsons chocolate factory, Wells Prison,

Bombay, 1935 (above left) (Bristol Aero Collection).

Advertisement from *Flight* (22 July 1943) showing the component sections of a Beaufighter (Rolls-Royce Heritage Trust). A structure like this was well-suited to the shadow factory system.

The 1000th aircraft, a Beaufighter, built at Weston-super-Mare, c 1944 (Bristol Aero Collection).

Highbridge Cheese Stores, Loxton Rectory, Tockington Manor, the bus garages on Winterstoke Road and Muller Road, the University of Bristol library, Ivor House and Wick House on the Downs, the Clergy Daughters' School, Woodhouse Manor, a Worcester railway arch, the Royal West of England Academy galleries, Clevedon Hall, a barn at Elberton and The Walton Park Hotel. Dispersal taught the directors of BAC that it was not essential to keep its employees all in one place in order to be productive, which allowed the company to become increasingly fragmented after the war when departments were based at different sites.

The main aircraft produced by BAC for World War Two were the Blenheim, a standard light bomber, the Beaufort, a standard torpedo strike aircraft, and the Beaufighter, a long-range fighter – all three of which were overseen by Leslie Frise as Chief Designer. These did not seem to achieve national acclaim in the way that the Supermarine Spitfire, Hawker Hurricane, de Havilland Mosquito, Avro Lancaster and Vickers Wellington did. This was partly because they did not fly in large formations and tended to be used in night flights, so the British public would not generally have been aware of them. They were also not associated with the Battle of Britain so lacked that prestige. Nevertheless, they made a significant contribution to the Allies' war effort and were well-respected by pilots and crew for their reliability, ruggedness and quality of build. A fitter wrote:

> They had a terrific reputation, those [Bristol] engines; they were simple to service and it was a pleasure to work on them. You knew that if they were well looked after they would never let you down.

> The same could be said for 'Bristol' aircraft, too. The old Blenheims established their reputation and the Beaufort added to it, but I think, and a lot of other ex-RAF types will back me up, that the Beaufighter was the greatest battle-wagon of the lot. The 'Beau' seemed to appeal to people's imaginations; it had a personality of its own. We used to talk of them as though they were alive... they were certainly always kicking the enemy where it hurt most.[24]

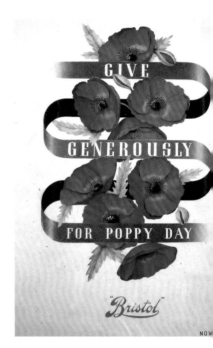

In addition to production, there were also BAC sites devoted to stripping-down damaged aircraft into their component parts and sorting out what could be re-used as it was, what needed repairing and what could be melted down. The re-usable components were then despatched to the production lines and the scrap metal sent off to the yards. The aircraft usually arrived on 18-metre (60 foot) lorries, known familiarly as 'Queen Marys', brought in from whichever airfield they had managed to limp to or crash-land at, accompanied on their journey by police escort. BAC employees were also working at RAF stations around the country carrying out maintenance, repairs and inspections on Bristol aircraft on site, some recruited locally, others being relocated from Filton for the duration.

Bomb being loaded onto Bristol T152 Beaufort, 1942 (Airbus).

War-time poppy appeal by BAC, c 1942 (Bristol Aero Collection).

An even greater contribution to the war effort was made by Bristol engines. BAC produced around 39 per cent of the UK's total engine output, excluding jet engines, between June 1939 and December 1945, mainly at the shadow factories and the agency factory at Accrington.[25] BAC's first engine for the RAF was the Jupiter IV, which entered service in the Hawker Woodcock II in May 1925. In March 1937 the Perseus VIII became the first sleeve-valve in military service. During the war, Allied agents were dropped from Mercury-powered Westland Lysanders into occupied France. Pegasus was used in the Fleet Air Arm's Swordfish and the Beaufort/Taurus bomber, and Hercules in the Armstrong Whitworth

War-time advertisements for the Lysander and Beaufort/Taurus (Rolls-Royce Heritage Trust) and Hercules engines (Fishponds Local History Society).

Albemale, Handley Page Halifax and the Lancaster. During the early days of the siege of Malta (1940-1941), Bristol-designed engines would have been in aircraft used by both the RAF and the Italian Royal Air Force: for the RAF, the Bristol Mercury VIIIA used in the Gloster Sea Gladiator; for the Italians, the Alfa Romeo AR126 – a version of the Bristol Pegasus built under licence that was used in the Savoia-Marchetti SM 79 (probably only one of many examples of inadvertently arming the enemy).

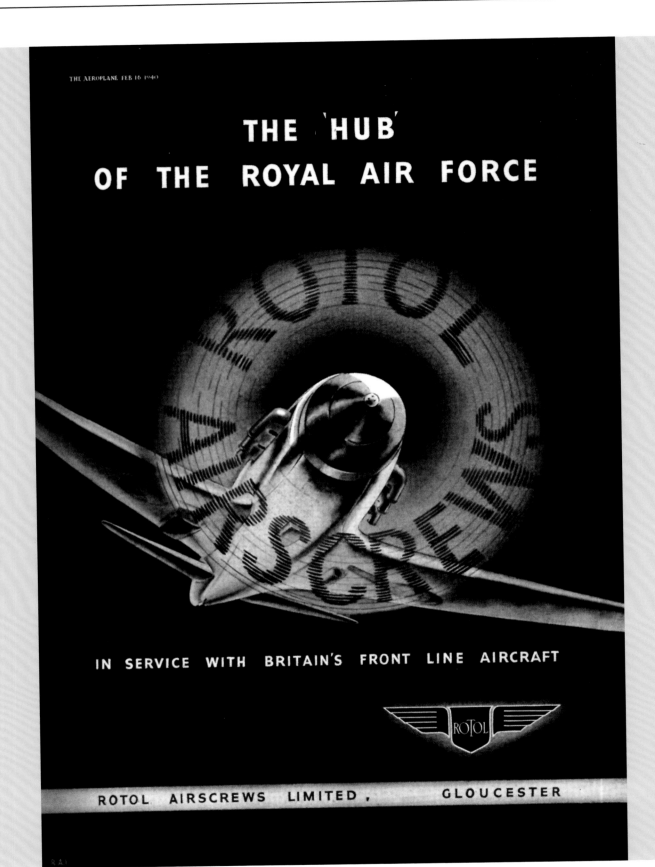

Rotol Airscrews had been set up in 1937 by Rolls-Royce of Derby and BAC at the instigation of Roy Fedden and others to manufacture variable-pitch, constant-speed propellers for the military aircraft of the time (the 'Ro' of the name being derived from Rolls, and the 'tol' from Bristol). The first Rotol propeller was demonstrated to the RAF on a Hawker Hart fitted with a Bristol Mercury engine. The company went on to produce the propellers for most marks of the Spitfires and Hurricanes and many types of bomber, notably the Wellington and the Halifax.

BAC's Armaments Division was an initiative dating from the rearmament period when the company directors realised they required a specialist facility separate from aircraft production. Its main function was to build power-operated gun-turrets and mountings for various aircraft, as well as hydraulic components such as undercarriage retraction gear. The Bristol BI dorsal turret, as used in the Blenheim, was the first power-operated turret to gain Air Ministry clearance. During the war, production was subcontracted to Daimler and Brockhouse, among other companies. Armaments later became one of the sections at the Weston Company, where work included the repair and electrical conversion of land and naval Bofors guns and aircraft gun-turrets, and the manufacture of naval mountings.

War-time advertisement for Rotol (facing page) (Rolls-Royce Heritage Trust).

A mechanical gun-turret test-rig that would have been used to train gunners before they flew, c 1940 (right) (Rolls-Royce plc).

As the result of concerted efforts by the government and industry, production of military aircraft in the UK rose from around 3,000 in 1938 to 15,000 in 1940. It had trebled by January 1942 and doubled again by March 1944.[26] However, the aviation sector was not immune to criticism. There were repeated complaints about weak management, a shortage of skills and experience and an over-dependency on overseas suppliers for components in both the rearmament and war-time periods. Ernest Bevin, the Minister of Labour, who had gained his early political experience as a union organiser for the carters operating in the docks at Bristol, described aviation as the one industry which had failed to improve its output in proportion to the amount of labour supplied.[27]

Before the war, BAC received specific criticism from the Air Ministry in a 1937 report:

> Considering the wealth, size and facilities possessed by this firm their performance was considered to be more disappointing than that of any other firm in the industry... Their manufacturing efforts were excellent for amateurs but could be very greatly improved by experienced men. It was considered that the time taken... to design the long nose of the Blenheim and also the Bolingbroke to be absolutely inexcusable. Neither had yet flown. It was anticipated that the Rootes Shadow Factory [at Speke] would turn out Blenheims at a very much less cost and therefore more efficiently than Bristol.[28]

Lieutenant Colonel Henry Disney informed William Douglas Weir, special adviser to Swinton, that the airframe side of the company was disorganised and needed a strong General Manager, with another to run the factory.[29] The criticisms were taken on board by William Verdon Smith who promised he would address them, but there was frustration on both sides. The Air Ministry was annoyed about production targets and delivery dates being missed, and by what they considered longstanding management weakness; BAC was annoyed by the lack of official appreciation of their efforts, unrealistic expectations on the part of ministers and a skills shortage that had resulted from compulsory redeployment. Smith did criticise a minority of the staff for absenteeism in his Directors' Report and Statement of Accounts for 1941, which was reported in *The Times* on 27 October 1942. But he said the faults were:

> basically due to the irresponsibility of the few [and] ought not to create prejudice against the genuine and whole-hearted readiness of the majority, many of them hitherto quite unfamiliar with industrial conditions, to work long hours, travel long distances, and frequently entirely subordinate personal considerations to the demands of their work. To young women and now increasingly married women on part-time work great credit is due.[30]

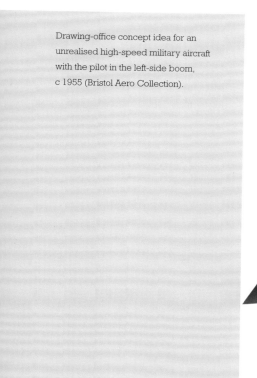

Drawing-office concept idea for an unrealised high-speed military aircraft with the pilot in the left-side boom, c 1955 (Bristol Aero Collection).

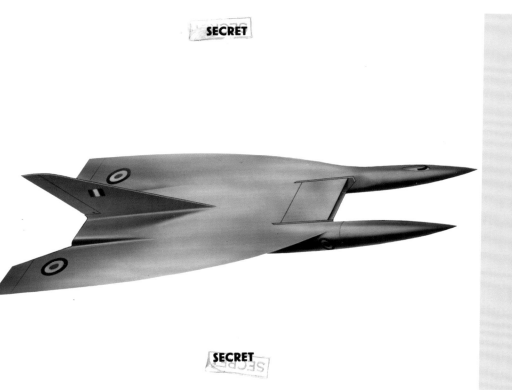

SECRET

SECRET

After the Second World War, there was a short-lived hiatus before the Cold War stoked up military demand once more. The North Atlantic Treaty Organisation (NATO) was formed on 4 April 1949 as a response to the Soviet threat to the West. As part of its research and development programme, BAC investigated the possibility of building an expendable, radio-controlled fibreglass bomber, code-named Red Duster, to contribute to the new war effort, as well as various swept-wing bombers, but these ideas never got off the drawing board. More successful were the development of helicopters, military conversion contracts and the missile programme, and there was a continuing demand for Bristol engines.

During the Korean War (1950-53) the Hawker Sea Fury was in action, powered by the Bristol Centaurus. Among other overseas customers, Sea Furies were sold to the Cuban Air Force. They were used by the dictator, Fulgencio Batista y Zaldívar, in his failed attempt to stop the advance of Fidel Castro's revolutionary army. The BAC manager in Cuba at the time, who was overseeing the overhaul of Proteus engines for the Britannia, was briefly under arrest once Batista fell because of the company's association with the previous regime. However, a Britannia was soon ferrying Castro, Che Guevara, Camilo Cienfuegos and other revolutionaries on triumphant speaking tours, so BAC was back in favour. Meanwhile, out at Whitchurch in the 1950s, BAC was overhauling Wright Cyclones under licence to the US Air Force for use at the American bases at Fairford and Greenham Common.

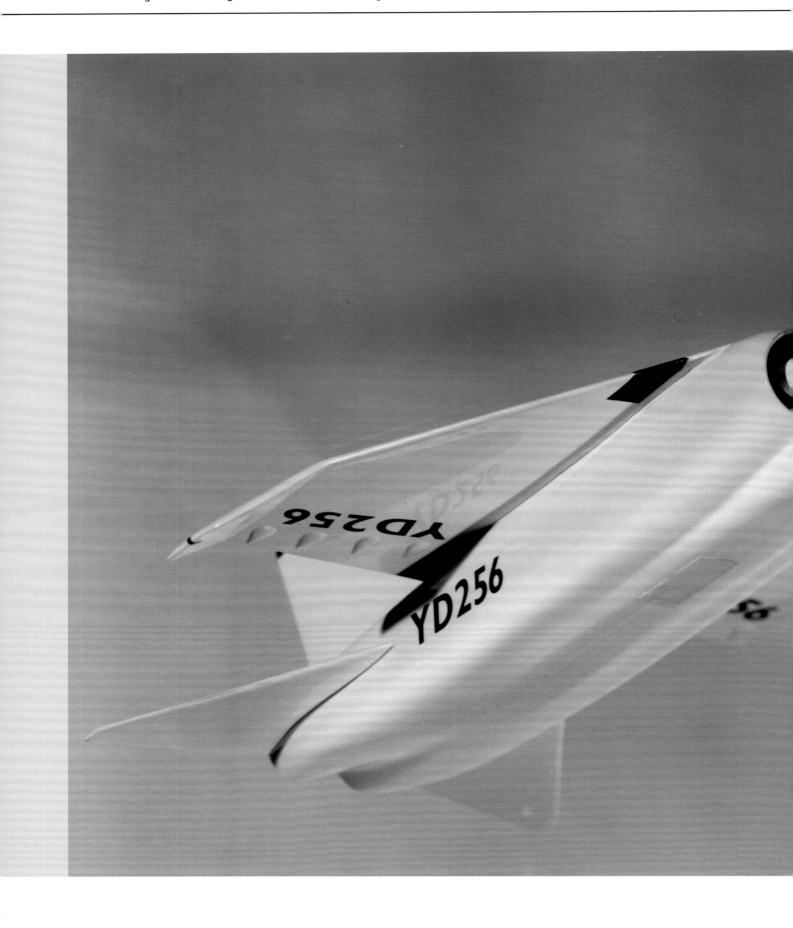

Vulcan flying over the coast, c 1975
(above) (Rolls-Royce Heritage Trust).

Artist's impression of the TSR2
aircraft in flight, c 1964 (left)
(Rolls-Royce Heritage Trust).

The Avro Vulcan, a delta-wing strategic bomber first delivered to the RAF in 1956, was fitted with the Bristol Olympus 101. The aircraft needed a power source for very high, very fast and very long flights. It also needed three sets of four engines in readiness for every aircraft in service, so this was a lucrative business for the company. The TSR2 (Tactical Strike and Reconnaissance), designed to fly low under radar, used the Olympus 320 and was first announced by the Ministry of Supply on 1 January 1958 as a joint initiative for Vickers Armstrong and English Electric. The two companies had been amalgamated into British Aircraft Corporation by the time the project was given the go-ahead. TSR2 had its first test flight on 27 September 1964 at the Aeroplane and Armament Experimental Establishment, Boscombe Down, Wiltshire but, despite election promises from the incoming Labour government, the project was cancelled in 1965 as it was running late and over budget. There were tentative plans to replace it with General

The Rolls-Royce RB 199-34R as made for the Panavia Tornado in No 2 shop at East Works, Patchway, c 1980 (right) (Rolls-Royce Heritage Trust).

Eurofighter 2000 prototype powered by two Turbo Union RB199 Mk104E engines pictured during a flight from British Aerospace's military aircraft facility at Warton, Lancashire, c 2000 (facing page) (Rolls-Royce plc).

Dynamics' F-111, but that deal was cancelled as well. Sir Sydney Camm, designer of the Hurricane, commented: 'All modern aircraft have four dimensions: span, length, height and politics. TSR2 simply got the first three right.'[31] As with other cancelled projects, it was poignant for employees to see the TSR2 jigs deliberately destroyed, ensuring it could not be revived.

The Folland Gnat, the standard advanced RAF trainer from the early 1960s to the late 1970s, was powered by the Bristol Orpheus. It was never used in its light fighter/bomber form by the RAF, but was built by Hindustan Aircraft Ltd on license and used by the Indian Air Force. Orpheus was also in the Etendard VI, Fiat G91 and Breguet 1001 Taon, other NATO light fighters. Following the Rolls-Royce/Bristol Siddeley merger, Patchway became the centre of Rolls' military aero-engine production, including Pegasus (used in Harriers), Turbo-Union RB199 (used in the Panavia consortium's Tornado, some of the cockpits and wings of which were built at Filton) and the Derby-designed Adour (used in BAe Systems' Hawk trainers and the Jaguar fighter). The EJ200 used in the Eurofighter Typhoon was jointly developed by the Eurojet consortium formed by Rolls-Royce, FiatAvio, MTU München and Industria de Turbo Propulsores. The Lockheed Martin F-35 Lightning II (the Joint Strike Fighter) uses Rolls-Royce's award-winning Short Take-Off and Vertical Landing propulsive LiftSystem®. As British military spending decreases, overseas customers with access to more generous budgets have become increasingly important, particularly India.

F-35B Lightning II with
Rolls-Royce LiftSystem®
(Rolls-Royce plc).

Bristol Fighter

British & Colonial's wartime profits were largely gained from the success of the Bristol Fighter, popularly known as the Brisfit. Frank Barnwell, working with Leslie Frise, based his design for the aircraft and its armament on the experiences he had gained at the front before his return to British & Colonial in August 1915.

King George V inspects a Bristol Fighter during a visit to the British & Colonial factory, 1917 (above) (Airbus). Employees who were presented to the king received a special commemorative medal.

Farndon's illustration of a Fighter in action from the 40th anniversary calendar (facing page) (Bristol Aero Collection).

The pilot could fire his Vickers machine gun through the propeller, its interrupter action synchronised to the spin of the blades so they did not get hit, while the observer/rear gunner operated a machine gun mounted on a rotating ring from his tip-up, two-way facing seat. The arrangement allowed the possibility of the men fighting back to back. The two cockpits were also close together so the rear gunner could easily tap the pilot's shoulder to warn of an attack.

The first government order for two prototypes and 50 production aircraft was received on 28 August 1916. The first prototype of the F2A version made its maiden flight on 9 September 1916. The production line for the aircraft was initially focused on Bristol Tramways' Brislington works, as the Filton factory was busy building BE2s. The first F2A deliveries were made on 20 December 1916, with the production order completed on 23 March 1917. The

aircraft first saw action with the No 48 Squadron at Arras on 5 April 1917. Four of the six on patrol were shot down, two of these by the German ace Manfred von Richthofen – the Red Baron. Eight more were lost over the next 11 days, but pilots quickly developed a new tactic of using the front gun for the main attack with the rear gun as back-up cover, which presented less of a target to the enemy.

An order for 200 of the improved, F2B version of the Fighter was received in November 1916. It had its maiden flight on 10 April 1917. The order had been increased to over 600 by July when the War Office decided to re-equip all of the RFC's fighter-reconnaissance and corps-reconnaissance squadrons with the aircraft. A second production line was started at Filton to meet an additional contract for 500 placed on 4 September, with a further order for 300 received in October shared between the two

Close-up of Fighter fitted with Falcon engine, 1917 (Bristol Aero Collection).

workshop sites. By the autumn of 1917, Canadian flying ace Lieutenant Andrew Edward McKeever had destroyed 20 enemy aircraft in his F2B. He was awarded the DSO in November for his action under attack from seven Albatros DVs and two two-seater fighters.

There was further expansion of the workforce and the Filton factory site to meet Fighter demand, but from November 1917 production was also subcontracted to Armstrong Whitworth, Austin Motors, Gloucestershire Aircraft, National Aircraft Factory No 3 and Standard Motor Company, among other companies. Of the 4,747 Fighters completed by the end of the war, 2,081 had been built at Filton, 1,045 at Brislington and 1,621 by subcontractors. British & Colonial was now having to manage a large number of sites, mainly staffed with novices to aviation.

The system required the provision of 'simple but effective jigs ensuring foolproof and rapid assembly and guaranteed interchangeability'.[32] The jigs were devised by John Daniel and Frank Davey. The subcontractors were supplied with a sample skeleton airframe, templates for the ribs, and photographs and drawings of the necessary jigs and tools.

The production of the frames outstripped supplies of the Rolls-Royce Falcon engine, most of which were being made under licence at Fishponds by Brazil Straker. Therefore modifications were made for using some generally unsatisfactory alternatives, including the Sunbeam Arab, Hispano-Suiza and Siddeley Puma. A Filton-built Fighter fitted with an Hispano-Suiza set an unofficial world altitude record over Dayton, Ohio on 18 November 1918, where the aircraft had an otherwise frustrating introduction. When the US entered the war after the sinking of the *Lusitania*, British & Colonial received a contract for 2,000 Fighters to be built under licence by Curtiss Aeroplane and Motor Corporation, Buffalo and fitted with Hispano-Suiza engines. The project was hampered by the Americans' insistence on using heavier Liberty engines, leading to several fatal accidents during tests and the cancellation of the contract after only 27 had been built. Among the fatalities was British & Colonial's first official test pilot, Captain Joseph Hammond.

Aviation companies increasingly turned to cabinet-makers for support in the war as they needed to engage a large number of skilled carpenters to keep up with the demand for airframes. The Fighter was of all-wood construction with fabric covering. Among those who helped in its production were the Bath Cabinet Makers at Bellott's Road, Bath which employed around 160 men and 200 women (a total of 2,128 men and 1,044 women in the city were employed producing munitions in World War One).[33] The Bath Cabinet Makers expanded into the Aircraft Flight Works at Twerton and, in addition to supplying Fighter ribs and other parts, made wings for de Havilland 10s and parts of the Sopwith Snipes. Complete aircraft were assembled in the Octagon, the Assembly Rooms' Ballroom and the County Rink and transported by road to the Acceptance Park at Filton for testing.

British & Colonial's final outstanding wartime Fighter contracts were cancelled on 20 September 1919. There continued smaller-scale production of new variants and modifications for various contracts, of which the most significant followed the RAF's decision to use the Fighter as the standard aircraft for its Army Co-operation squadrons. Some stockpiles were converted to fully dual-controlled Tourers for the civil market, while others were sold to foreign air forces including those of Greece, Mexico, Peru and New Zealand. In September 1920 a Major W F Vernon converted one into a seaplane with twin floats.

The Fighter continued in service with the RAF for several years after the war, including seeing action on the North West Frontier and in Iraq. It was used as a trainer with the University Air Squadrons at Oxford and Cambridge until 1931. The last to be scrapped in overseas services were those of the Royal New Zealand Air Force, which continued using the Fighter until 1938. BAC therefore had a steady business in reconditioning aircraft and supplying spares after production had ended.

A vintage Bristol Fighter running on the ground waits to be joined by the Bristol Bulldog, c 1964 (Bristol Aero Collection).

Women in wartime

Portrait of Ada Smith wearing her mop cap and overalls, 1918 (private collection).

Until the modern era, the main area where women were employed in aviation was in clerical, secretarial and administrative posts in environments that ranged from the typing pool, where there were hundreds of women, to individual departments or sections with only one female employee. War time brought more varied opportunities.

In March 1915 the UK Board of Trade launched a campaign to encourage women to register for war service. Around 124,000 signed up. Employers were generally enthusiastic about female recruitment during the war because women usually accepted lower wages than their male counterparts. The women were mainly offered unskilled positions at aircraft factories as part of the process of breaking down previously complex, skilled work into its basic constituent parts to increase production. One of the jobs they took on was stringing, making wood and wire frames over which canvas was stretched as tightly as possible and then stitched by hand to form the structure of the wings and fuselage. They then applied a substance called dope to the fabric to tighten it further on the frame and make a smooth surface. The dope also acted as a form of varnish. It was highly toxic – non-poisonous dope was not available in the UK, though it was in use elsewhere

– and the women were given milk to counter the effects of giddiness, headaches and fatigue. Women also assisted those skilled workers who had been retained because they provided an essential service, such as the carpenters. To protect their members' interests, the National Amalgamated Furnishing Trades Association and other craft unions blocked the Ministry of Munitions' attempts to train women for more skilled work. According to surveys, some women said they enjoyed their new independence in the workplace, but gender divisions were reinforced after the war.

At Filton in July 1916 a new, separate canteen and restroom were built for women joining the company. This was part of the war-time expansion programme. The War Office also contributed £30,000 towards the cost of erecting a new assembly hall with fabric and dope shops where many women were employed. At Brislington, women worked in the Final Assembly Hall, in the Carpenter Shop and Cabinet Shop and as wing assemblers. Some were retained until well into 1919 as there was still some demand for aircraft and it took several months for the men to return and resettle after the war.

During World War Two the Extended Employment of Women Agreement of 1940 confirmed that women war-time workers and other 'dilutees' were to be considered only temporarily employed to avoid concerns about them permanently taking over skilled male jobs. The agreement was backed by the Amalgamated Engineering Union. In January 1941 the government encouraged more women between the ages of 18 and 40 to register voluntarily for war work, but the response was not as enthusiastic as anticipated. The social research organisation Mass Observation, which recorded everyday life in Britain, said this was because women felt they were being ordered to sign up rather than being appealed to, which they resented. They also wanted information about rates of pay before making a decision and this was not forthcoming at the registration offices because of the uncertain situation. The War Cabinet soon decided compulsory registration was the answer rather than appealing to the women's better

War-time Rotol advertisement showing female mechanics attaching a propeller – as made by men to 'maximum reliability' – to an aeroplane with 'maximum simplicity' (Rolls-Royce Heritage Trust).

nature, and by 1943 'it was almost impossible for a woman under 40 to avoid war work unless she had heavy family responsibilities or was looking after a war worker billeted on her'.[34] Ernest Bevin as Minister of Labour implemented nursery provision in munitions factories to make it easier for women to work, though responsibility for the nurseries fell upon local authorities and in reality 'most children of war workers never saw the inside of one'.[35] There was the equally pressing problem of how women could do the family shopping if they were out at work all day.

Women were offered more varied jobs in the Second World War than they had had in the First, and got their hands onto heavy tools like riveting guns, but the work still tended to be 'repetitive and boring'. As before, 'their

War-time BAC employees (Bristol Aero Collection).

jobs were [typically] broken down into short operations which could be mastered in a very short time simply by watching the toolsetter perform the work'.[36] The 1942 Mass Observation report *People in Production* showed that 39 per cent of the war-time women employees interviewed 'really liked' their work and that 36 per cent were 'fascinated' by it, but it also reported that a fairly long period of the women's day was spent not working (chatting in the cloakroom, for example) and a later report referred to a lot of 'clock watching'.[37] There was also a higher incidence of absenteeism and reported slacking among women than men.[38]

Women were normally paid on a piece-work rate which was set lower than for their male counterparts, as was the hourly rate. Such differences were seen as 'unfair and inexplicable'.[39] It was particularly difficult for those women classified as mobile who were sent away to other towns to work and had to pay their way there as well as send money home. A Mass Observation report of 1944 showed 'that less than twenty-five per cent of women working in factories wanted to continue in their present job' and that although many of those who had been working part-time 'found the arrangement by and large suited them', most 'took a different attitude, tending to regard wartime work as a necessary evil, a temporary interlude'.[40] The unions were keen for them to return to the home once war was over, sticking to the terms of the 1940 agreement which stressed they were temporary employees.

Women also had the opportunity to contribute to the war effort by joining the Air Transport Auxillary (ATA). This was formed on 9 September 1939 from a nucleus of civilian pilots with a minimum of 250 hours of flying time. Initially this meant those who were considered too old for the RAF or fell short of the medical requirements, hence the nickname Ancient and Tattered Airmen. Women were grudgingly accepted into the group, with the first eight joining in January 1940. Female pilots were mainly from well-heeled families since they were the only ones who could afford private tuition and flight time in order to get their wings. Originally the ATA was envisaged as a messenger service, but the pilots were soon being used for transporting aircraft from factories, including Filton and the BAC shadow factories, to the RAF, Fleet Air Arm and other forces in the UK and overseas. This required the introduction of systematic training for handling the different aircraft types. By 1944 there were 659 ATA pilots, of whom 108 were women, in addition to male and female ATA engineers, ground crew and other back-up staff. Thirty other countries contributed pilots to the service, of which the largest contingent came from the US. Eventually, 22 ferry pools had been built up, including No 2 Ferry Pool at Whitchurch. Most pools were mixed but

Lettice Curtis pictured in a Spitfire just after World War Two (Rolls-Royce Heritage Trust). She was one of the first pilots in the ATA to qualify to fly four-engined bombers.

some were all-female. By the end of the war the ATA had ferried over 309,000 aircraft. Among over 170 pilots to lose their lives on ATA missions was the record-breaking aviatrix Amy Johnson, who ditched into the Thames estuary in heavy fog in an Airspeed Oxford on 5 January 1941. Her body was never found.

The bombing of BAC

BRISTOL AEROPLANE COMPANY LTD
AIR RAID PRECAUTIONS
THE COLOUR OF YOUR GROUP IS **BLACK.**
YOUR SHELTER NO. IS   817.
YOUR LEADER IS Mr J. Morgan
DEPARTMENT   Inspection
CLOCK NO.   05790.
SIGNATURE   W R Dyer.

Air Raid Precautions Card issued by BAC stating the employee's group colour, shelter number and leader, c 1940 (private collection).

The most destructive war-time bombing raid on the BAC site took place on 25 September 1940. It was also the first major daylight raid in the Bristol area – a prelude to the devastating Bristol Blitz which began in November that year.

The attack by three *gruppen* of Heinkel bombers was led by Major Friedrich Kless. Information was used from a pre-war German reconnaissance flight made by the Graf-Zeppelin D-LZ-127 which had taken aerial photographs of the factory, recorded its map co-ordinates and made detailed notes about the buildings. Weston-super-Mare, recognisable by its pier, was used as the outer marker guide for the bombers' flight path. Coming over Portbury, one of the lead aircraft was brought down by the anti-aircraft guns positioned there, crashing near Failand to the West of Bristol at 11.45am. The crew bailed out and were captured by farmers.

No 501 Squadron, equipped with Hawker Hurricanes, and No 263 Squadron, equipped with Gloster Gladiators, had been based at Filton airfield at the start of war, but at the time of the raid there were no squadrons in the area. BAC was therefore left with only barrage defence and the surrounding anti-aircraft batteries, at least one of which (Purdown) was being serviced at the time. The drawback of balloon barrage defences was that it made it difficult to deploy fighter aircraft from the ground.

BAC had introduced its own warning system to avoid unnecessary disruption to production when the local sirens sounded to announce attacks on the city of Bristol rather than the immediate vicinity of the factory (the Air Ministry shadow factory within the BAC site still continued to respond to the general alarm). There was a specially-trained Air Raid Precautions unit on site, an underground emergency hospital, and a large fire and ambulance service. With the first sounds of approaching aircraft on the morning of the raid, the tune 'Marching through Georgia' was played through the factory's speakers and employees began to make their way to cover (the all-clear signal was 'Colonel Bogey').

Employees were dispersed across different shelters so a department would not lose all its workers if one was hit. The shelters were narrow, concrete tunnels with bench seats along the sides and a dedicated warden assigned to each. Some employees are said to have preferred to make for the nearby railway tunnel, which they felt was safer. Ironically, the distinctive rectangle formed by the railway lines was one of the markers used by the bombers to pinpoint their target.

The bombing of BAC

GB 74 52 b
(2. Ang.)
Nur für den Dienstgebrauch
Bild Nr. F 908 b/40/016 (Lfl. 3)
Aufnahme vom 27. 9. 40

Filton

Werk für Flugzeugzellen
„The Bristol Aeroplane Co. Ltd."

Länge (westl. Greenw.): 2° 34' 30''   Breite: 51° 30' 50''
Mißweisung: — 11° 36' (Mitte 1940)   Zielhöhe über NN 65 m

Maßstab etwa 1 : 14 600

Genst. 5. Abt.   November 1940

Karte 1 : 100 000
GB/E 32

Ⓐ GB 74 52 Werk für Flugzeugzellen „The Bristol Aeroplane Co. Ltd."
Ⓑ GB 73 52 Flugmotorenfabrik „The Bristol Aeroplane Co. Ltd."

Luftwaffe aerial photograph of Filton with the two main targets, the airframe
sheds and engine works, marked (Special Collections, Bristol Central Library).

At 11.48am the 57 German bombers began to drop their loads over the factory. Over 100 bombs were dropped from approximately 4,500 metres (15,000 feet) in less than a minute into an area approximately one mile square. Officers at Yatesbury near Calne in Wiltshire witnessed the attack on their radar; they did not realise at the time what they were seeing as the technology was so new. There were direct hits to six of the shelters and considerable damage to the flight sheds, the main engine shops, the Rodney Works and the shadow factory. The BAC Minute Book refers to the cost of repairing the damaged premises as an estimated £30,000. Nine hundred homes were destroyed or damaged in the surrounding area. A total of 149 people were killed, some in and some outside the factory, and Filton Church became a temporary mortuary. It is a long-established local myth that one of the shelters that had been hit was left untouched with the bodies buried inside.

504 Squadron (Hawker Hurricanes) arrived at Filton on 26 September and were ready the next day when the Germans returned for a second daylight raid. The last major attack on the Bristol area took place on 11 April 1942 when the main building in the aircraft works was hit by a single bomb. During the course of the war many local people, including firemen, went to London to share their expertise on civil defence, along with local builders who contributed to rebuilding projects in the capital.

One of the worse-hit departments at Filton in the September raid was the Tool Room, which despite the policy of using separate shelters lost more than a dozen employees. An unexploded bomb at the Patchway Tool Room, which took five weeks to be defused, meant the workers there had to be sent home on full pay and some of these volunteered to transfer to the airframe works until the vacancies could be filled.

Hurricane, c 1940 (top) (Bristol Aero Collection).

One of the maps that formed part of the German flight plan for the raid (facing page) (Special Collections, Bristol Central Library).

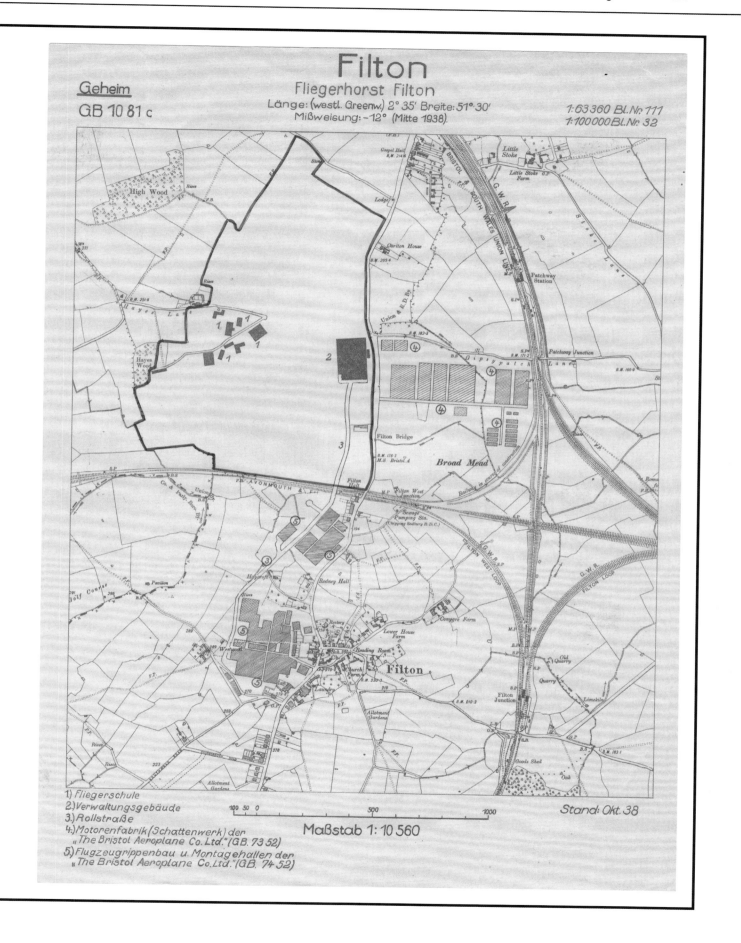

Geheim
GB 10 81 c

Filton
Fliegerhorst Filton
Länge: (westl. Greenw.) 2° 35′ Breite: 51° 30′
Mißweisung: −12° (Mitte 1938).

1:63 360 Bl. Nr. 111
1:100 000 Bl. Nr. 32

1.) *Fliegerschule*
2.) *Verwaltungsgebäude*
3.) *Rollstraße*
4.) *Motorenfabrik (Schattenwerk) der "The Bristol Aeroplane Co. Ltd." (GB. 73 52)*
5.) *Flugzeugrippenbau u. Montagehallen der "The Bristol Aeroplane Co. Ltd." (GB. 74 52)*

100 50 0   500   1000

Maßstab 1: 10 560

Stand: Okt. 38

Spring Quarry

With an increasing risk of air raids after the fall of France, Lord Beaverbrook, Minister of Aircraft Production, advised the aviation industry to move part of its operation underground. Underground stores were already being used as ammunition depots at that time.

It was originally proposed that the whole of BAC's engine development and production department and most of the airframe construction department should be housed in an underground facility, for which an initial budget of £1m was allocated for building work, fittings and others costs. The first site considered was Monk's Park Quarry near Corsham in Wiltshire, which was used for the quarrying of Bath stone. Interest then switched to the larger Spring Quarry between Corsham and Box tunnel. Construction of the facilities (sometimes referred to as the Hawthorn Engine Factory) started in April 1941 with estimated costs now at £2.34m (by 1945 they were close to £20m). Thousands of Irish navvies were drafted in to move some two million tons of stone debris to create the workspaces.

The initial plan was to have 12,000 employees on site working in shifts around the clock with 6,000 to 7,000 additional staff brought in daily by bus, but it was decided complete relocation would be too disruptive to essential production. The German bombing threat had also receded by this stage, so the project was scaled down. In the event, only the development department and a small production programme were moved to the underground site, which was now 'reclassified as a *shadow* rather than a *dispersal* scheme', reducing the need to relocate large numbers of BAC employees.[41]

Many of those who did move to the area lived in Government-funded housing estates that had been built on former farmland around Corsham and Chippenham. The estates' facilities included a cinema, community centre, school and shops. They were designed to accommodate those employed in the local munitions industry which, in addition to BAC, included Birmingham Small Arms. Other workers came in from Patchway by company coach, adding two hours or more travel time to the standard, 12-hour working day.

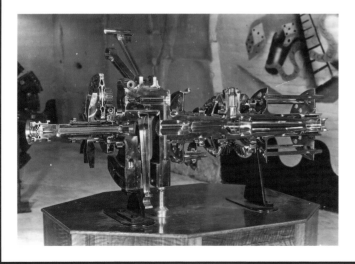

A sliced-through Pegasus crankshaft on display at the Spring Quarry site with a mural by Olga Lehmann visible in the background (Rolls-Royce Heritage Trust).

One of the surviving Lehmann murals, c 2007 (Bristol Aero Collection).

The first complete Spring Quarry engine emerged in September 1943. There had been an expectation at one time that the factory would turn out 260 Centaurus engines a month, but only 42 a month were produced. Of the 100,932 Bristol engines built in World War Two, only 523 came from the underground factory – a tiny percentage when the costs and upheaval are taken into consideration. Parnall Aircraft and Dowty were also due to move to the site, but that plan was shelved despite much of the clearing and building work being completed. At the end of the war, the factory was taken over as a Naval Depot (which it remained until 1995), with BAC completing the transfer of its equipment and production lines by 1946.

Many of the BAC employees found the factory damp, cramped, badly lit and confusing in its layout. Air vents located in the floor proved a problem for female workers wearing skirts and dresses. However, others enjoyed the novelty of working over 30 metres (100 feet) below the earth's surface in what was effectively an immense complex of caves with an artificially controlled temperature, neither too hot nor too cold. The canteen areas were decorated with colourful murals by Olga Lehmann, a Chilean educated at the Slade who was best known as a costume designer. The paintings were on various themes including the circus, mermaids and sports. They were commissioned by Reginald Verdon Smith, with the architect David Aberdeen acting as intermediary.[42]

Blenheim

Bristol Blenheims were used on a reconnaissance mission to observe German ports on 3 September 1939 within an hour of war being declared.

Artist's impressions of Blenheims in action for use in BAC war-time advertising (Bristol Aero Collection).

The first Allied bombs of the war were dropped on 4 September by a long-nosed Blenheim IV (N6204) piloted by Flight Lieutenant Kenneth Christopher Doran. The target was the German fleet at Wilhelmshaven. On the same day, Sergeant George Booth became the first British Prisoner of War when his Blenheim was shot down in action.

The first flight decorations of the war were awarded on 10 October 1939 to Blenheim pilots Flight Lieutenant Doran (110 Squadron) and Flight Officer McPhearson (139 Squadron). Blenheims made the first Fighter Command raid on a German base (Borkum) on 28 November 1939

The team responsible for the design, manufacture and development of the Type 142, 1935 (Bristol Aero Collection). Reading from left to right, front row: William Morgan, Mr Dunn, Frank Barnwell, Herbert Thomas (by then Assistant Managing Director), Mr Grant, Leslie Frise, Mr Sibley; back row: Mr Powell, Mr Adams, Mr Ebbels, Mr Whitmore, Mr Murray.

and Blenheims sank the first U-boat for the RAF without surface support on 11 March 1940. On the night of 22 July 1940, a Blenheim converted for night fighting became the first aircraft to intercept and destroy an intruder using the airborne interception Mark III radar facility. The Blenheim won more VCs than any other aeroplane. It was noted for its versatility and served 26 RAF squadrons in every theatre of war. This is an impressive record considering the aircraft was initially thought by pilots to be under-powered, under-armed, an easy target for German fighters, difficult to handle and with an inconvenient cockpit layout.

The Blenheim was derived from Frank Barnwell's Bristol Type 142, which made its maiden flight on 12 April 1935. The Type 142 was a high-speed, twin-engined, all-metal, cantilever-winged monoplane. It was one of the first examples of what is now known as the executive jet and, at the time, was the most advanced aeroplane in Europe, if not the world. It had been developed by BAC from an earlier design, the Type 135, as a private aircraft for the newspaper magnate Lord Rothermere, proprietor of the *Daily Mail*. In early 1934, at a luncheon held for his editors, Rothermere had announced his intention to commission the building of Europe's fastest commercial aeroplane. Bob Lewis, editor of the *Bristol Evening World* and an advocate for the local aircraft industry, approached BAC through Roy Fedden, encouraging the directors to take on this challenge.

When the government announced its rearmament programme, Lord Rothermere presented his Bristol Type 142 to the nation for extended trials that might

lead to its development as a light bomber. He gave it the patriotic name Britain First. The aircraft was sent to Martlesham Heath in June 1935 for its official trials, where it proved it could fly 50mph faster than the RAF's latest prototype fighter, the Gloster Gladiator. It was damaged the following month when its landing gear failed to lock, and was eventually scrapped in 1944 having served as an instructional airframe for a number of years.

BAC developed a military version of Britain First, the Type 142M, which had its maiden flight on 25 June 1936, though large orders had been received from the government as early as September 1935 because the aircraft was so impressive on paper. The biggest change between the original Type 142 and what became the Blenheim was the

raising of the wing from a low to a mid position to allow room for the bomb bay. Space for a navigator was made beneath the pilot's seating area in the now fully-glazed nose cone. There was a Browning machine gun by the port wing and a Lewis or Vickers gun in the hydraulically-powered turret. At the time, Blenheim was the biggest aircraft built in quantity at Filton. The 1916 erecting hall and flight sheds were enlarged to accommodate it. The monocoque system presented a challenge for draftsmen used to frame structures and Archibald E Russell became involved in the project, applying his expertise in stressed-skin construction.

Blenheim gave the Air Ministry initial confidence in BAC's military capabilities, though this relationship later became strained. The myth of the aircraft's ability, based almost

Bristol Type 142 in its original configuration
(facing page) (Duncan Greenman: Bristol AirChive).

The layout of the Blenheim cockpit with the pilot
position to the left and the observer/bomb aimer
position on the right, 1938 (above) (Airbus).

Member of WRAF refuelling a Mark 1 Bristol Blenheim
from an Air Transport Auxiliary fuel tank, c 1942 (right)
(Eric Viles).

entirely on the Type 142's speed, became self-perpetuating and soon two new production lines had to be set up as orders for still more aircraft were placed. The first deliveries to the RAF were made in March 1937. In 1938 large contracts for Blenheim IVs were placed with shadow factories run by Avro (by now a subsidiary of Hawker Siddeley) at Chadderton and by Rootes Securities Ltd at Speke on Merseyside. Sales of the Blenheim to foreign governments flourished prior to the outbreak of war, with orders from Finland, Romania, Portugal, Yugoslavia, South Africa and Egypt, among others. Over 650 Blenheims were made under licence in Canada as the Bolingbroke by Fairchild Aircraft Limited, Montreal. Later variations had American engines, seaplane floats and ski landing gear.

BAC was less successful with the Buckingham, a medium bomber derived from the Beaufighter as a replacement for the Blenheim. The first prototype was flown on 4 February 1943 and the aircraft went into production later that year, more than 12 months overdue and already obsolete. The delay had been partly caused by BAC's inability to solve problems relating to the Centaurus supercharger.[43] Potentially, the Buckingham might have been more useful in the Japanese war than the de Havilland Mosquito because its monocoque, aluminium construction meant it was less likely to warp in the tropical heat and humidity.

Beaufighter

The Beaufighter, nicknamed by the Japanese 'Whispering Death', was a versatile long-range fighter devised for offensive and defensive roles.

The RAF was aware it was deficient in long-range cannon-armed fighters at the time of the Munich crisis, when the service was put on a war footing. Roy Fedden had three guided tours of German aircraft and engine facilities in 1937, and had reported back on how production for the Luftwaffe was set to outstrip that of the UK industry but his warnings had been ignored.

In October 1938 at a meeting at the Air Ministry, Fedden and Leslie Frise said that the design for the Bristol Beaufort bomber could be converted into a fighter and argued that it made sense for the company to concentrate on that project instead of building more Beauforts. The Ministry staff eventually agreed to the proposal being carried forward as a private venture. The Beaufort adaptation – which became the Beaufighter – probably saved BAC having to join a subcontractors' group making Stirling bombers.

The first Beaufighter prototype made its maiden flight on 17 July 1939. It had Beaufort-type wings, undercarriage and tail with a smaller fuselage and more powerful Hercules engines (the Beaufort used Taurus). In April 1940 the first two prototypes were delivered to the RAF for trials and Beaufighter was cleared for squadron service on 26 July. In September No 29 and No 25 fighter squadrons became the first to be re-equipped with the aircraft, which

Artist's impression of Beaufort in action at Cherbourg for use in BAC war-time advertising (Bristol Aero Collection).

were fitted with airborne interception radar, four cannon and six Browning machine guns. Four bombs were added to the arsenal in late 1941. On 4 April 1943 a torpedo-armed coastal version had its first successful action when it sank two German supply ships off the Norwegian coast. The aircraft was used against Japanese shipping in the war in the East until it was replaced by the Bristol Brigand.

Beaufort division factories in Australia switched to Beaufighter production in 1944 and the aircraft was used in the advance to recapture the Dutch East Indies. By this

A Bristol Beaufighter fitted with two Bristol Hercules sleeve-valve radial engines, c 1940 (Rolls-Royce Heritage Trust).

time, production at Filton had ended but the Weston-super-Mare shadow factory was completing 87 a month on average. By the end of war, a total of 5,564 Beaufighters had been built at home and 363 in Australia.

One of the most audacious incidents involving a coastal Beaufighter was the dropping of a 'Tricolore' in a roof-top-level daylight flight over occupied Paris by pilot Flight Lieutenant Ken Gatward and observer Flight Sergeant George Fern on 12 June 1942. The flag fell upon the tomb of the unknown soldier and was collected by members of the French Resistance. The aircraft made two circuits, the first attracting little attention, the second drawing astonished Parisians and Germans into the street. The only shots to be fired by the aircraft were cannon shells aimed at the building that housed the German headquarters. In addition to being chased by German tracer fire, the pilot had to contend with a startled crow smashing into the radiator, causing erratic readings on the oil gauge, and a swarm of flies which splattered across the windscreen, obscuring the view.

British poet Gavin Ewart was called up in June 1940 and in May the following year was commissioned in the Royal Artillery, serving in anti-aircraft batteries in North Africa and Italy. Among the poems he wrote while in the service was 'When a Beau goes in', an ironic take on the expendability of aircrew in war time and the need to carry on without emotion:

When a Beau goes in,
Into the drink,
It makes you think,
Because, you see, they always sink
But nobody says 'Poor lad!'
Or goes about looking sad
Because, you see, it's war
It's the unalterable law.

Although it's perfectly certain
The pilot's gone for a Burton
And the observer too
It's nothing to do with you
And if they both should go
To a land where falls no rain nor hail nor driven snow –
Here, there, or anywhere
Do you suppose *they* care?

You shouldn't cry
Or say a prayer or sigh.
In the cold sea, in the dark,
It isn't a lark
But it isn't Original Sin –
It's just a Beau going in.[44]

Artist's impression of Beaufighters in action in Bay of Biscay for use in BAC war-time advertising (above) (Bristol Aero Collection).

Farndon's illustration of the Beaufighter from the 40th anniversary calendar (facing page) (Bristol Aero Collection).

Helicopters

Cuneo painting of a Bristol Belvedere lifting the new spire onto Coventry Cathedral, c 1956 (Westland Helicopters Ltd).

Heavier-than-air flight by moving wing developed through the flapping-winged ornithopters to the spinning blades of the autogyros and helicopters, in which the rotors act as wing and propeller, providing both lift and thrust.

The autogyro was invented by the Spanish designer Juan de la Cierva in the 1920s. On a modern autogyro, the engine drives a propeller for thrust and also starts the rotors turning. Once the rotors are spinning fast enough to generate lift, the engine is disconnected from them. The propeller thrust keeps the autogyro moving forward and this forward flight keeps the blades rotating freely. Sadly, de la Cierva, who believed moving wings were safer than fixed ones, was killed in a crash in a fixed-wing aircraft.

The first-ever helicopter flight probably took place in 1907 when the Frenchman Paul Cornu managed to get airborne for about 20 seconds, but the first modern helicopters emerged in the 1930s. Helicopters are more manoeuvrable than most other aircraft as they can fly in any direction – straight up, straight down, backwards and forwards – and also, unlike the autogyro, hover in one place. They were used in post-war reconstruction, humanitarian efforts and civilian land and sea rescues as well as military activity.

Helicopter design and manufacture began in earnest at BAC in 1944 when Raoul Hafner, the Austrian-born designer of the Hafner gyroplane, joined the company. Hafner had been employed at the Airborne Forces Experimental Establishment on rotorcraft design, and was effectively made redundant once the D-Day preparations were completed and it was decided that rotating wings would not be needed. BAC had formed a helicopter design department based in No 3 Flight Shed at Filton, with offices in Fairlawn Avenue, and Hafner and his technical team were released to form the nucleus of this new enterprise.

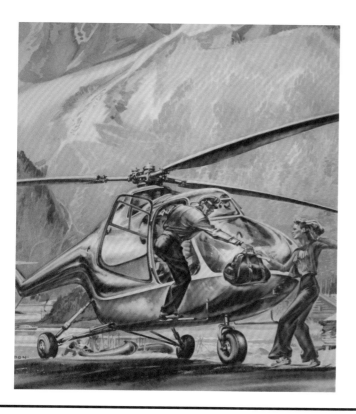

BAC's Type 171 was the first all-British designed and built helicopter. It went through a two-year design phase before the first prototype had its maiden flight on 27 July 1947. The Pratt and Whitney Wasp Junior 450hp engine was chosen for the first two prototypes. On 25 April 1949 the second prototype Mark 1 (G-ALOU) became the first British helicopter to be granted a Certificate of Airworthiness, which it needed to fly to the Paris Salon in May. The prototype Mark 2, which had a 550hp Alvis Leonides engine, was the first to have BAC-designed and built blades, the Mark 1 having had blades produced by the specialist firm Hordern Richmond. The Mark 3 was the first production aircraft and a total of 23 were built. Now named Sycamore, the helicopter entered service with the RAF in April 1953. The Mark 4 was in production from May 1953 until April 1959. Demonstration and trial flights for the aircraft included lake and mountain rescues in Switzerland and tests in the heat and humidity of the jungles of Malaya. Mark 4s were built in all variants, of which 87 were supplied to the RAF as the Sycamore HR14, 50 to the West German armed forces as the Mark 52, ten to the Royal Australian Navy as the HR51 and three to the Belgian Government.

The Sycamore was described by *The 'Bristol' Quarterly* as 'a basic vehicle which is capable of a wide variety of tasks, and the user – whatever his wants – has an aircraft which can be converted from one role to another with the least delay and with the minimum of difficulty'.[45] Its versatility was shown in its ability to operate in rescue mode, ambulance mode, as a passenger transporter with a four- or five-seat configuration and as an aerial crane. Among the many examples of the difficult and unorthodox tasks it could tackle were transporting surveyors and materials for a hydroelectric project in largely uncharted territory in south-west Tasmania, undertaking major airlifts for industrial projects in British Columbia, helping steeplejacks in Anglesey erect an offshore beacon and

Farndon's illustration of the Sycamore from the 40th anniversary calendar (Bristol Aero Collection).

A Belvedere twin-rotor helicopter lifting a Bristol/Ferranti Bloodhound, complete with its ground movement trolley, c 1959 (left) (Westland Helicopters Ltd).

Shot of the bare shell of the interior of the second prototype Bristol 173 twin-rotor helicopter, c 1953 (above) (Bristol Aero Collection).

British Army Apache (Rolls-Royce plc).

filming aerial footage over Almeria in southern Spain.[46] Three Sycamores formed part of the Navy squadron that was involved in ferrying passengers and carrying supplies during the extensive flooding of the Netherlands in the early 1950s. A Sycamore also took part in BAC's Civil Defence exercise in October 1953, evacuating 'casualties', carrying out reconnaissance and transporting personnel.

The Bristol Type 173 was the only twin-engine, tandem-rotor passenger aircraft built in the UK. On 3 January 1952 the first prototype made its first hovering flight using two 550hp Alvis Leonides radial engines. At the time it was 'the only helicopter in the world designed for safe flight with one engine shut down': if one engine failed, the other could automatically switch to driving both rotors, the power transferring from the engine to the rotors through the transmission.[47] The second prototype had stub-wings to increase lift and reduce power demands, thereby making fuel savings. It was operated by manual controls; Hafner preferred these to power ones, which he suspected of hiding potential defects, though at one time it was proposed there should be a system whereby the pilot could revert from power to manual in an emergency.

BAC hoped to enter the commercial helicopter market with the Type 173 being used as an inter-city transporter, but the military value of this design soon became apparent.

New government specifications for more advanced twin-rotor helicopters led to the ship-borne, general-purpose Bristol Type 191, the land-based, general-purpose Type 192 and the Type 193, a variant on the 191 for the Royal Canadian Air Force. Only the Type 192 entered production, although the Royal Navy put in an order for 100 Type 191s which was subsequently cancelled. The Type 192 had its first flight on 5 July 1958, powered by two Napier Gazelle free-turbine engines. The RAF took 26 Type 192s, even though some of the features were at this stage more appropriate for a naval role, including sonar for submarine detection, a torpedo carriage and landing gear designed for aircraft carriers. The helicopter was named the Belvedere when it entered service.

The BAC Helicopter Division moved into the former BAC Beaufighter shadow factory at Old Mixon, Weston-super-Mare in March 1955. The move was encouraged by the local council, which wanted to build up the town's industry. Employees who transferred from Filton and Patchway went to the head of the waiting list for the new council estates being built in the area and BAC paid for some of their furnishings once they had settled into their new homes. Initially, wooden blades for the rotors continued to be made at Filton and transferred down to Weston.

BAC's Helicopter Division became part of the Westland Aircraft group in 1960, with Hafner becoming Technical Director (Research). Some staff were transferred to the new company to continue work on the Belvedere but, as was customary, the jigs were destroyed once the existing orders were fulfilled. Today, Rolls-Royce engines built at Patchway are used in the Lynx (Gem), Merlin, Apache and NH90 (Turbomeca RTM322) helicopters. The Gem has retained the world's helicopter speed record of 400.87kph (around 250 mph) since 1986.

V/STOL

In January 1957 Gordon Lewis, a Bristol Aero Engines project engineer, and Michael Wibault, a French aircraft designer, took out a provisional patent for an engine suitable for vertical or short take-off and landing (V/STOL). Wilbault had an idea of building engines in which the exhaust gas could be diverted through 'two pairs of centrifugal blowers with rotatable... casings' to produce either downward or rearward thrust.[48]

Artist's impression of an unrealised concept for a slow-speed wingless vehicle capable of lifting various objects into difficult areas by means of downward-facing exhaust nozzles, c 1950s (Bristol Aero Collection).

He was advised to bring his idea to Patchway where, with guidance from Stanley Hooker, it was combined with elements from the Orpheus and Olympus engine designs to create the turbofan Pegasus. The development was jointly funded with the Mutual Weapons Development Programme in Paris. Pegasus has two pairs of directional exhaust nozzles which can swivel through 98.5 degrees, providing vertical exhaust thrust to send an aircraft straight up and horizontal thrust to send it forward like a normal jet. The nozzles must swivel in the same direction at the same time or the pilot might lose control of the aircraft.

Pegasus was fitted to the first prototype of Sir Sydney Camm's P1127 for its first tethered hover on 21 October 1960. The P1127 was built by the Hawker company in Kingston-on-Thames, Surrey. Early in 1964 the aircraft, now called Kestrel, underwent Tripartite Squadron evaluation and Pegasus entered the next stage of its development. The design of the airframe formed the basis of the Harrier 'Jump Jet' built by what was now Hawker Siddeley. The RAF's No 1 Squadron received its first Harriers on 18 April 1969, which entered service the following month. Pegasus was also used in the British Aerospace Sea Harrier, which saw action in the Falklands War in 1982.

Harrier landing on the deck of a ship, c 1997 (above) (Rolls-Royce plc).

Turbine blades of a Pegasus engine being checked in a Spanish Navy Harrier, c 1998 (right) (Rolls-Royce plc).

A high ratio of crashes of Harriers in service with the American Marines led to the redesign of the engine training programme, a project overseen by Rolls-Royce's Reginald John Philips, who wrote the report for the Pentagon. Philips had joined BAC's engine department in 1932 as a shop boy. The Harrier was renamed the Matador for the Spanish market. It was sold by Hawker Siddeley to McDonnell Douglas Aircraft Manufacturing in the US, who in turn sold it to the Spanish Navy to get around the UK boycott of arms deals with the fascist regime.

On 14 August 1989 a Harrier with Pegasus 11-61 engine set time-to-height records to 3,000 metres (9,482 feet) in 36.38 seconds, 6,000 metres in 55.38 seconds and 9,000 metres in 81 seconds. It was flown by Andy Sephton, Rolls-Royce's Chief Test Pilot, for the 3km and 9km records, and by Heinz Frick for the 6km record.

Bloodhound

BAC's Guided Weapons Department was formed in 1949 at the request of the UK government. The Bristol/Ferranti Bloodhound was the RAF's only long-range, surface-to-air transportable anti-aircraft missile and it remained in front-line operation until 1993.

In 1957 it achieved the first direct hit by a British surface-to-air guided missile of a Firefly pilotless target aircraft (the Firefly was later superseded by the Anglo-Australian Jindivik drone for target practice, which was built at Filton). With the merger of Bristol Aircraft Company, English Electric and Vickers, the headquarters for guided missile activity moved to the English Electric site at Stevenage, but Filton and Patchway continued to be heavily involved in the programme, which proved highly profitable for the company.

During the early years of the Cold War, the main risk to North America and Australia was thought to be long-range missile attacks by the Soviets. Western Europe was thought to be more at risk from short-range attacks because of its proximity to the Soviet Bloc. An article in *The 'Bristol' Quarterly* explained: 'the short-range attack can be delivered by a variety of means and at almost any altitude. Such an attack can be heavier, more prolonged and more closely-controlled than attacks directed against more remote objectives.'[49] Bloodhound was designed to meet that threat as an anti-aircraft defence system that could respond quickly with a high rate of lethal fire-power delivered with accuracy. The Ferranti partnership was suggested by the Ministry of Supply. Ferranti was responsible for the missile's electronic equipment, control and guidance systems. These were built into the missile itself and provided a semi-active homing device as an alternative to command guidance, whereby the missile would be guided from controls on the ground. BAC developed the weapon itself, with its unique moving-wing configuration, and the Thor ramjets to propel it.

As ramjets cannot operate at low speeds, ramjet-powered vehicles 'are usually launched by rocket booster units that accelerate the vehicle to a speed at which the ramjet can be started and thence take over the job of propulsion'.[50] BAC began its ramjet work with a Ministry of Supply contract to build the Twin Ramjet Test Vehicle. The chief designer on what became the Thor project was David Farrar, who had been involved in the structural design of Brabazon. A large extension was built at Patchway for the project's test plant. Tests also took place at the artillery range at Larkhill, at ranges at Aberporth owned by the Ministry of Supply and at the Woomera range belonging to the Weapons Division of BAC's Australian subsidiary.

The first successful short-range Bloodhound flight took place on 19 July 1951. This was 'the first sustained supersonic flight to be made by a British designed and built ramjet powered missile'.[51] Shortly afterwards Bloodhound made its first successful long-range flight. The Thor ramjet at that time was the most highly developed power unit of its kind in the UK. There was a later project to develop a hypersonic ramjet capable of Mach 4 and higher, but this was cancelled by the government. Bloodhound I passed its acceptance trials in 1958 and production began at Bristol Guided Weapons Division's Cardiff factory. That same year the first order from Sweden was received, with the first order from Australia coming the following year.

Other missiles developed at Filton included the Rapier mobile air defence system, the Swingfire, the Sea Dart, the Sea Eagle, the Sea Skua and the Sea Wolf.

Bristol Bloodhound II, c 1983 (Rolls-Royce Heritage Trust).

A400M

The wings of the Airbus A400M military transporter were designed at Filton. They are partly built there before being transported to Seville for final assembly at the European Aeronautic Defence and Space (EADS) facilities. They have the largest area of top skin made primarily from composite materials of any wing in the world.

Airbus A400M's first flight, 2009 (above) (Airbus).

Delivery of A400M wings from Filton to Seville for assembly at the EADS factory, 2007 (facing page, top) (Airbus).

TP400-D6 turboprop used in the Airbus A400M (facing page, bottom) (Rolls-Royce plc).

According to *Flight* magazine, the A400M project had been rumbling away for decades before formally coming under the Airbus umbrella in 1996. It was conceived as a European competitor to the Boeing C-17 Globemaster and Lockheed Martin C-130 Hercules. It made its maiden flight on 11 December 2009 and it is currently estimated that it will be available for delivery in late 2012. By January 2010 it had been purchased by the governments of Belgium, France, Germany, Luxembourg, Spain, Turkey and the UK.

Rolls-Royce at Patchway is part of the Europrop International consortium, which is supplying the aircraft's TP400-D6, the most powerful engine of its kind in the world. This contract covers the development and production of more than 750 engines to be delivered from 2009 onwards for the A400M fleets, and the production of additional engines for potential export customers. Rolls-Royce's areas of responsibility include the overall engine performance, air and oil systems, the intermediate casing, the six-stage high-pressure compressor and the low-pressure shaft.

Naval projects

Sir George White had demonstrated an early interest in marine engineering with the work of Lieutenant Burney in Department X on the unsuccessful hydrofoil project.

Many years later, BAC's plastics division had contracts for various components to be supplied to the Navy, including gun-shield turrets for frigates. In addition to the plastic dinghies and cruisers previously mentioned, the division made a motor torpedo boat in 1946. This was powered by the Hercules and it was in the field of marine engines that BAC and its associated companies made their most significant contribution to naval projects.

The Marine Proteus, adapted from the Proteus 755 turboprop aero-engine, was used in the Royal Navy's motor torpedo boats HMS *Brave Swordsman* and HMS *Brave Borderer*. These were small, high-speed coastal-patrol craft commissioned from Vospers at Porchester in the late 1950s. According to *The 'Bristol' Quarterly*, the 'gas turbine is more reliable and simpler to maintain than the ultra-light high speed piston engine'.[52] The Proteus was also considered more economical than other engines because it had originally been developed for the civil market, which demands longer life between overhauls and greater fuel economy than does the military one. This is largely because keeping costs down is more critical in a civil context where there is an expectation of commercial profit. The Marine Proteus, which was noted for its flexibility, was also used in Vosper's *Ferocity*, a prototype fast attack craft, and *Mercury*, a luxury motor yacht commissioned by a Greek shipping magnate.

HMS *Brave Swordsman* and HMS *Brave Borderer*, both powered by 3,500hp Bristol Pegasus gas turbines, c 1958 (Rolls-Royce Heritage Trust).

Artist's impression of Naval Type 45 Destroyer powered by WR-21 turbine engines (Rolls-Royce plc).

The Type 82 destroyer HMS *Bristol*, launched by Swan Hunter in 1969, was powered by two Bristol Siddeley Olympus TM1A gas turbines. It was withdrawn from service in 1991 after a serious onboard fire, but continued in commission in a permanent berth at Whale Island, providing training programmes and accommodation for cadet and reserve forces. Other naval ships powered by the marine Olympus are HMS *Invincible*, *Illustrious* and *Ark Royal*.

During the 1980s, following the acquisition of Sperry Gyroscope at Bracknell, some underwater systems projects were transferred to Filton. These included various initiatives relating to the detection of enemy mines and submarines, and the building of Consub, a remotely controlled underwater vehicle for inspecting pipelines and oil-rig structures. The underwater systems unit was eventually merged with Marconi and moved to Portsmouth.

Prior to its merger with Bristol-Siddeley in 1966, Rolls-Royce's naval projects included a marinised version of the Merlin engine which was fitted in Royal Navy prototype motor torpedo boats in 1938. In 1953 two Rolls-Royce RM60s were fitted to HMS *Grey Goose*, a former steam gun boat, in a successful test of the viability of gas turbines for marine use. Today, Patchway is home to Rolls-Royce's Naval Marine division, providing a wide range of products for around 70 navies worldwide.

The division is responsible for marine gas-turbine development, manufacture and support. Assembly and testing of the MT30, the world's most powerful marine gas-turbine, is undertaken at the Patchway site. The forthcoming DDG1000 Zumwalt class multi-mission destroyer for the US Navy will be powered by this engine, a derivative of the Aero Trent 800. MT30 will also be installed in the new, Queen Elizabeth-class aircraft carriers for the Royal Navy. Rolls-Royce was part of an international consortium that designed and manufactured the WR-21, an advanced marine gas turbine engine installed on the Royal Navy's Type 45 Destroyers.

Computer-generated image of
A350 XWB (Airbus).

Section 6:
Into the Future

Imagine it is 2030. An oil tanker is making its way across the open waters of the sea, unaware that it is being pursued by pirates. It's a dark, moonless night.

An unmanned, long-endurance surveillance aircraft is flying overhead. It has been loitering, tirelessly and silently, at a height of more than 20,000 metres for the last few days, watching and waiting. It has a hybrid power system: gas turbines for generating high-power density during take-off, climbs and when speed is of the essence, and an energy-efficient fuel-cell generating sufficient electrical power for cruising.

The aircraft's radar picks up the presence of the pirate boat. It has the capability to assess a situation as suspicious and to decide to investigate. Its onboard integrated control system automatically selects the most appropriate power source for the job in hand and switches from the fuel-cell to the aircraft's gas turbines so it can swoop down quickly, with a blast of thrust, and get a closer look at what is happening below.

The control system is also able to change the shape of the aircraft's wings: it is like an albatross when it is cruising, like a hawk when it is flying fast. Unfortunately, as it dives, the aircraft hits a real flock of migrating birds and an engine is damaged. The sensors on the engine tell the control system the extent of the damage so it can decide how to continue the mission. It sends a message to the Rolls-Royce Operations Centre in Bristol, ordering replacement engine parts for when it returns to base so it can swiftly be repaired and resume its work.

At the same time, the aircraft sends its surveillance information regarding the pirates to a naval ship out at sea. The ship is too far from the tanker to intervene directly in the potential raid, but it launches a high-speed Unmanned Combat Air Vehicle (UCAV) with an integrated power system. The vehicle's integrated power system has at its heart a variable cycle turbofan which can be in 'hot-rod' mode when needed (for example at take-off) and a more efficient 'quiet' mode at other times. The UCAV zooms to the location given by the surveillance aircraft and drops a bomb close to the pirates' boat to disable it. The pirates had no idea it was coming as it could not be seen with their infrared binoculars or picked up with their radar equipment. That is because it uses the latest in sophisticated stealth systems. These shield the heat coming from the engines and hide the aircraft from radar, thereby making it difficult to detect at night.

The combat aircraft returns to the naval ship, which has by now also launched a new, high-speed compound helicopter from its deck which drops commandos onto the boat to arrest the pirates. The helicopter uses a combination of jet thrust and rotors to travel faster than standard models.

Computer-generated image of Mantis, unmanned demonstrator surveillance aircraft, 2009 (facing page) (BAE Systems).

Analysts, engineers, designers and scientists in some of the aviation companies that are associated with BAC are already working on the technology that can make this future scenario possible. They are experimenting with advanced computerised control systems, unmanned aircraft, integrated power systems, stealth systems and advanced helicopter engines. They are also working on more energy-efficient turbine engines that will use less fuel and produce less CO_2 (carbon dioxide) than present-day designs, as well as on materials for airframes that are more environmentally friendly and on more efficient manufacturing processes. These new technologies are maturing at different rates, so some will be well-established by 2030; others will only just be coming into operation.

Unmanned autonomous vehicles are advantageous for missions that are dirty (for example, in locations contaminated by nuclear fallout), dull (such as long-term surveillance or reconnaissance operations) and dangerous (like coming under heavy enemy fire). Potentially there is a cost saving to be made by not needing to train or pay pilots to fly the vehicles, but there are additional technological costs that need to be taken into consideration when assessing the long-term economic benefit of these programmes.

BAE Systems, Rolls-Royce and EADS are members of the consortium engaged in the Autonomous Systems Technology Related Airborne Evaluation and Assessment (ASTRAEA) programme, which is exploring controls-technology for use in unmanned aircraft. They are trying to anticipate what a control system would need to be like if there were no pilot in the vehicle to monitor, anticipate and respond to variations in performance and information received. The programme aims to make unmanned aircraft systems safe, routine and unrestricted in their use. This is a generation beyond so-called 'fly-by-wire', in which a pilot works alongside a computerised system in assessing a situation and acting promptly. That type of dual control was seen, for example, in the Airbus A320 that made a successful emergency landing in the Hudson river in January 2009.

Mantis is a pioneering unmanned demonstrator surveillance aircraft which made its maiden flight on 21 October 2009 at the Woomera range in Australia, a facility that was used by BAC in the development of the Bloodhound and other missiles. It is the largest fully autonomous unmanned aircraft to have been built in the UK. Phase 1 of the Mantis programme focuses on the evaluation of the control systems. These allow the aircraft effectively to fly itself throughout a mission, automatically detecting and managing all target information. Future phases may look at possible civilian applications, armed versions and sensor packages.

The Phase 1 Mantis is powered by two Rolls-Royce Model 250 turboprops. The company has already gained experience of these types of propulsive systems through its work on the US Department of Defense's Global Hawk and Fire Scout. Mantis is the first time Rolls-Royce at Patchway has not only supplied the engine of an aircraft but also designed the pod that encases it and integrated all the associated systems, such as electrical generators, cooling systems and the propeller. Normally these are separate elements that come together during assembly, but the company is moving towards integrated power systems responsible for the management and control of the gas-turbine propulsion, the electrical systems and the cooling systems.

Taranis is a technology demonstrator being developed by a consortium led by BAE Systems. It will form the basis for building the first unmanned high-speed, low-observable, front-line strike aircraft. It is expected to make its maiden flight by the end of 2010. A demonstrator is not intended to be the prototype of a future aircraft but a means of testing the technology that will be needed for that future project. Rolls-Royce at Patchway is responsible for designing and building the Taranis' propulsion system. Compared to an existing fighter engine, such as the Eurojet EJ200, a future stealthy UCAV will need a turbofan which has better fuel economy and a cooler exhaust (so it is harder to observe by infrared technology), and which is compact enough to fit into the aircraft's slender flying-

Computer-generated image of Taranis unmanned combat air vehicle (facing page) (BAE Systems).

wing shape. Rolls-Royce is leading a three-year, Ministry of Defence-funded programme called ENTAPS (ENgine Technologies for Aircraft Persistence and Survivability) to develop the technologies for such an engine.

Another key priority in developing new technology today is minimising future environmental impact, a consideration that would never have been anticipated in Sir George White's time. A major concern is the increase in CO_2, one of the greenhouse gases in the earth's atmosphere that trap the heat of the sun. An increase in greenhouse gases upsets the natural balance, raising the earth's temperature and precipitating climate change, with some places getting hotter, some cooler, some wetter, some drier. In addition to the likely loss of species, there will be less land suitable for growing crops and for grazing, and sea levels will rise, displacing communities. Carbon dioxide is produced by both natural and human activity. Approximately 25 per cent of CO_2 increase has been attributed to deforestation resulting from logging activity and the clearing of land for other uses (trees absorb CO_2). Other major contributors to the increase are heating and lighting buildings, car travel and power stations that burn fossil fuels. Around two to three per cent of the increase is attributed to the aviation industry.[1]

Ferranti Merlin measuring system with a Renishaw TP2 MIH probe in use at Component Coating and Repair Services Ltd (CCRS). CCRS Ltd specialises in the repair of gas turbine components and the application of coatings that enhance the efficiency of the compressor section of the engine.

CO_2 emission is taken seriously by the industry. It is committed to working closely with all stakeholders to develop an effective response to climate change through new approaches, based on a thorough understanding of the science. In recent decades, most companies have taken an interest in the environmental impact of the materials they use from a health and safety perspective – another development from White's day – but increasingly in the last few years the wider environmental impact has also been considered.

Rolls-Royce, for example, is working to produce more fuel-efficient and environmentally friendly engines. The more efficient an engine, the less fuel needs to be burnt to power it and therefore the less CO_2 is produced through the exhaust. Total efficiency is a combination of thermal efficiency and propulsive efficiency. Improved thermal efficiency in a gas turbine comes mainly from increasing the pressures and temperatures within the core of the engine and improving the aerodynamic and thermodynamic efficiency of individual components. The development of advanced materials plays a vital role in achieving these goals. Propulsive efficiency is improved by optimising how much the engine accelerates the surrounding air in order to generate thrust. In the case of commercial jet airliners, this has led to engines with higher bypass ratios which take a larger amount of air and accelerate it by a smaller amount. Careful studies are needed to consider the engine as part of the complete aircraft system. For example, it would be of no benefit if gains in engine fuel efficiency came at the cost of increasing aircraft weight and drag which then, paradoxically, increased the total amount of fuel burnt. One approach to addressing this dilemma is the open rotor turbine engine, referred to below. Whatever the proposed improvement, it must be achieved with an engine which is mechanically sound and reliable.

The Environmentally Friendly Engine programme aims to develop UK aerospace capabilities in terms of technologies relating to high-temperature materials, high-efficiency turbine components, low-emission combustion, and improved engine controls and nacelle aerodynamics, among other areas. Advancing UK AeroSpace Defence and Security Industries says:

> The environmental effects of burning fossil fuels are clearly a significant issue and whilst alternative power generating systems are being developed for land and marine use there is little long-term alternative to oil based fuels for air travel. It is therefore vitally important that the most efficient and clean way of producing the power is developed.[2]

The Environmentally Friendly Engine programme is a demonstrator programme led by Rolls-Royce at Derby, with assembly and testing at Patchway. It aims to contribute to industry targets of reducing CO_2 emissions by 50 per cent, nitrous oxide (another greenhouse gas) emissions by 80 per cent and noise by 50 per cent by 2020 from baseline figures of 2000. These reduction goals have been set by the Advisory Council for Aeronautics Research in Europe (ACARE). The experience gained from this work will be used in the next generation of gas turbines.

There is an on-going search for alternative fuels. Currently, most gas-turbine aero-engines burn kerosene produced from crude oil. An alternative is to create a synthetic petroleum substitute using natural gas (as in the Airbus A380 trials of 2008), coal (more plentiful in the US than crude oil) or biomass, for example coconut oil. The process of conversion

(called Fischer-Tropsch) unfortunately requires high energy input which could release significant CO_2 into the atmosphere. Biofuels are an attractive alternative for some as the growth of plants by photosynthesis removes carbon dioxide from the atmosphere, but their sources need to be sustainable. Others think hydrogen would be the greenest solution as it does not release CO_2 during combustion in the engine. However, most of the processes used to produce hydrogen require high levels of energy input. Hydrogen also has a number of issues associated with storage and handling which would need to be addressed if it were to be a serious contender as a replacement for kerosene. In addition, the low density of hydrogen would require a major change in the design of aircraft.

All of these engine-fuel alternatives are at different states of development, with aviation companies either actively involved in the research or keeping a watching brief on what is a complex subject. Other side-products of combustion can also have a damaging effect on the environment. Rolls-Royce has had considerable success in the design of combustion chambers which substantially reduce the production of soot and nitrous oxides. These

Airbus A380, powered by the Rolls-Royce Trent 900, being filled with liquid fuel processed from natural gas at Filton, 2008 (facing page) (Rolls-Royce plc).

designs are incorporated into the latest marks of commercial and military engines and could potentially be retrofitted to older engines.

At the moment, the gas turbine is unrivalled in terms of the amount of thrust or power it can produce in relation to weight. It is, however, less fuel-efficient than some other types of engines, such as diesels. Considerable work is being undertaken to improve gas-turbine fuel-efficiency, but at the same time alternatives to the gas turbine are being explored. Fuel-cells using hydrogen are potentially a more efficient means of generating onboard electricity, which in turn could be used to drive a fan or propeller to produce thrust. At present, the weight of such a system would rule it out from most aircraft with a practical payload. Solar cells for flight are also still only in their early research stages and the possibility of an aircraft being powered by solar energy alone is a long way off, not least because solar cells are not yet able to produce enough power to bear a fully functioning aircraft's weight. In addition, there is the problem of storing enough energy so that the aircraft can function at night. Despite these issues, a number of light-weight experimental aircraft, including manned aircraft, have been put on trial which use a combination of solar power, batteries and/or fuel-cells.

Similar research work is taking place in developing more environmentally friendly materials, moving away from a dependence on nickel, chrome and aluminium to increased use of composites and ceramics. New materials are usually more expensive in the short-term, but through-life analysis can demonstrate their long-term benefit, particularly with regard to environmental impact. 'Through-life' refers to the period from the moment a product is created to the moment it is disposed of. Traditionally, a company would be given a specification by a customer for an aircraft or aero-engine and would then decide how to fulfil it and how much it would cost. Now the supplier has to think of the bigger picture, which includes environmental concerns.

The National Composites Centre (NCC), based in the Bristol area and fully operational by 2011, will help deliver the next phase of research and development that will lead to the rapid manufacture of composite products. GKN is one of the industry partners in the Centre. It is currently embarking on major technology investment and development plans in response to the demands of its customers, such as Airbus and Rolls-Royce (both also partners in NCC), as well as to the demands of their ultimate customers – the airlines and their passengers. Much of this work has focused on the use of composite and titanium light-weight material in airframes and aero-engines, and on the use of the latest manufacturing technology. Reducing weight and improving performance has an immediate effect on fuel consumption and emissions, and ultimately on cost. Among its projects, GKN is producing composite winglets for new and existing aircraft which significantly improve aerodynamic performance and has formed a joint venture with

Rolls-Royce to develop and manufacture light-weight composite gas-turbine fan blades. GKN's new facility at Severn Beach has five auto fibre placement (AFP) machines used in the manufacture of composite wing spars for the forthcoming Airbus A350 XWB. The AFP process allows a more complex shape to be achieved through automated means and reduces manufacturing time. In addition, GKN at Filton is working with the company's Munich facility to investigate new microwave processing techniques which will reduce energy consumption in manufacturing processes, among other benefits.

Ideas have a tendency to come around again as improvements in technology and materials turn something that was overtaken by events or did not previously achieve its potential into a conceivably viable proposition. The idea of resurrecting large airships for use as cargo carriers or military reconnaissance is regularly revisited. The advantage of the airship is that it is basically a big bag of gas which stays up with little effort. The airship's 'moment' as the most popular form of passenger air transport passed when they proved to be slower and less reliable than the new intercontinental airliners that were coming in and not as

comfortable as the existing ocean liners. Airships require a light gas such as hydrogen or helium to provide sufficient lift. Since the infamous Hindenburg disaster, inert helium is the gas of choice. Despite being one of the most abundant elements in the universe, industrial quantities of helium on earth are becoming more scarce and expensive. In the past, extreme weather has caused the loss of a number of large airships through structural failure. The modern-day airship designer would look to use the latest light-weight, high-strength materials and digital control systems to ensure safe and economical operations.

Another idea that is coming to the fore again, albeit under a different name, is that of the open rotor, a form originally seen in turboprops such as BAC's Proteus. The main difference with the latest open-rotor design is its ability to operate efficiently at the high subsonic speeds of today's turbofan-powered airliners, as opposed to the somewhat slower speed of turboprop-powered aircraft such as the BAC Britannia. The component units (for example, turbines) at Rolls-Royce at Patchway are working with colleagues in Derby to improve engine propulsive efficiency through the use of open rotors (also sometimes referred to as unducted fans) as a contribution towards ACARE's 2020 targets. Open rotors use less fuel and are expected to produce 30 per cent less CO_2 than modern turbofans with only a minimal increase in journey times. They operate in either a pusher or puller configuration.

Open rotors were last under serious consideration by the industry in the 1980s, when the primary motivation was concern about rising fuel costs and fuel shortages rather than environmental damage. Among the challenges being addressed in current research and development programmes is the potential for increased engine noise, as there is no casing around the rotor blades to help absorb sound. Open rotors are likely to be a little noisier than the next generation of turbofans, but they are also likely to be quieter than present-day ones. Those involved in this development are keen to stress that they are not looking to return to the conventional turboprop, as the twenty-first century open rotor will incorporate new technologies that have emerged over the intervening decades: advanced compressors, low-emission combustors, improved control systems, light-weight structures and advanced propeller blades.

In the future scenario that opened this chapter, the Operations Centre at Rolls-Royce played a crucial role in sharing and acting upon information received. This is symptomatic of an industry shift between supply and support. The centre already runs Mission Ready Management Solutions, developed in response to the changing environment of its military customers, notably falling defence budgets. The Ministry of Defence wants to concentrate its resources on the practicalities of front-line operations and leave questions of the maintenance and support of the hardware it purchases to those with the

An airship powered by Rolls-Royce engines built by Brazil Straker at Fishponds, c 1919 (facing page) (Rolls-Royce Heritage Trust). Rolls-Royce turboshaft engines could be suitable for future airship designs.

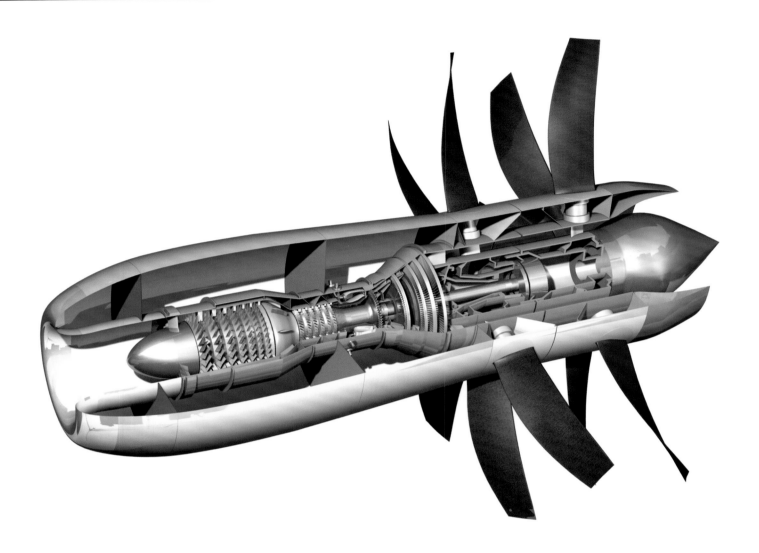

Computer-generated image of
pusher open rotor (Rolls-Royce plc).

necessary expertise. This is a departure from the traditional business arrangement that
BAC would have been involved in, where a product was sold to a customer who then
took full responsibility for it, with possibly a separate service agreement being set up to
cover maintenance. Now customers are offered a range of packages, with varying levels
of support, and choose the one that best meets their needs and budgets. Rolls-Royce is
extending the service it offers through the development of MissionCare™, which will
provide its customers with an even wider range of support. It also means that there is an
even greater incentive for Rolls-Royce to ensure the engines it supplies meet their life
expectancy, as the customer relationship does not end with the sale.

An example of a service-orientated package is the AirTanker programme. AirTanker is a
UK company with five shareholders: Cobham, EADS, Rolls-Royce, Thales UK and VT
Group plc. It was created as part of the 27-year Future Strategic Tanker Aircraft initiative.
This will entail delivering a service that provides safe, reliable, efficient and comprehensive

The first of the Future Strategic Tanker Aircraft on its maiden flight at Toulouse, 2009 (Airbus).

air-to-air refuelling and air transport capabilities to the Royal Air Force. It will use a fleet of new, multi-role tanker transport aircraft derived from Airbus A330-200 commercial airliners and powered by the Rolls-Royce Trent 700 engines. The fleet will be owned by AirTanker and provided when needed by the customer, with Rolls-Royce responsible for engine servicing, ensuring spare parts are available and planning each stage of the product's through-life.

Moving away from technology, there are other issues that will have an impact on future flight. One area is the predicted long-term increase in passenger travel. This will occur despite some people opting to reduce the number of flights they take in order to reduce their carbon footprint, and despite the prospect of high-speed rail routes and the use of teleconferencing to limit the necessity of travelling to business meetings. For the first 50 years of aviation, aircraft provided transport to a select few, whereas air travel is now considered an affordable means of travelling the world, within the means of many. It brings the advantages of experiencing different cultures and different landscapes first-hand and communicating face-to-face instead of virtually, as well as reducing travel times.

Bristol International Airport, which was founded in 1930, is addressing how it will be able to handle an estimated ten million passengers per annum by 2020. It anticipates some of the increase will come from people choosing to use their local airport rather than travelling to London. Proposals to balance economic benefits with environmental initiatives were included in the planning application submitted to North Somerset Council in June 2009 for the airport's future development. The proposals had been developed following extensive consultation. The airport has committed to maintain CO_2 emissions at or below 2007 levels, with 20 per cent of the additional energy required by the proposed development coming from on-site renewable sources. Flight emissions will be capped at 2005 levels from 2012. Public transport services will also be extended. An economic impact assessment submitted as part of the planning application estimates that the development will create over 3,500 new jobs in the South West and will have contributed total additional income of up to £2 billion to the region by 2020, as well as addressing travel issues such as congestion. Airline companies with fleets of aircraft built by Airbus and powered by Rolls-Royce engines will be among those using the new facilities.

Another issue which will have an impact on the aviation industry is the potential shortage of skills. There are a number of initiatives to ensure that companies have the right type and level of technical ability and intellectual capacity to meet the challenges of the future. These include encouraging more young people to consider a career in manufacturing and engineering, directing graduate-level expertise into the industry and retraining existing employees. For the descendants of BAC, these measures are needed to maintain the West of England's pre-eminence as a dynamic, globally significant centre of excellence.

In facing the future, the industry will be taking practical lessons from the experiences of the past. In 1910 Sir George White set in motion a process by which innovative solutions in design and manufacture were developed for what were then new materials, new methods, new products and a new type of business. Those early pioneers, facing considerable financial and physical risk, had the courage to grow and to overcome the challenges that faced them. They served as an inspiration to those who followed and provided an exciting legacy for the future.

Computer-generated aerial view of
extended Bristol International Airport
(BIA).

Endnotes

Introduction:

1   Figures from the West of England Aerospace Forum. Despite its name, this body covers the whole of the South West, not just the West of England.

2   'A "Bristol" Anniversary' *The Aeroplane* 16 February 1940 (pp 196-210), p 196 and 198.

3   This timeline has been compiled from the general background research for this book. In addition, other chronologies have been specifically consulted including *Chronicle of Aviation* (1992, J & L Publications), Charles H Gibbs-Smith's *Aviation: an Historical Survey from its Origins to the End of the Second World War* (HMSO 1985, Science Museum 2003) and the websites www.century-of-flight.net, www.rafmuseum.org.uk/milestones-of-flight and www.aviationarchive.org.uk.

Section 1:

1   Davy, M J B (1931) *Henson and Stringfellow: Their Work in Aeronautics* HMSO: London p 9.

2   Davy p 10.

3   A hang glider was indeed created from a number of his sketches and flown cautiously but successfully for Skysport Engineering in 2003. See the *Times* Online article at http://is.gd/5NTbB.

4   Public confidence in this form of transport plummeted with the *Hindenburg* disaster of 6 May 1937. This hydrogen airship operated by the Zeppelin company was engulfed in flame as it attempted to dock at Lakehurst Naval Air Station, New Jersey following an Atlantic crossing. Radio broadcasts, film footage and photographs of the disaster spread the news around the world.

5   For further details of some of these pioneers, see the computer CD of material entitled 'Eilmer the flying monk of Malmsbury, Courtney's flying leap of the Avon Gorge, Pocock charvolant material' deposited in the local studies reference section of Bristol Central Library. This was prepared by Bristol resident Paul Chapman, who researched accounts of early flying in the city for a lecture on 'Eilmer, the flying monk of Malmsbury' which was given to the Bristol Branch of the Royal Aeronautical Society in 2006. He made extensive use of rare records found in the Bristol Central Library and copied some of these to CD to make access easier.

6   Davy p 12.

7   The patent's full title was 'Locomotive Apparatus for Air, Land, and Water: Certain Improvements in Locomotive Apparatus and Machinery for conveying Letters, Goods and Passengers from Place to Place through the Air, part of which Improvements are applicable to Locomotive and other Machinery to be used on Water or on Land'.

8   Davy p 29.

9   Penrose, Harald (1988) *An Ancient Air: a Biography of John Stringfellow of Chard, the Victorian Aeronautical Pioneer* Airlife Publishing Ltd: Shrewsbury p 73.

10   Davy p 74.

11   Ronald M Birse, 'Stringfellow, John (1799-1883)', rev, *Oxford Dictionary of National Biography*, Oxford University Press, 2004 [accessed online 22 May 2009].

12   Mackersey, Ian (2003) *The Wright Brothers: the Remarkable Story of the Aviation Pioneers who Changed the World* Little Brown: London p 176. For a detailed biography of Alexander, read Gordon Cullingham's *Patrick Y Alexander* Cross Manufacturing Company: Bath (1984).

13   Cody also made the first flight of more than a mile in Britain on 14 May and, on 8 September 1909, the first flight of more than an hour.

14   Harper, Harry 'Bristol "Flash-back"' *Bristol Review* Christmas Issue 1952 (pp10-11, 28) p 10.

15   Barnes, C H (1988) *Bristol Aircraft Since 1910* (3rd edition) Putnam: London p 13.

16   Harvey, Charles and Press, Jon (1989) *Sir George White of Bristol 1854-1916* Bristol Branch of the Historical Association p 28.

17   'A "Bristol" Anniversary' *The Aeroplane* 16 February 1940 (pp 196-209) p 197.

18 'Fifty Bristol Years: the Bristol Aeroplane Company's
    Golden Jubilee' *Flight* 12 February 1960 (pp 205-212)
    p 206. The scroll was used on the Bristol trams from 1920
    to commemorate the building of Bristol Fighters at the
    Brislington tramway works during World War One.

19 Barnes p 14.

20 Copies of flyers carrying the original statement are in the
    local studies reference section at Bristol Central Library,
    catalogue reference B20078.

21 Barnes pp 28-29.

22 Barnes p 30.

23 Harvey and Press (1989) p 30.

24 For a biography of Sir George White, we recommend
    Tramlines to the Stars: George White of Bristol published
    by Redcliffe Press (1995), by his great-grandson, the
    current Sir George.

25 Charles Harvey and Jon Press 'Sir George White and
    the Urban Transport Revolution in Bristol, 1875-1914' in
    Harvey, Charles E and Press, Jon (ed) (1988) *Studies in the
    Business History of Bristol* Bristol Academic Press: Bristol
    (pp 109-163) p 139.

26 Harvey and Press (1989) p 4.

27 Letter to *Bristol Mercury* 17 October 1878 quoted in
    Harvey and Press (1989) p 7.

28 Harvey and Press (1989) p 15.

29 According to Harvey and Press (1989) p 8.

30 Harvey and Press (1988) p 155.

31 Editorial *Bristol Review* Spring 1952 p 2.

32 Harper p 28.

33 'Bristol Biplanes on the Downs' *Bristol Times and Mirror* 19
    November 1910.

34 Barnes p 19.

35 For further details see Norman C Parker's monograph
    for the South Wiltshire Archaeological Society entitled
    'Aviation in Wiltshire: A Historical Survey', May 1982.

36 The Commonwealth War Graves website lists a Captain
    Henry Maitland Maitland of the Intelligence Corps who
    died on 10 November 1918 and was buried at Tourlaville
    Communal Cemetery. Although it cannot be confirmed,
    this is likely to be the same Maitland as was at Brooklands.
    There is no record of an H M Maitland gaining an RAC
    certificate, so possibly he gave up flying after his accident.

37 Grey, C G 'Forty Plus Years of the "Bristol" Company'"
    Bristol Review Christmas Issue 1953 (pp 6-7, 36) p 6.

38 See the Aviation section of *Salisbury Plain: a Second
    Selection* Chalford Publishing Company: Stroud (1997)
    compiled by Peter Daniels and Rex Sawyer for archive
    photographs of these pilots and others.

39 Barnes p 18.

40 Barnes p 20.

41 From the Military Trails section in Parker's monograph.

42 'The *Flight* Century' *Flight* 6-12 January 2009 (p6-34) p 6.

Section 2:

1   Barnes, C H (1988) *Bristol Aircraft Since 1910* (3rd edition)
    Putnam: London p 32.

2   Glyn Stone 'Rearmament, War and the Performance of
    the Bristol Aeroplane Company, 1935-45' in Harvey,
    Charles E and Press, Jon (ed) (1988) *Studies in the
    Business History of Bristol* Bristol Academic Press: Bristol
    (pp 187-212) p 196.

3   A "Bristol" Anniversary' *The Aeroplane* 16 February 1940
    (pp 196-210) p 197.

4   'Fifty Bristol Years: the Bristol Aeroplane Company's
    Golden Jubilee' *Flight* 12 February 1960 (pp 205-212)
    p 207.

5   'A "Bristol" Anniversary' p 202.

6   Referred to in Russell, Sir A (1992) *A Span of Wings: an
    Autobiography* Airlife Publishing Ltd: Shrewsbury.

7   Barnes p 158.

8   Barnes p 192.

9   These and other tests recalled in Phillips, Reginald John
    (1989) *Bulldog to Matador 1915-1980 (an Autobiography)*
    John Reginald Phillips: Llandeilo pp 51-55.

10 'Developments in Plastics: Research and Practical
    Applications' *The 'Bristol' Quarterly* Spring 1954 Vol 1 No
    3 (pp 81-84) p 82. Obviously claims made in a journal
    designed to promote the company have to be taken
    with a certain degree of healthy scepticism, but they can
    generally be relied upon to have at least a grain of truth.

11 'Structure Testing: Important Contributions to Aeronautical
    Science' *The 'Bristol' Quarterly* Spring 1957 Vol 2 No 4
    (pp 104-108) p 104.

308   Take Flight: Celebrating Aviation in the West of England Since 1910

12 'Structure Testing' p 105.

13 'A "Bristol" Anniversary' p 198.

14 Barnes p 171.

15 'Freighter: Success Story of a Private Venture' *The 'Bristol' Quarterly* September 1953 Vol 1 No 1 (pp 10-13) p 13.

16 Barnes p 40.

17 James, Derek (2001) *The 'Bristol' Aeroplane Company* Tempus Publishing Ltd: Stroud p 183.

18 Barnes p 379.

19 James p 184.

20 Barnes p 30.

21 Wixey, Ken (1995) *Gloucester Aviation: a History* Alan Sutton Publishing Limited: Stroud p 73.

22 Later knighted, Robert Brooke-Popham was Commander-in-Chief Far East Command in World War Two, responsible for the defence of Singapore, Malaya, Burma and Hong Kong. He had learnt to fly at the Bristol Flying School at Brooklands.

23 Stone p 188. The 16-year agreement with Gnome-Rhone began 5 Feb 1922 and was terminated early, finishing on 18 July 1934.

24 Stone p 189.

25 Stone p 188.

26 Quoted in Davy, M J B (1931) *Henson and Stringfellow: Their Work in Aeronautics* HMSO: London p 12.

27 Frise is particularly remembered for the introduction of the differential displacement of ailerons. With equal-deflection ailerons, the one going down generates more drag than the one going up. This can cause the aircraft to yaw unintentionally, so the pilot has to apply the rudder to correct it. Frise's aileron used a set-back hinge so that the nose of the down-going aileron projected a little into the airstream under the wing. This equalised the drag, allowing for continued air flow, and eliminating the yaw effect.

28 'Proteus: The Advantages of Turboprop Power' *The 'Bristol' Quarterly* September 1953 Vol 1 No 1 (pp 20-22) p 20.

29 For a detailed biography of Fedden, read Gunston, Bill (1998) *Fedden: the Life of Sir Roy Fedden* Rolls-Royce Heritage Trust: Derby.

30 Kings Norton, 'Fedden, Sir (Alfred Hubert) Roy (1885-1973)', rev. Robin Higham, *Oxford Dictionary of National Biography*, Oxford University Press, 2004 [accessed online 2 Sept 2009].

31 Stone p 189.

32 Kings Norton.

33 'Higher and Higher' *Flight* No 1489 Vol XXXII 8 July 1937 (pp 41-42) p 41.

34 Referred to in Wixey p 62-63. The record was set by Meteor IV.

35 Referred to in Croucher, Richard (1982) *Engineers at War 1939-1945* Merlin Press: London p 329.

36 'Aluminium Buildings Production: Rapid Development of a Post-War Project' *The 'Bristol' Quarterly* Summer 1954 Vol 1 No 4 (pp 109-112) p 109.

37 'Aluminium Buildings Production' p 110.

38 Harper, Harry 'Bristol "Flash-back"' *Bristol Review* Christmas Issue 1952 (pp 10-11, 28) pp 10-11.

39 'Village that was Razed for Nothing' *The Gazette* January 2 1971.

40 Brace, Keith (1971) *Portrait of Bristol* Robert Hale: London p 180.

41 Barnes p 40.

42 Barnes p 328.

43 Russell, Archibald E (1992) *A Span of Wings: an Autobiography* Airlife: Shrewsbury.

44 Jason Tomes, 'Russell, Sir Archibald Edward (1904-1995)', *Oxford Dictionary of National Biography*, Oxford University Press, Sept 2004; online edn, May 2008 [accessed online 4 Sept 2009].

45 Jason Tomes.

46 'Developments in Plastics' p 81.

47 'Cabin Atmosphere Control: Comfort for the Passenger' *The 'Bristol' Quarterly* Winter 1956 Vol 1 No 8 (pp 208-211) p 208.

48 *The Concise Oxford English Dictionary*, Twelfth edition. Ed. Catherine Soanes and Angus Stevenson. Oxford University Press, 2008. *Oxford Reference Online*. Oxford University Press. [accessed online 4 September 2009].

49 *A Dictionary of Space Exploration*. Ed. E. Julius Dasch. Oxford University Press 2005. *Oxford Reference Online*. Oxford University Press. [accessed online 4 September 2009].

50 *World Encyclopedia*. Philip's, 2008. *Oxford Reference Online*. Oxford University Press. Bath and North East Somerset Libraries. [accessed online 4 September 2009].

Section 3:

1   'Down on Filton Farm' *Bristol Review* Autumn 1951 pp 22-23.

2   'A "Bristol" Anniversary' *The Aeroplane* 16 February 1940 (pp 196-210), p 201.

3   Glyn Stone 'Rearmament, War and the Performance of the Bristol Aeroplane Company, 1935-45' in Harvey, Charles E and Press, Jon (ed) (1988) *Studies in the Business History of Bristol* Bristol Academic Press: Bristol (pp 187-212) pp 189-190.

4   Barnes, C H (1988) *Bristol Aircraft Since 1910* (3rd edition) Putnam: London Barnes p 34.

5   Barnes p 35.

6   Barnes p 35.

7   First Things First' *Bristol Review* Vol II No 4 Autumn 1951 p 2.

8   Chris Wrigley, 'Brown, George Alfred, Baron George-Brown (1914-1985)', *Oxford Dictionary of National Biography*, Oxford University Press, Sept 2004; online edn, Oct 2008. [accessed online 24 July 2009].

9   *A Dictionary of Human Resource Management.* Edmund Heery and Mike Noon. Oxford University Press, 2008. *Oxford Reference Online*. Oxford University Press. [accessed online 7 September 2009].

10 BAC had the smallest percentage share in the new business, but it was said that the name British Aircraft Corporation was agreed by the three partners so the world-renowned initials remained in circulation.

11 http://www.bawa.biz/htm/php/what_is_bawa.php.

12 See Harvey, Charles and Press, Jon (1989) *Sir George White of Bristol 1854-1916* Bristol Branch of the Historical Association p 26.

13 Referred to in Richardson, Mike (2000) *Trade Unionism and Industrial Conflict in Bristol* ESRU: UWE p 25.

14 Croucher, Richard (1982) *Engineers at War 1939-1945* Merlin Press: London p 9.

15 See Richardson p 33.

16 'How Bristol Cars Are Built: Attention to Detail in the Pursuit of High Quality' *The 'Bristol' Quarterly* Winter 1956 Vol 1 No 8 (pp 203-207) p 207.

17 'The Type 404: A Blending of Elegance and High Performance' *The 'Bristol' Quarterly* Spring 1954 Vol 1 No 3 (pp 68-72) p 68.

18 http://www.bristolcars.co.uk/BristolFighter.htm.

19 'Type 405: The First Bristol Four-Door Saloon' *The 'Bristol' Quarterly* Winter 1954 Vol 1 No 5 (pp 119-122) p 119.

Section 4:

1   Barnes, C H (1988) *Bristol Aircraft Since 1910* (3rd edition) Putnam: London p 14.

2   'Flying in India' *Flight* April 22 1911 p 358.

3   According to Harvey, Charles and Press, Jon (1989) *Sir George White of Bristol 1854-1916* Bristol Branch of the Historical Association p 29.

4   'A "Bristol" Anniversary' *The Aeroplane* 16 February 1940 (pp 196-210), p 198. The article lists 25 countries who have bought aircraft and 45 who have bought engines.

5   Stroud, John 'Imperial Record' *Flight* 16 April 1954 (pp 487-489) p 487 for these and other dates. See also the History sections of http://www.imperial-airways.com.

6   Grey, C G 'Forty Plus Years of the "Bristol" Company'' *Bristol Review* Christmas Issue 1953 (pp 6-7, 36) p 36.

7   'Britannias in Service: The Background of Preparation' *The 'Bristol' Quarterly* Spring 1957 Vol 2 No 4 (pp 96-99) p 96.

8   'Britannia Progress' *Bristol Review* Spring 1952 (pp 6-7) p 6.

9   Hooker, S G 'The "Bristol" Free-Turbine' *Bristol Review* Christmas Issue 1952 p 9.

10 'Proteus: The Advantages of Turboprop Power' *The 'Bristol' Quarterly* September 1953 Vol 1 No 1 (pp 20-22) pp 21-22.

11 'Britannia Progress' p 7.

12 James, Derek N (2001) *The Bristol Aeroplane Company* Tempus: Stroud p 169.

13 'The *Flight* Century' *Flight* 6-12 January 2009 (pp 6-36) p 19.

14 'Gathering Momentum: A Review of Britannia Production' *The 'Bristol' Quarterly* Spring 1954 Vol 1 No 3 (pp 63-67) p 64. The first five were completely constructed in the Filton shops; for the remainder, most of the jigs were dispersed to the subcontractors.

15 'Furnishing Engineering: A Significant Element in Aircraft Design' *The 'Bristol' Quarterly* Autumn 1957 Vol 2 No 6 (pp 152-155) p 155.

16 See BBC Bristol's commemorative website including archive footage of crash site http://is.gd/5ObV0.

17 'Structure Testing: Important Contributions to Aeronautical Science' *The 'Bristol' Quarterly* Spring 1957 Vol 2 No 4 (pp 104-108) p 106.

18 Brace, Keith (1971) *Portrait of Bristol* Robert Hale: London p 181.

19 'The *Flight* Century' p 20.

20 This and other information taken from http://www.airbus.com/en/aircraftfamilies/a380.

Section 5:

1 Glyn Stone 'Rearmament, War and the Performance of the Bristol Aeroplane Company, 1935-45' in Harvey, Charles E and Press, Jon (ed) (1988) *Studies in the Business History of Bristol Bristol* Academic Press: Bristol (pp 187-212) p 187.

2 Harper, Harry 'Bristol "Flash-back"' *Bristol Review* Christmas Issue 1952 (pp 10-11, 28) p 10.

3 Barnes, C H (1988) *Bristol Aircraft Since 1910* (3rd edition) Putnam: London p 19.

4 Barnes p 21.

5 Grey, C G 'Forty Plus Years of the "Bristol" Company' *Bristol Review* Christmas Issue 1953 (pp 6-7, 36) p 7. Grey was a Fascist sympathizer in the 1930s.

6 Patrick Parrinder, 'Wells, Herbert George (1866-1946)', *Oxford Dictionary of National Biography*, Oxford University Press, Sept 2004; online edn, Jan 2008 [accessed online 17 Sept 2009].

7 Thetford, Owen G and Riding, E J (1946) *Aircraft of the 1914-18 War* Harborough Publishing: Leicester p 3. Later the authors describe the BE2C as being 'virtually defenceless and incapable in combat... [It] was responsible for more casualties in a given period than any other type of aeroplane with the RFC... short-sighted authorities continued to send them out to France until 1917, long after the machine had become obsolete' p 4.

8 Explained in Barnes pp 24-25.

9 'A Bristol Anniversary' *The Aeroplane* 16 February 1940 (pp 196-209) p 203.

10 'A Bristol Anniversary' p 203.

11 Croucher, Richard (1982) *Engineers at War 1939-1945* Merlin Press: London p 2.

12 Croucher p 4.

13 Croucher p 4.

14 Barnes p 34.

15 Croucher p 4.

16 Quoted in Stone p 196. From Public Record Office (PRO) AIR 6/44 White (G Stanley) to Swinton (Lord) 31 March 1936.

17 Despite this precaution, the company was almost bankrupted during the war because it was owed millions of pounds by the Ministry.

18 Figures presented in Stone p 191 from Bristol Aeroplane Company *Annual Report and Accounts*.

19 Stone p 199. From PRO AVIA 10/5 Minute, Freeman to the Chief of Air Staff 29 April 1938.

20 Stone p 202. From PRO AIR 6/44 32nd Progress Meeting with the Bristol Company 13 March 1936.

21 Stone p 203. From PRO AIR 6/44 White to Swinton 31 March 1936.

22 Stone p 203. From PRO AIR 6/46 Secretary of State's Progress Meetings: Meeting with the Bristol Aeroplane Co Ltd 17 July 1936.

23 Stone pp 203-204. Various original references given.

24 Russell, D A (ed) (1946) *Book of Bristol Aircraft* Harborough Publishing Company Limited: Leicester p 4.

25 Quoted in Stone p 202.

26 John Gooch, Angus Calder, J. M. Lee, M. R. D. Foot, Keith Jeffery, Charles Messenger, Tony Lane, Peter Stansky "UK" *The Oxford Companion to World War II*. Ed. I. C. B. Dear and M. R. D. Foot. Oxford University Press, 2001. *Oxford Reference Online*. [accessed online 26 May 2009].

27 Quoted in Stone p 194.

28 Stone p 197. From PRO AIR/1790 Air Ministry Report 27 August 1937.

29 Quoted in Stone p 197.

30 *The Times* 27 October 1942 p 8. In looking back, historians need to resist being 'enticed into the atmosphere of nostalgic patriotism' in which the war effort is presented as a united front; in the workplace, 'Foremen and managers who were seen as "little Hitlers" were given just as short shrift as the foreign enemy' according to Croucher p iii, p iv. A Ministry of Aircraft Production (MAP) survey of the effects of strikes and industrial action on aircraft

production between 1 January and 30 September 1943 accounted for the loss of around 60 bombers and 15 fighters, leading to a reduction in Bomber Command's capabilities. In the summer of 1943 MAP began running training courses for management and foremen to improve industrial practice, and took direct action by replacing the senior management at Short's.

31 Various references but original not traced. See, for example, *Daily Telegraph* 7 June 2005 at http://is.gd/aU7LM.

32 Barnes p 27.

33 Figures provided by Museum of Bath at Work.

34 Gooch et al.

35 Croucher p 17.

36 Croucher p 254.

37 Reported in Croucher pp 254-256.

38 Referred to in Croucher p 267.

39 Croucher p 283.

40 Croucher p 297.

41 McCamley, N J (1998) *Secret Underground Cities* Leo Cooper: Barnsley p 160.

42 See *Western Daily Press* article at http://is.gd/5QUj0 and the BBC Wiltshire article at http://is.gd/5QUcA [both accessed 22 July 2009].

43 Stone p 208.

44 Stallworthy, Jon (ed) (1988) *The Oxford Book of War Poetry* Oxford University Press: Oxford pp 272-273. Reproduced by permission of Margo Ewart.

45 'Sycamore: The Only All-British Helicopter in Series Production' *The 'Bristol' Quarterly* September 1953 Vol 1 No 1 (pp 17-19) p 19.

46 'Sycamore Variety: A Selection of Unusual Charter Operations' *The 'Bristol' Quarterly* Spring 1957 Vol 2 No 4 (pp 92-95).

47 'Rotorcoach: Prototype of the Inter-City Commercial Helicopter' *The 'Bristol' Quarterly* September 1953 Vol 1 No 1 (pp 23-25) p 23.

48 James, Derek N (2001) *The Bristol Aeroplane* Company Tempus: Stroud p 171.

49 'Bloodhound Capability: A European Weapon of Universal Application' *The 'Bristol' Quarterly* Winter 1958/9 Vol 3 No 1 (pp 3-6) p 4.

50 'The Ramjet: A Simple Power Unit Simply Explained' *The 'Bristol' Quarterly* Spring 1954 Vol 1 No 3 (pp 77- 80) p 80.

51 'Flight Development of Ramjets: The Basic Importance of Test Vehicles' *The 'Bristol' Quarterly* Autumn 1956 Vol 2 No 3 (pp 67-72) p 72.

52 'Marine Proteus: A Development of the Turboprop for Shipboard Installation' *The 'Bristol' Quarterly* Winter 1956 Vol 1 No 8 (pp 221-224) p 221.

Section 6:

1 This figure is acknowledged in the 2009 Oxford Economics Report *Aviation: The Real World Wide Web*, which promotes the direct economic benefits of the aviation industry and argues that constraining air transport will not necessarily lead to lower emissions.

2 http://www.sbac.co.uk/pages/35232180.asp [accessed 5 February 2010].

Index

Numbers in **bold** indicate illustration. Note aircraft and engines produced by British & Colonial, BAC, Bristol Aircraft or Bristol Siddeley are grouped together under 'Bristol'.

Acknowledgements

Special thanks to Elfan ap Rees, Paul Chapman, Linda Coode-Smith, Will Erith, Duncan Greenman, David Hall, Patrick Hassell, John Heaven, Bob Hercock, Bill Morgan, Jackie Sims, Barry Taylor and Sir George White Bt for their help with fact-checking and proofreading; the authors take responsibility for any errors that remain. Some of these people also provided help with obtaining images, and additional thanks for this support goes to Andrew Appleton, Christopher Balfour, Melissa Barrett, John Battersby, Jim Bishop, Gerry Brooke, Oliver Dearden, John Penny and Tom Vine. Many of the images in this book were sourced using Aviation Archive: www.aviationarchive.org.uk. For providing information about their companies' future projects and suggestions for topics to address in the Into the Future section, thanks go to Frank Bamford (Senior VP Business Development and Strategy, GKN), John Bradbrook (Advanced Projects, Rolls-Royce – who also provided the scenario which opens the section and provided considerable help with proofreading), Mike Collins (Public Affairs Manager, Airbus), Alan Dean (CEO, Component Coating and Repair Services Ltd) and James Gore (Head of Communications, Bristol International Airport).

BAC 100 is a partnership project. We are grateful for the support of the companies and organisations listed opposite, who have provided funding to the overall project. A great debt is owed to Arts Council England, Bristol City Council and GWE Business West, who make up Bristol Cultural Development Partnership and Bristol Creative Projects, for all their support in the development and management of BAC 100. Particular thanks go to Alan Dean and David Rowlson of Component Coating and Repair Services Ltd for their work in sponsoring this book.